IN PURSUIT OF ALASKA

153

IN PURSUIT OF ALASKA

AN ANTHOLOGY OF TRAVELERS' TALES, 1879–1909

Jean Morgan Meaux

UNIVERSITY *of* WASHINGTON PRESS

Seattle

Composed in New Caledonia, a typeface designed by
William A. Dwiggins.

University of Washington Press
uwapress.uw.edu

Visit this book's website at www.inpursuitofalaska.com

Library of Congress Cataloging-in-Publication Data

Meaux, Jean Morgan.
In pursuit of Alaska : an anthology of travelers' tales, 1879-1909 / Jean Morgan Meaux.
pages cm
Includes bibliographical references and index.
ISBN 978-0-295-99288-4 (paperback : alkaline paper)
1. Alaska—Description and travel—Anecdotes.
2. Travelers' writings. 3. Frontier and pioneer life—Alaska—Anecdotes.
4. Alaska—History—1867-1959—Anecdotes. I. Title.

F904.6.M43 2013 917.98'03—dc23 2013000510

The paper used in this publication is acid-free and meets the minimum requirements of American National Standard for Information Sciences—Permanence of Paper for Printed Library Materials, ANSI Z39.48–1984.∞

White men appeared before us on the surface of the great waters in large ships which we called canoes. Where they came from we knew not, but supposed that they dropped from the clouds. The ships' sails we took for wings, and concluded that, like the birds of the air, they could fly as well as swim.

Chief Toy-a-Att,
Sitka Indian, Wrangel, Alaska (1878)

Campsite with man and woman standing in front of tent, 1900.
Alaska State Library, P41-035. P. E. Larss Photograph Collection.

"Alaska, 1910," Ralph S. Tarr and Frank M. McMurry, *New Geographies*, 2nd ed. (New York: The Macmillan Company, 1910). Obtained online at Maps, Etc. and used with permission of Florida Center for Instructional Technology, map #02058, http://etc.usf.edu/maps/pages/2000/2058/2058.htm, accessed September 22, 2010. Modified and adapted by Steven Villano.

ALASKA 1910
Scale of Miles
0 100 200 300 400
Cities with over 10,000 Nome
Cities with 1,000 to 10,000 Juneau
Smaller Places Circle
Capital
Other Places
Comparative Area
PENNSYLVANIA
45,215 Square Miles
Beaufort Sea
OCEAN
Gulf of Alaska
ALASKA
CANADA
Mt. McKinley 20,300
Mt. Wrangell 17,500
Mt. St. Elias 18,024
Fairbanks
Dawson
Juneau
Sitka
Skagway
Valdez
Seward
Kodiak
Circle
Eagle
Ft. Yukon
ARCTIC CIRCLE
ENDICOTT RANGE
ALASKAN RANGE
KLONDIKE REGION
ALEXANDER ARCHIPELAGO

CONTENTS

FOREWORD BY STEPHEN HAYCOX

Given Alaska's exotic character in the American imagination, there ought to be more anthologies of historical first-person travel accounts than there are. Those accounts that Jean Meaux has collected here focus on a fascinating if underappreciated transition period in the region's history. In the late nineteenth century, the territory evolved from being "Darkest Alaska," as Robert Campbell has styled it, when the popular conception was of a land mysterious and forbidding, to becoming post–Gold Rush Alaska by the early twentieth century, when journalists describing the Klondike, Nome, and Fairbanks gold rushes dispelled much ignorance with their reportage and literary portraits of pioneer settlers planting civilization in the wilderness.

With a discerning and comprehensive eye, Meaux has gathered over two dozen firsthand impressions published over thirty years, the generation between 1879 and 1909, which she has grouped into three categories: tourists, explorers, and gold seekers. Together they provide the reader with arresting and insightful impressions of the territory's Native life, geography, and economic development, and with stories of the challenges faced by travelers and settlers alike in that transitory period. Many of Meaux's selections will be unknown even to persistent readers of Alaskana. The result is seductive and rewarding for scholar and casual reader alike.

The 1880 US Census recorded an Alaska population of under 30,000, almost all Natives—a mere 435 non-Natives were officially counted. Perhaps half of those were trapper/prospectors deep in the middle of the Yukon basin, and the remainder could be found mostly in a few coastal communities. The 1910 census would record twice the number of inhabitants—about the same 30,000 Natives, but now also 30,000 non-Natives. Reading the richly detailed passages presented here, one gains a vivid sense of how rapidly Alaska was changing, how expansive were some people's aspirations for it, and yet how primitive most of the territory still was. In the following selections, the reader can witness Alaska's transformation from a forbidding wilderness into a land that becomes increasingly imaginable and accessible.

PREFACE

Jumping Off the End of the Earth

Even the idea of Alaska is daunting, the way it flexes its mountain ridges and spreads its glaciers at the top of the globe, one edge running alongside desolate Canada, the other nearly touching frozen Siberia. It's too vast and too wild to take in all at once.

The Russians, who began hunting sea otters in the Aleutians in 1743, occupied Alaska for little more than a century. Focused on maritime fur trade, they settled mainly on islands, and at the mouths of rivers and the heads of bays. They were able to gain little headway in controlling the place and had mixed results in their efforts to manage the indigenous peoples. Their greatest success—if one can call it that—was with the Aleuts, whom they brutalized into providing labor, sex, and companionship. There is one particularly barbarous tale about a tyrant named Solov'ev who, American cultural historian Stephen Haycox tells us, was nicknamed "the deadly nightingale."[1] The fellow is said to have lined up a number of Aleuts, one behind the other, and then fired a bullet into the chest of the first to see how many of them it would penetrate. Even if the story is apocryphal, as it well may be, it captures the brutal determination of the Russian fur trappers to wrench profits from Alaska by whatever means it took.

The Russians encountered more resistance when they tried to subjugate the fiercely independent Tlingits in southeast Alaska. The two cultures, Russian and Indian, would eventually develop a mutual—if somewhat uneasy—alliance. Despite tensions, the Natives were enticed by the trading goods the Russians offered—cooking pots, knives, heavy woolen coats, and beads—while the Russians needed the deer meat and potatoes that the Tlingits could supply. The greatest number of colonists the Russians ever had on Alaskan soil was 823 and, given that limited manpower, they were never in a position to develop the vast resources of the mainland. Thus, the Inupiats and the Athabaskans, occupants of more remote regions, were left largely alone.

Aside from the companionship of the Natives and the cold winter wind, there was little in the New World for the *promýshlenniki*, the Russian fur hunters. All manufactured goods—window glass and building materials, writing materials and candles—had to be shipped from the motherland. The yearlong sea journey, via Tierra del Fuego or Cape Horn on through to the North Pacific, was so treacherous that it was soon abandoned as a supply route. Meanwhile, the overland trek across Siberia was of even greater duration and could take as long as two years. By the time supplies reached Alaska, Haycox says, "most of the butter was rancid, the flour filled with worms and lice."[2]

Supplying the colony would be an ongoing issue, but the Russians would give up on the New World for other reasons. They were unable to defend their territory on the North American continent and, although fully aware of the value of Alaska's coal, fish, gold, and ice, were unwilling to expend the funds and efforts necessary to develop those resources. So, in the end, they packed their valises and sold their claims in North America to the United States.

It was 1867, and the United States was occupied and preoccupied with post-Civil War reconstruction. Some might have perceived the Alaska territory as a land of ice and snow inhabited by strange, wild beasts, but, as Robert Campbell, historian of the American West, points out, all that "nonsense" about "Seward's Folly," "Walrussia," and "Icebergia" was the product of un- and ill-informed minds. Those in the know, those foresighted enough to recognize Alaska's potential and promise, knew better.[3]

At that time, secretary of state William Seward was still serving in the position to which he had been appointed by his great friend, the late Abraham Lincoln, and Seward had a vision of Alaska's role on the world stage and its future in American domination of the Pacific. To at least a portion of the citizenry, the acquisition of Alaska would be a first step toward the incorporation into the United States of Canada—or, at the very least, British Columbia. As the *New York Times* proclaimed, such a move would release British Columbians from their "bondage" to Great Britain.[4]

Senator Charles Sumner was an especial fan of the idea of acquiring Alaska. He had perused all of the Russian and European scientific reports about Alaska, including accounts of more than sixty Russian scientific voyages. In a three-hour peroration on the Senate floor, Sumner was so persuasive that the final vote in favor of the purchase was an astounding thirty-seven to two. On October 17, 1867, the day before the Russian flag was lowered and the Stars and Stripes hoisted in its place at Sitka, the *New York Times* proclaimed Alaska to be "our Northwest bargain."[5]

A bargain and a land of potential and promise it may have been, but for another fifteen years or so, that was about all it was. Travelers to Alaska in those days would have to have not merely good but *really* good reasons to go there. Government-sponsored scientists and soldiers were generating essential and path-finding reports, but most early visitors were business people and missionaries. These came forewarned, knowing they should carry along whatever they needed—or learn to do without. Once they ventured farther than the southeastern coastal panhandle, they would encounter few non-Native residents and none of the comforts of home. As late as 1874, according to Haycox, there were a mere thirty-two Caucasians spread along the three major rivers of the interior—the Yukon, the Tanana, and the Kuskokwim. Needless to say, supplies and groceries, if one ran low, were impossible to find.

The southern and southeastern coastal regions had benefitted from eighteenth-century mapping and exploring expeditions led by two English captains, James Cook and George Vancouver, and, at the conclusion of the Russians' tenure, the coastlines were fairly well defined. On the other hand, the interior—the vast heart of the mainland—was still largely unmapped and unknown—except by its Native inhabitants.

In 1880, gold was discovered along Gastineau Channel. The Treadwell mine opened on Douglas Island and began to provide jobs and attract settlers. A decade later, Juneau boasted a newspaper, hotels, restaurants, drugstores, and—inevitably—saloons and breweries. But travelers who exchanged the homeyness of Juneau for the wilds of the Kenai Peninsula or the banks of the Yukon River would have searched in vain for a hotel or boarding house—much less a confectioner or a blacksmith.

Most of the gold near Juneau (after the quick depletion of that found lying around) was lode ore—ore still encased in rock—and would have been difficult to recover without the Treadwell's huge stamp mills. Until the discovery of more easily recovered placer gold (gold that had been eroded into stream and river beds) in the regions of Fortymile River (1886) and Birch Creek (1893), there was a slow drip, rather than a trickle, of newcomers into Alaska. The 1880 census could track down only 435 non-Natives in the 600,000 square miles of the territory, and some of those were Russian holdovers. Given that small number of non-Native residents, Congress was understandably unwilling to fund a civil government or territorial structure for Alaska. Those who perceived what Alaska historian Morgan Sherwood has called "conspiratorial neglect" on the part of Washington were mainly denizens of the only area of Alaska populated by whites, the southeast. Ironically, when the government started paying attention and sponsoring military explorations of the interior, the Sitka *Alaskan* objected to such spending, arguing that the money should be spent "nearer home" instead of in a part of the territory so sparsely populated by whites.[6]

Inevitably, things changed. By 1910, Alaska's population of non-Natives had increased nearly a hundredfold, and visitors and newcomers were still arriving. Why, after centuries of what might be termed—at most—a sort of benign neglect, did Alaska become a place to which people traveled for excitement, adventure, and fortune? The writers in this collection provide us with some of the answers.

During the last decades of the nineteenth century, America's perception of Alaska and the role of Alaska on the national scene underwent profound alteration. That change resulted from a plethora of news accounts about the gold rush and gold rush towns and from the publication of widely read firsthand accounts by early travelers. For the first time, readers had access to information about a place that had been, until then, largely inscrutable. Those who had considered Alaska uninviting and uninhabitable were disabused of the notion. Those who had already known otherwise learned more. Significantly, Alaska became a desirable destination—alluring, exciting, and different.

Why was Alaska different? Fundamentally, there was all that natural beauty. Early visitors to Alaska were often well-heeled and well-traveled, but their nineteenth-century eyes would see sights unlike any they had seen before. Even an experienced traveler such as naturalist John Muir, himself a man who knew a thing or two about wilderness, was hyperbolically rhapsodic in his descriptions of Alaska. He called it "the very paradise of poets, the abode of the blessed."[7]

There were grizzly bears, caribou, whales, and golden eagles—and salmon packed so tightly in the rivers that it seemed a person could cross on their backs. Glaciers, unseen and unheard, calved icebergs—some as big as hotels or railcars—into empty bays. Waterfalls, springs hot enough to boil an egg, rainforests, the crumbling remains of Russian occupation, and Indian villages with totems awaited.

Forget the scenic wonders, the skeptic might say. Wasn't Alaska just like the rest of the American wilderness had been twenty-five, fifty, or a hundred years earlier—raw and wild? Alaska would shrug off the comparison. The southern American frontier had been fairly well trod by its original inhabitants before the white men appeared, but some of Alaska's vast spaces were unfamiliar even to the Native peoples whose ancestors had roamed the land for thousands of years. English hunter Agnes Herbert wanted Yupiks to guide her upriver from their home at the mouth of the Kuskokwim River, but their chief pooh-poohed the idea. His people had never been that far from home. Likewise, Lieutenant Joseph Herron's Indian guides urged him to abandon a trip that took him and them deeper and deeper into the wilderness. They finally deserted him because "they 'saveyed' ... the country no further."[8]

The vastness and scope of Alaska's unknowns, combined with other factors—the climate, the geography, and the environment—made exploration difficult. But forays into the wilderness were made less daunting by the friendliness of the Natives. Military explorers, accustomed to the conduct of the Indians on other parts of the American frontier, were to be pleasantly surprised by the hospitality afforded by Alaskan Natives. There were exceptions to this general geniality, to be sure. The Chilkats jealously guarded the southern passes at the head of Lynn Canal until the American army made clear that it intended to take control, and at least one party of Russians was known to have been massacred by Copper River Indians for unknown reasons. For the most part, however, expeditions in Alaska were welcomed with shelter and victuals—albeit the humble moose nose and beaver entrails—by Natives who were themselves starving.

Alaska is set apart from the rest of the country by the intractability of its landscape and the harshness of its environmental conditions. Nowadays, a farmer in Matanuska Valley may have to harvest his pumpkins with a forklift, but such extraordinary growth is exceptional. The growing season in Alaska lasts a mere forty-five to ninety days (depending on the latitude), half the territory is treeless, and where trees do grow, they do so slowly. According to environmental historian Roderick Nash, only a little more than 5 percent of Alaska's land is suitable for farming and grazing, and he relates how 1930s' visitor Robert Marshall "found knee-high spruces over a century old" in the Brooks Range.[9]

As hard as it is on plants, Alaska can be even tougher on animals. The climate is often brutal, and competition for survival is fierce. According to Nash, Alaska has less harvestable game per acre than does Oregon. He suggests that the justly deserved reputation of the place for animal viewing may be as much a product of the plentitude of its wilderness as of its wildlife.[10] Military leader Henry Allen and his men, who had hoped to "live off the country" on their

1885 exploration of the Copper River, could find no game and grew so weak from hunger that they staggered around like drunks.[11] As one old-timer said, Alaska is "a hungry country."[12]

Such subtleties could have easily escaped some of Alaska's nineteenth-century visitors. But they would not have failed to notice the nascent aura of romantic intrigue. In the late 1800s, the nation had to grapple with the fact that the rest of the American frontier had vanished. "Fears of howling wilderness," writes Robert Campbell, were giving way to the "terror" of urban living, mechanization, and industrialization.[13] The perceptions of savageness and wildness were no longer threatening and became, instead, enticing ideas. The primitiveness of Alaska, with its perceived status as "the last frontier," drew travelers north.[14]

At the head of a long train of visitors to Alaska came a California nature-lover and incipient hippie named John Muir. Already known as a wilderness defender, Muir arrived in Alaska in 1879 by the only method available—the monthly mail boat. He canoed the waters of southeast Alaska that summer and fall and, liking what he found, returned the following year. While exploring, he carried along a pocket compass, a barometer, and the map drawn by Captain Vancouver a century earlier.

Muir's euphoric dispatches about the "pure" wilderness he found in Alaska were widely read, first in California and then around the nation. Those popular accounts of Alaska's beauty captivated the public and, according to Nash, inspired commercial carriers to begin offering tours.[15] Many early excursionists returned home to write up accounts of their voyages, and those accounts, in turn, inspired others to visit.

Mail boats gave way to first-class steamers and colorful captains dedicated to excursionists' pleasures. Tourists could anticipate a sail through the placid waters of the Inside Passage and (as visitors called them) the "emerald isles" of southeast Alaska, a climb over a glacial moraine (wearing hobnailed boots was a good idea), and a visit to the Treadwell mine (a regular stop on the tourist agenda, glowingly described in travel books and promotional brochures). Guidebook author Eliza Scidmore assured her readers that the Treadwell's owners had no objection to tourist visits, but she hastened to add that work in the mines would not be suspended nor would guards or guides be provided. In those pre-OSHA days, Scidmore urged visitors "to exercise great caution in entering tunnels, where trains are always moving; pits, where blasts are being fired; and [the] mill, where no voice can be heard to warn them of belts and cogs."[16] At the end of a visit to the Treadwell, early tourist Charles Taylor and his companions were invited to fill their pockets with gold dust.[17] If travelers were looking for an unusual experience, in Alaska they would find it.

While tourists were rambling around the southeastern panhandle, the blank places on the map of Alaska's interior were calling out to adventure seekers—like the Sirens who sang to Ulysses. One of those adventure seekers was English explorer Harry de Windt, a man who believed that some feats remained unachieved not because they were impossible but simply because no one had managed to do them. De Windt was determined to be the first to journey by whatever means it took—foot, ship, boat, railroad, reindeer, horse, or dog sled—from New York to Paris by way of Alaska. When asked what he hoped to gain by risking his life and enduring such hardship, de Windt's answer was simple: he wanted to do something that had never been done.[18]

And what can be said of the cool indomitability of a man like army captain William Abercrombie? During "twenty-nine consecutive hours of practically continuous work, without sleep, rest, or shelter," Abercrombie and his men crossed Valdez Glacier, first in fog, then in rain, sleet, and snow. When they arrived at their destination, they were coated in ice. Abercrombie concluded the route was impracticable for travelers, but, never losing his sang-froid, he wryly summed up the trip: "Like all other nights, this one came to an end."[19]

If the tourists were curious and the adventurers determined, a third group of early travelers—the prospectors—were hungry. Many of them were surprised, when they reached Alaska, to find that the ground wasn't covered with gold. Hadn't the newspapers and magazines said anyone could go to Alaska and return a millionaire? All that hard-earned cash wasted on supplies, all that claptrap junk bought from hucksters in Seattle and San Francisco—and then it dawned on them: how were they to get home from Skagway or Nome or Valdez, flat broke and sick with scurvy?

Without exception, the people who went to Alaska in those days were out of the ordinary. Their ideas and dreams—some of them cockamamie, others merely far-fetched—drew them north. Tourists, adventurers, and gold seekers all went to Alaska filled with anticipation and a fair amount of trepidation, whether packing a sealskin coat and a fur muff for a tramp across the glacier or carrying a pack as big as a baby elephant for a trek into the wilderness.

Some of their plans would come to naught; some were changed by the experience; some were glad to escape with their lives. When few people voiced a desire to see Alaska, the writers in this collection wanted—desperately—to go there. Whatever they were looking for—new sights, new adventures, or newly found gold—they were all on a quest.

Was Alaska different? Let's put it this way: while the white-gloved populace of New York was setting out in their carriages for concerts at Carnegie Hall, in Alaska, volcanic islands were erupting from the sea.

In 1971, my then husband (I'll call him "P.") and I were on sort of a quest ourselves. He was job hunting and had answered a three-line ad in the *New Orleans Times-Picayune* that read, "Accountants wanted, Anchorage, Alaska," followed by a phone number in Houston. We each had our own romantic notion of what life in Alaska would be.

When P. was a child, his family had owned a single volume of Funk and Wagnalls *New World Encyclopedia*—volume "A"—and he had been enchanted with the article on Alaska. In my house, we had subscribed to *National Geographic*, and, like the magazine's readers a century earlier, I found the stories about Alaska especially appealing—that giant, distant territory, part of America, yet foreign and strange. I remember a glossy pictorial spread of Anchorage stretched cozily along the foot of the Chugach Mountains, houses covered with a blanket of snow, windows warmly lit in the dusky purple twilight.

Neither P. nor I had been farther north than Chicago, and leaving home would mean saying good-bye to the world we knew—south Louisiana, with its humidity, swamps, colorful politicians, and our families. At the same time, there was something oh-so exciting about venturing to an exotic place far, far away. Our dreams were fairly generic: P. hoped to fill the larder with big game, and I thought of a cabin built on a mountainside beside a clear stream. My little French grandmother, with her conscripted world view, asked if there were any Americans "in that place."

In the end, we were captivated by the idea of no more mosquitoes, no more swamps, and, the job offer having included such generous remuneration, we were led on by that universal motivator: "We'll be rich!" Holding our breaths, we said yes. We might as well have jumped off the end of the earth.

Anxious to begin seeking his fortune, P. set out to cover the nearly 5,000 miles between New Orleans and Anchorage in our Chevrolet Impala. He was shod in penny loafers and wore his yellow cotton windbreaker—as I remember, the only coat he owned. Although it was October, the Impala wore no studded tires. The snow met up with P. in Canada, and, somewhere on the Alcan Highway, he acquired a set of chains.

A month later, I flew from New Orleans to Chicago and then on to Anchorage. Having traveled on a commercial flight once before, I was an experienced traveler. On the extravagantly named Northwest Orient Airlines, I chose a window seat over the wing where the thrum of the engines droned on and on, later to reverberate in my brain in the days that followed. The plane, meanwhile, flew into the night over dark, frozen Canada, and then over dark, frozen Alaska.

It all seemed rather daring until I stumbled out into the November cold, with its snowy drifts, carrying an eleven-month-old baby in one arm and a diaper bag in the other. I was twenty-four years old and wearing double-knit maternity pants with an elastic waist, since I was—ta da!—once again pregnant. Would there be a competent physician to deliver our baby? We'd soon find out.

In the darkness, the air-conditioned Impala fishtailed out of the airport parking lot as the vehicles around us puffed plumes of foggy, grey exhaust into the night sky. One day followed another, and I watched from the window of our tiny apartment as a flat, pale, lemon-colored disk of sun rose late in the morning in the hazy southeast. It made a low pass over the horizon and, in the early afternoon, dropped off the face of the earth again. And that was on the days when there was sunshine.

The Impala wended its way between the dirty snowbanks that edged the roadways. The car had an automatic transmission, but I kept one foot on the gas pedal and the other hovering over the brake in the event that I hit a patch of glare ice. "Don't worry," P. would say. "You'll get used to it." And, in a way, I did. At least for a time.

A dozen or so years later, I was still in Alaska. By then, I had three children, was still married to P., and, after a stint composing obituaries, was freelancing for the *Anchorage Daily News*. In the depths of another grey winter, I paid a visit to the windowless little room which then housed the rare book collection at the University of Alaska Anchorage's Consortium Library. At random, I pulled Robert Dunn's *The Shameless Diary of an Explorer* off the shelf and found the extraordinary tale of a 1903 Mount McKinley expedition gone awry—agony, adventure, and unforgettable characters, such as spoiled Simon, who hogged more than his share of the condensed milk, and the pompous Professor, who fiddled with his theodolite when it was time to saddle the horses. Who could resist a book that begins, "This is the story of a failure"?

I turned to Dunn's neighbors on the shelves—other writers in the section designated by the Library of Congress as "Alaskan History," all those F901–951s. As I read the stories about Alaska in the late 1800s and early 1900s, I discovered a time and a place that no longer existed except between the covers of those books. Many of the authors were strong-minded individuals, buoyant, self-confident travelers with original voices. Although those books had been widely popular when they were published, when I first read them in 1983 they were no longer even in circulation. I decided that these writers were too good to ignore and started collecting their works. Today, some of these books have been reprinted, and that's a good thing, for they are as interesting and enjoyable now as they were when they were written.

This collection results from my affection for twenty-seven writers whom I found to be the most engaging of their kind. The vignettes presented here, which occurred between 1879 and 1909, all took place on Alaskan soil. A couple of these travelers, Mary Hitchcock and Robert Kirk, may have had the Klondike as their final destination, and another, Harry de Windt, was ostensibly headed three-quarters of the way around the world. No matter where they were going, they all wrote at length about their time in Alaska; those portions of their works are—at least to my mind—the most interesting parts. All of these writers would add to the history of Alaska by achieving what was, in one way or another, unimaginable in their day. When these works appeared in print, they gave the nation its first firsthand accounts of a place that most Americans would never see. And, while they were changing the nation's view of Alaska, they were also changing Alaska.

How were early travelers such as these, without the advantages of modern technology and traveling as they did on foot or by boat and dogsled, able to change a place as vast as Alaska? Historian Stephen Haycox provides a litany of what had taken place in Alaska by the end of the first decade of the twentieth century. Among other things, trees along riverbanks had been clear-cut to provide fuel for river boats and for the construction of cabins. Tailings from the "diggings" littered areas of the landscape, and the mercury that had been used to separate gold from other minerals polluted the streams.

The lives most seriously affected by this influx of visitors may have been those of the original residents, the Native population. In some ways, missionaries of various denominations ameliorated the situation by teaching Native children and treating diseases. However, they also encouraged Natives to abandon their traditions and customs, to wear cotton instead of fur, and to call themselves silly names like Miss Sally Shortandirty and Mrs. Monkey Bill.[20] The newcomers provided a market for Native arts and crafts, which allowed them to earn incomes, and boats plying waterways created jobs for Athabaskan woodcutters and river pilots. At the same time, Natives with incomes at their disposal grew dependent, in Haycox's words, on the "white goods and the white economy." Some of them left their homes and migrated to the towns;[21] others developed alcohol dependence or turned to prostitution. Smallpox had been imported by the Russians and had affected Native populations, but other diseases, such as measles and syphilis, were brought in with the gold rush and caused further epidemics and more deaths—as many as a quarter to a third of those deaths in Alaska's western and northern regions caused by the "great sickness" of 1900.[22]

By 1910, increased attention from the federal government meant that educational programs were offered for both Native and non-Native children, and private land ownership was provided for. Better maps of Alaska were available, and a telegraph line connected non-Native settlements with the outside world. A wagon trail from Valdez on the coast wended its way through the wilderness to Fairbanks, smoothing the delivery of goods and people inland. On balance, were these changes improvements? It depends on your perspective.

Alaska has now been part of the United States for nearly one hundred fifty years. In that span of time, the pace of life there has been changed by automobiles and pickup trucks, recreational vehicles, cruise ships, tour buses, developers, snowmobiles, off-road vehicles, oil fields, pipelines, logging, hydraulic mining, fishing camps, fixed-wing airplanes, commercial jetliners, military installations, and hunters with high-powered binoculars and rifles with long-range scopes who track animals from the seats of their ATVs. Alaska's Native peoples have gained political and economic clout but continue an ongoing struggle to retain their heritage while living in a modern age. Depending on one's philosophical bent, development and innovation may be good or bad, and any Alaskan can quickly tell you which.

No matter the viewpoint and in spite of these changes, the character of the wilderness of Alaska—its quintessence—isn't all that different from what it was one hundred fifty years ago. Despite the inroads of civilization, huge tracts of Alaska's land—millions of acres—remain untouched. From the window of a plane, the towns and cities of Alaska are merely man-made clutter sprinkled at the feet of mountain ranges that spike the skyline. Rivers are filled with migrating salmon. Streams are so clear that you can see their bottoms. Old growth forests have been spared the axe. Puddles of lakes are sprinkled across the vast plains of tundra stretching to the horizon. When seen from the air, the few highways of Alaska—some of them still gravel—look like pencil lines drawn across miles and miles of wilderness. On many backcountry trails, a hiker is more likely to encounter evidence of bears than of another human. As the Alaska tourism ads say, there are more miles of glacier than of roadway, and more sheep, caribou, and eagles than people.

Alaska stolidly remains. Not hostile, just indifferent, unyielding, demanding, and—perhaps—unforgiving.

Today, the places that these early travelers struggled to reach can be visited at significantly less peril to life and limb, and in relative ease. The White Pass and Yukon Route Railway that Charles Taylor rode in 1900 still chugs up the switchback trail where thousands of pack horses dropped dead or (it is said) jumped off a cliff to avoid further torture. Alaska is the only place on American soil with Russian remains, such as the green-domed Russian Orthodox Saint Michael's Cathedral in Sitka. The structure burned and was rebuilt in 1996, but Sunday services there are still conducted in Slavonic, Aleut, Yupik, and Tlingit. In 1975, a group of young men built a raft at Lake Bennett and spent two years floating the entirety of the Yukon River in a recreational version of the trek taken by the gold rushers in the late 1800s and early 1900s. That modern-day saga was so novel that it was reenacted, filmed by PBS, and broadcast on national television. Each winter, there are long-distance dog-team races through silent wilderness in subzero temperatures, with mushers yelling "Gee!" and "Haw!" just as Hudson Stuck did at the dawn of the twentieth century.

As for P. and me, the lives we led in Alaska little resembled our fantasies. The mosquitoes were—if anything—fatter, fiercer, and more ubiquitous than in the south. The swamps were just as swampy, and there were lots more of them. Need I mention Alaska's colorful politicians?

P. never shot a bear or a moose, and, despite our hopes of early riches, we lived through a dismal period later referred to as "the years of near starvation," since the salary that had sounded so extravagant barely covered our basic necessities. Had I paid enough attention to my history book before migrating north, I would have realized something the Russians had learned long before. By the time foodstuffs—milk and bananas, meat and potatoes—crossed my threshold and the lumber and nails had been cobbled into my dwelling, they had traveled fifteen hundred miles and more, and someone—in this case, me—had to pay the freight. As it turned out, the hospital and obstetrician were fine, and I realized I could tote two babies—one on each hip.

We did grow rich, not in the way we had hoped, but in friendships with wonderful people who laughed and cried with us through fourteen long winters and fourteen short summers. We feasted on king crab and red salmon and wild blueberry jam and built up a store of memories of camping trips in endless summer sunlight, of singing "I've Been Working on the Railroad" to fend off bears, of bracing against rushing currents in hip boots and long johns with a big fish flopping around on the line. As an old pioneer friend of mine used to say, what "diff" did it make if much of these times were spent in the rain? We were in Alaska, weren't we?

I've been lucky. I've hiked part of the trail Addison Powell helped build through Keystone Canyon in 1899, a place with mounds of bear scat and inclines so steep that the men who broke the trail had to hang on to the bushes with one hand while swinging an axe with the other. In the summer of 2011, I had plans to camp near Childs Glacier, where Henry Allen started up the Copper River in 1885, and where I understand there is a warning sign about the danger of being washed off the viewing platform. I got a last-minute phone call from the National Park Service saying the river was trying to change course and had washed out the only road into the area. So, instead, we camped in Cordova, where the typical sixty-mile-an-hour winds threatened to blow the lid off of our rented RV.

I still have hopes of floating the Brooks Range's Huluhulu River and of climbing at least a part of Chilkoot Pass, where that ragtag bunch—those prospective prospectors—mounted the Golden Stairs in 1898 and 1899. Then there is what is, for me, the ultimate Alaskan experience: standing somewhere in the six million acres of wilderness that surround "the mountain" (McKinley or Denali, whichever you prefer) and imagining, like writer Robert Dunn used to do, that I am the only human being on earth.

Everybody who goes to Alaska has a reason. Few head north on a whim. Once there, some find they can't leave. Others can't get away soon enough. In the mid-1980s, a switch flipped in my brain that made it impossible for me to get warm unless I filled the bathtub with water nearly straight from the hot water tank and submerged my body until my skin turned as pink as a boiled crab. In the depths of my soul, something told me that I could not shovel snow in the dark in below-zero temperatures for another winter and retain my sanity at the same time. It was time for me to go someplace where I could wear white cotton until mid-November.

For heaven's sake, you might say. Get a grip! What did I have to complain about? I had an engine block heater in my car and a fancy fluorescent-lit grocery store just around the corner. My troubles were pfff!—nothing—compared to what these early travelers went through.

I've thought about that—a lot. Perhaps the severity of their trials toughened them. Having gone to Alaska at a time when it was nearly impossible to get there, much less to survive, many of Alaska's early visitors decided that they could do anything—whether it was write a book or chase after Pancho Villa. So they did.

Notes

1 Stephen Haycox, *Alaska: An American Colony* (Seattle: University of Washington, 2002), 58.

2 Ibid., 91.

3 Robert Campbell, *In Darkest Alaska: Travel and Empire Along the Inside Passage* (Philadelphia: University of Pennsylvania Press, 2007), 5.

4 "Our New Possessions on the Pacific Coast—Peaceable Annexation," *New York Times,* October 22, 1867.

5 "Our Possessions in the Northwest—The Resources of Alaska," *New York Times,* October 17, 1867.

6 Morgan Sherwood, *Exploration of Alaska, 1865–1900* (New Haven: Yale University Press, 1965), 134–35.

7 John Muir, *Travels in Alaska* (Boston: Houghton Mifflin, 1915), 14.

8 First Lieutenant Joseph Herron, *Explorations in Alaska, 1899, for an All-American Overland Route from Cook Inlet, Pacific Ocean, to the Yukon* (Washington, DC: Government Printing Office, 1909), 32.

9 Roderick Nash, *Wilderness and the American Mind*, 3rd ed. (New Haven: Yale University Press, 1967), 274.

10 Ibid.

11 Lieutenant Henry T. Allen, *Report of an Expedition to the Copper, Tananá, and Kóyukuk Rivers in the Territory of Alaska in the Year 1885* (Washington, DC: Government Printing Office, 1887), 51.

12 Nash, *Wilderness and the American Mind*, 274.

13 Campbell, *In Darkest Alaska*, 53.

14 Roderick Nash, "Tourism, Parks, and the Wilderness Idea in the History of Alaska," in *Alaska in Perspective*, vol. 4. no. 1, ed. Sue E. Liljeblad (Anchorage: Alaska Historical Commission / Alaska Historical Society, 1981), 10–11.

15 Nash, "Tourism, Parks, and the Wilderness Idea," 6–7.

16 Eliza Ruhamah Scidmore, *Appletons' Guide-Book to Alaska and the Northwest Coast* (New York: D. Appleton and Company, 1893), 86.

17 Charles M. Taylor, Jr., *Touring Alaska and the Yellowstone* (Philadelphia: George W. Jacobs & Co., 1901), 184.

18 Harry de Windt, *From Paris to New York by Land* (London: Thomas Nelson & Sons, n.d.), vii.

19 Captain William Abercrombie, "Report of Captain W. R. Abercrombie," in *Reports of Explorations in the Territory of Alaska (Cooks Inlet, Sushitna, Copper and Tanana Rivers), 1898* (Washington, DC: Government Printing Office, 1899), 307.

20 Hudson Stuck, *Ten Thousand Miles with a Dog Sled: A Narrative of Winter Travel in Interior Alaska* (New York: Charles Scribner's Sons, 1914), 24.

21 Haycox, *Alaska, An American Colony*, 209.

22 Ibid.

ACKNOWLEDGMENTS

This work would have been greatly impoverished without the benefit of well-thumbed and extensively highlighted copies of Stephen Haycox's *Alaska: An American Colony* and two works by Roderick Nash, *Wilderness and the American Mind* and "Tourism, Parks, and the Wilderness Idea in the History of Alaska." I especially owe a debt of gratitude to Nash for pointing out that the word "travel" stems from "travail," and for his observation that it is "easier to stay home." I relied on the late Morgan B. Sherwood's *Exploration of Alaska, 1865–1900* for his thorough explication of the nineteenth-century expeditions that made the unknowns of Alaska known. Other good guides to the Alaska of the late 1800s and early 1900s are Pierre Berton's *The Klondike Fever* and *The Life and Death of the Last Great Gold Rush*, Robert Campbell's *In Darkest Alaska: Travel and Empire along the Inside Passage*, and David Wharton's *The Alaska Gold Rush*.

In considering this work for publication, the University of Washington Press asked two readers to review and comment on the manuscript. The identities of these persons are—at least to me—unknown, but I am nonetheless indebted to them for valuable insights that helped shape the final draft.

I thank these known authors and anonymous readers for their keen interest in Alaska and its history. My task was made easier by the hard work each of them has done.

I also am deeply grateful to my husband, Jerry Ballanco, who has been unwavering in his affection for Alaska, his interest in these writers, and his support for my work. My creative and enthusiastic daughter, Amy E. Despalier Meaux, was the best proofreader I could have hoped for, and my son, Jared Meaux, and his search program saved me endless hours in the revision process. Steven Villano patiently revised the 1910 map of Alaska and fielded my photography questions. Amy D. Meaux read and made suggestions to the introduction, and Laura and Travis Polk were enthusiastic supporters.

I can never adequately thank poet Thomas Sexton for suggesting that I take a look at the UAA Consortium Library's Alaskana collection and for making me believe I was a writer. The late William Siemens, along with other staff and faculty at UAA—Catherine Innes-Taylor, Peggy Michielsen, and Stephen Haycox—assisted in more ways that I can count with the first version of the manuscript in 1983 and 1984. Patrick Dougherty, James Macknicki, and M. A. Mariner, my editors at the *Anchorage Daily News*, gave me the privilege of writing for the *News*, and taught me much about good writing, and I thank them.

David Kessler of the Bancroft Library at the University of California, Berkley; Carla Rickerson in Special Collections at the University of Washington's Allen Library; and Sandra Johnston of the Alaska State Library were of invaluable assistance. I owe much gratitude to my friend and coach, James Nolan, who encouraged me to pick up this project after it had lain fallow for many years. I also thank Carolyn Perry, Grace Frisone, Celeste Berteau, Maurice Ruffin, Don Downey, Joe Barbara, Amy Conner, and Bruce Nesbitt, who read and critiqued parts of this work. And I am grateful, for the many ways they have offered encouragement and assistance, to Woodrow and Laura Morgan, Elaine and Ed Cordova, Peggy and Dick Welch, Gail and Dick Barnes, Gail Pittenger, Becky Sencial, Sandra Jones, Don Sparrow, Patrick Meaux, Laurie Honold, and Kerrie Maynes.

Finally, I thank Marianne Keddington-Lang of the University of Washington Press, whose enthusiasm for and support of this project made my heart feel like it would burst.

NOTE ON ORIGINAL SOURCES

Many of the first editions of the works that make up this collection can be read online at http://openlibrary.org or at www.archive.org. Lieutenant Henry Allen's *Report of an Expedition to the Copper, Tananá, and Kóyukuk Rivers in the Territory of Alaska in the Year 1885* and M. Clark's *Roadhouse Tales* are accessible at http://www.hathitrust.org. Reprints of almost all of the works excerpted here can be ordered through Internet sources, the best being photocopies of the original works rather than scanned reprints. Original first editions of some of these works can still be purchased through Internet sources. The highly readable and enjoyable 1900 *Compilation of Narratives of Explorations in Alaska*, which includes reports by many early Alaskan military men, has been scanned and posted online by Harvard University at http://pds.lib.harvard.edu/pds/view/8502870.

The works in this collection are divided into three groups of early Alaskan travelers: tourists, adventurers/explorers, and gold seekers. Within each section, the writings are arranged chronologically by date of publication. A selection begins with an overview of the author and his or her work, followed by an excerpt from the original source, and concludes with a brief coda. If additional relevant information about the author was available, I've tried to include that.

The only selection not taken from a book is the 1880 *Daily Evening Bulletin* article by John Muir, and that is because his best work about Alaska, *Travels in Alaska*, was not published until after his death. Arthur Dietz's *Mad Rush for Gold in Frozen North* and Hudson Stuck's *Ten Thousand Miles with a Dog Sled*, were both published in 1914, and the publication date of John Stacey's *To Alaska for Gold* is unknown. That said, all of the stories collected here are accounts of events that took place in Alaska between 1879 and 1909.

My goal was to select the best story each author had to tell and, in order to present cohesive vignettes, it was sometimes necessary to condense. While there was no need to shorten the selection from Robert Dunn's *The Shameless Diary of an Explorer*, Mary Hitchcock's *Two Women in the Klondike* contains much peripheral detail, including information from a guidebook.

Thus, paragraphs could be eliminated from Hitchcock's passage without loss of continuity. Nonetheless, I strived to maintain the integrity of the author's voice and style by making as few internal cuts as possible and by making no changes to grammar. While cutting, I attempted to delete only unnecessary facts and confusing asides, and, to increase readability, have not interrupted with ellipses. For clarity, I deleted errant commas, semicolons, and paragraphing, and also added such devices when appropriate. The authors' spellings and syntax have been retained except where a word was clearly misspelled or where the original led to confusion. I've provided the page numbers in the notes for readers who wish to view the original selections in their entirety on the Internet.

The names of some Alaskan landmarks have changed over time and, where available, I've included the modern place name in brackets in the text. Assistance with place names can be found in Donald Orth's *Dictionary of Alaska Place Names* (Washington, DC: Government Printing Office, 1971).

Finally, it's important to remember that these writers were recording firsthand experiences and impressions. Sometimes they display a xenophobic attitude that was typical of the day. While these are good stories about a special place in a special time, these authors, like most of the rest of us, are not without their flaws.

IN PURSUIT OF ALASKA

“Nothing grows in Alaska,” Lover’s Lane, Sitka, 1887. Alaska State Library, P88-19. William H. Partridge Photograph Collection.

PART I

ROMANTIC VOYAGE

A Tour of Southeastern Alaska

Three hundred and fifty dollars cannot be
more profitably spent for a summer vacation, and this is
more than it costs from New York to the icebergs and back.
Think of it! Hardly the price of a French costume,
a ring, or a bracelet, and yet the memory of
such a trip will outlive them all.

Septima Collis,
A Woman's Trip to Alaska, 1890

When John Muir first went to Alaska in 1879, there was no such thing as an Alaskan tourist. Although Muir had a hand in changing that, it didn't work out in quite the way that he had hoped.

In his 1880 photograph, the forty-one-year-old Muir's face already displays the twin qualities of openness and intensity for which he would later become known. He had studied glacial remnants in the California Sierra Nevada and wanted to observe the still-living rivers of ice in Alaska. His Native guides became his friends and led him to glaciers that he was one of the first whites to set eyes on. With his strong sense of adventure and his zeal for new experiences, Muir was in a way himself a tourist. However, his fearlessness and willingness to encounter the unknown set him apart from the early Alaskan excursionists who followed him.

On two early trips, one in 1879 and a second the following year, Muir reached Alaska by the only method that was then available—the monthly mail boat. As the vessel wended its way from Victoria into and through the Alexander Archipelago, Muir was enchanted by the mountains that descended to

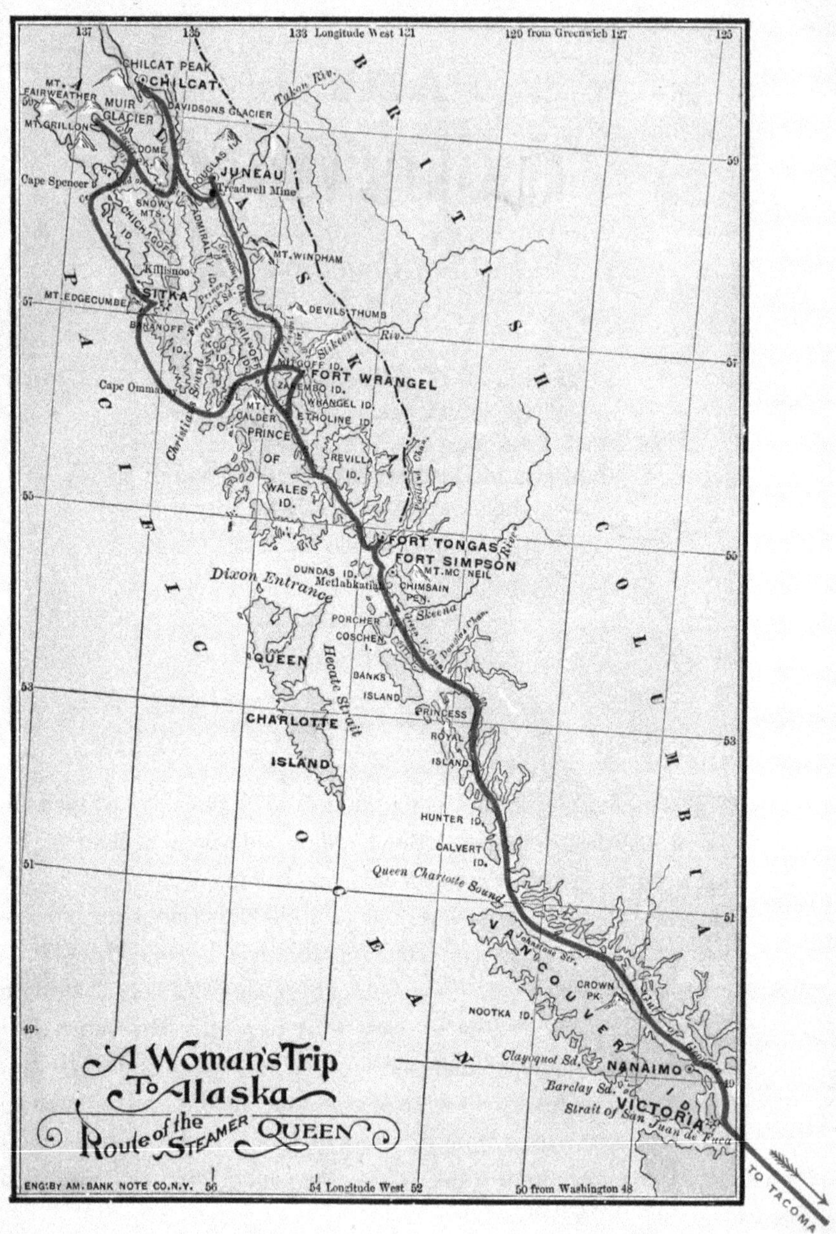

Route of the steamer *Queen.* From Septima M. Collis, *A Woman's Trip to Alaska* (1890).

the water's edge, giant spruces so close he could see cones clustered in their branches, granite cliffs, sea and bird life, verdant islands—and, best of all, all of it was undeveloped and unexplored.

Before he'd left California, Muir had arranged to work as a freelance journalist for a San Francisco newspaper, the *Daily Evening Bulletin*. After scribbling notes in his journal, he sat down to write enthusiastic accounts that he dispatched south on the mail boat. Describing the "pure" wilderness he'd found in Alaska, he encouraged others to visit.

Reader response to Muir's articles was so keen that, in 1881, railroad magnate Henry Villard offered the first excursion through the Inside Passage[1]—the nearly thousand-mile stretch of protected waters lying between the narrow strip of the North American mainland and the 1,000 islands of the Alexander Archipelago. The eighty passengers on that trip included the members of a military band and an army general named Nelson Miles, the man who would later be the prime mover behind several important military explorations of Alaska.[2]

After the success of that voyage, Villard's Northern Pacific Railway began carrying travelers to the west coast, where they were loaded onto ships that sailed to ports in southeast Alaska and to Glacier Bay before returning south. The Pacific Coast Steamship Company (PCSC), which had until then been strictly a commercial carrier, imitated Villard's excursions, and the route through southeastern Alaskan waters soon became a standard tour.

Wealthy Americans saw the voyage to Alaska as an exciting alternative to their usual summer European jaunt. Muir's prediction—"Were one-tenth part of the attractions that this country has to offer made known to the world, thousands would come every year"[3]—was proved correct. Excursions were conducted only during Alaska's short summers but were nonetheless so popular that between 1884 and 1890, more than 25,000 travelers booked passage.[4] By 1890, the PCSC had several ships plying the waters of southeastern Alaska, each carrying as many as two hundred passengers, who paid fares of around one hundred thirty dollars apiece. The round-trip between San Francisco and Glacier Bay took thirty days,[5] and shorter trips were available from more northerly ports such as Seattle and Victoria. One 1893 advertisement boasted, "Novelty and startling incidents … may well make the trip the object of a lifetime." Truly, there was nothing like it.[6]

Impressed visitors went home to sell accounts of their trips that were published as books and printed in newspapers and magazines. These garnered a wide audience, since those with neither the time nor the money to pay a visit to Alaska could vicariously enjoy the thrills experienced by those who had. As historian Robert Campbell said, these popular writings "helped to fix a particular vision of the north in the national imaginations of Americans."[7]

If there was anyone who was less than enthusiastic at this turn of events, it would have to have been John Muir. While Muir had hoped to inspire travelers like himself, it would be decades before people went to Alaska, as he did, in search of encounters with raw nature. Many nineteenth-century Alaskan visitors hoped instead for the "long, blithesome holiday" described by Muir's contemporary Charles Hallock.[8] To Muir's chagrin, when he returned to Wrangell in 1890, only eleven years after his first visit, he found "shops … jammed and mobbed, [with] high prices paid for shabby stuff manufactured expressly for tourist trade."[9] He would write of this kind of tourist as an "arm chair" wonder and despair over the Kodak wrappers he saw dropped on the glaciers.[10] So much, it might be said, for wilderness experiences.

By then, however, it was too late for Muir to rewind the skein he had unraveled, and it was left to Nature herself to take matters in hand. In 1899, a massive earthquake caused miles of glacial ice to collapse into Alaskan waters, clogging Glacier Bay and blocking access. As a result, cruises to southeast Alaska stopped for nearly half a century. In turn, tourists were forced to turn their attention to less accessible, more remote parts of Alaska.[11]

These days, southeast Alaska is definitely back on the tourist circuit, and Glacier Bay is a big draw. Millions of visitors have followed basically the same route taken by Muir and the other tourists represented here. If Muir were to know that the National Park Service now imposes a limit of two cruise ships per day into Glacier Bay,[12] he might wince. And, as those massive tour boats, some of them longer than two football fields, slice through Alaska's still-pristine waters, few passengers are aware that they sail the same seas traveled by John Muir in a red cedar canoe almost a century and a half ago.

Notes

Epigraph: Septima M. Collis, *A Woman's Trip to Alaska; Being an Account of a Voyage Through the Inland Seas of the Sitkan Archipelago in 1890* (New York: Cassell Publishing, 1890), 190.

1 Ted C. Hinckley, *The Americanization of Alaska, 1867–1897* (Palo Alto: Pacific Books, 1972), 147.

2 Robert Campbell, *In Darkest Alaska: Travel and Empire Along the Inside Passage* (Philadelphia: University of Pennsylvania Press, 2007), 94.

3 John Muir, "Alaska Land," *Daily Evening Bulletin,* September 25, 1880, reprinted in *Letters from Alaska by John Muir,* eds. Robert Engberg and Bruce Merrell (Madison: University of Wisconsin Press, 1993), 66.

4 Morgan B. Sherwood, *Exploration of Alaska, 1865–1900* (New Haven: Yale University, 1965), 71.

5 Roderick Nash, "Tourism, Parks, and the Wilderness Idea in the History of Alaska," in *Alaska in Perspective,* ed. Sue E. Liljeblad (Anchorage: Alaska Historical Commission / Alaska Historical Society, 1981), 7.

6 Eliza Ruhamah Scidmore, *Appletons' Guide-Book to Alaska and the Northwest Coast* (New York: D. Appleton and Company, 1893), inside cover.

7 Campbell, *In Darkest Alaska,* 12.

8 Charles Hallock, *Our New Alaska; or, The Seward Purchase Vindicated* (New York: Forest and Stream Publishing Company, 1886), 36.

9 John Muir, *Travels in Alaska* (Boston: Houghton Mifflin, 1915); 276.

10 Stephen Haycox, *Alaska: An American Colony* (Seattle: University of Washington Press, 2002), 198.

11 Nash, "Tourism, Parks, and the Wilderness Idea," 8.

12 "Glacier Bay National Park and Preserve," National Park Service, August 6, 2012, http://www.nps.gov/glba/parkmgmt/cruise-ships.htm.

The great Muir Glacier, ca. 1891. Alaska State Library, P214-104. Leslie E. Keeley Photograph Collection.

Indian totems at Kasaan, n.d. Alaska State Library, Kasaan-04. Alaska State Library Collection.

Tourists on moraine at Muir Glacier, n.d. Alaska State Library, P88-33. William H. Partridge Photograph Collection.

Juneau, largest mining town in Alaska, ca. 1887–1889. Juneau-Views-General-1887-89-11. Alaska State Library Photograph Collection.

Tlingit women and boy sitting on wood bench at Wrangell, n.d. Alaska State Library, P297-0012. Early Prints of Alaska Photograph Collection.

Greek Russian church at Sitka, n.d.
Alaska State Library, P39-201.
Case & Draper Photograph Collection.

Chilkat Indians in old dancing costumes, Klukwan, ca. 1895. Alaska State Library, P87-008. Winter & Pond Photograph Collection.

Parade grounds, Sitka (jail and wharf in background), ca. 1884. Alaska State Library, P297-103. Early Prints of Alaska Photograph Collection.

John Muir portrait, by I. W. Taber and T. N. Boyd, ca. 1880. John Muir Papers, Holt-Atherton Special Collections, University of the Pacific Library.

1

JOHN MUIR

Fort Wrangel, Alaska,
August 8, 1879

> How delightful it is, and it makes one's pulses bound to get back again into the heart of this grand old northland wilderness, with its giant mountains, glaciers, forests, cataracts.... and its lifegiving air without dust or taint.... How truly wild it is, and how joyously one's heart responds to the welcome it gives.

John Muir was still a young man when he went to Alaska in 1879, but he had already begun making a name for himself as a defender of wilderness and the environment by trying to convince California lawmakers to ban clear-cut logging in the Sierra Nevada[1] and by agitating for the creation of national parks.[2]

Raised by a stern, religiously orthodox father in the woods of Wisconsin, Muir had dropped out of college and was working in a wagon parts factory in Indiana when his eye was pierced with a file. He was temporarily blinded in both eyes and feared that the loss might be permanent. When his fear proved unfounded and his eyesight was restored, Muir set out on a thousand-mile walk cross-country, from north to south. On the cover of his journal, he inscribed his name and address as "John Muir, Earth-Planet, Universe."[3]

Muir made his field notes in a notebook tied to his waist, dated or not, sometimes at the front and other times at the back of the book. To his mind, hiking in the rain meant that his clothes would be clean. He was untroubled by mismatched garments, tangled hair, or an unkempt beard. As the product of an abstemious upbringing, he could survive on little, sometimes spending a whole day snacking on the crackers or bread he carried in his pocket and on the huckleberries and blueberries he found on the trail.

Influenced by geologist Louis Agassiz, Muir believed that the Sierra Nevada valleys had been formed by glacial action rather than by uprisings in the earth's crust. In Alaska, he would test his hypothesis, watching ice advance and recede from one day to the next, climbing over crevasses, planting stakes to check glacial movements, and examining bedrock and moraines. His accounts of hiking, canoeing, and camping in Alaska—filled with praise for the extraordinariness of what he'd found—appeared first in a newspaper in San Francisco and were subsequently published around the country.

Muir went to Alaska a total of five times, later venturing further afield. On his early trips, in 1879 and 1880, he remained in southeastern Alaska, often traveling with Tlingit Indian guides and a Presbyterian missionary named Hall Young. The Tlingits, who eventually became Muir's friends, at first found him strange. To their minds, only a witch would go out, as Muir did, to explore alone in heavy rains and sludgy snow. Meanwhile, Young was an amicable companion, despite the two men's different concepts of religion. Young thought that the Lord's Day should be spent resting in camp, while Muir preferred to spend the Sabbath, as Morgan Sherwood, says, "flying before the winds He sent, in order to hear what He had to say."[4] Young traveled, in part, to preach the gospel to the Natives; Muir, after a visit to one of his "noble ice rivers," would say that he had been to church and seen God. Muir's observations of whatever was put in his path—landforms, rocks, plants, weather, animals, and people—show that the divine was, for him, in all of it, that it all had merit and beauty.

"I care to live only to entice people to look at Nature's loveliness," he would later write,[5] and, in focusing the nation's attention on Alaska, he did just that. The response to his early newspaper stories about Alaska was so overwhelming that, according to historian Roderick Nash, they "almost single-handedly ... transformed the wilderness of Alaska from a liability to an asset so far as tourism was concerned."[6]

Muir's first stop in Alaska was at a place then called Fort Wrangel, now known as Wrangell and located on the island of the same name. The following piece was written shortly after he arrived on July 14, 1879. It first appeared in the *Daily Evening Bulletin* on September 6. When he stepped ashore, Muir found Wrangell so desolate that he was homesick for a bit, but he quickly recovered. After all, all that wilderness was out there waiting for him.

JOHN MUIR

Fort Wrangel, Alaska, August 8, 1879[°]

Wrangel Island is one of the thousands of picturesque bits of this cool end of the continent carved out of the solid by the ice of the glacial period—not by separate glaciers such as now load the mountain tops and flow, river-like, down the valleys, but by a broad, continuous ice-sheet that crawled slowly southward, covering all the land and much that is now sea, grinding on unhalting through unnumbered seasons, and modeling the comparatively simple and featureless pre-glacial landscapes to the marvelous beauty and variety of the present day.

The island is about fourteen miles long, separated from the mainland by a narrow channel or fiord, and trending north and south in the direction of the flow of the ancient ice sheet. From the tops of its highest hill down to the water's edge all around it is densely planted with coniferous trees that never suffer thirst in all their long century lives, that never have been wasted by fire, and have never yet been touched by the ax of the lumberman. Abundance of snow keeps them fresh and lusty through the winter, abundance of rain and soft, shady clouds makes them grow luxuriantly through the summer, while the many warm days, half cloudy, half clear, and the little groups of pure sun-days, enable them to ripen their cones and perpetuate the species in surpassing strength and beauty.

Wrangel is a rough place, the roughest I ever saw. No wildcat mining hamlet in the grizzly gulches of California, or in the remote recesses of the Sagebrush State, approaches it in picturesque, devil-may-care abandon. It is a moist dragglement of unpretentious wooden huts and houses that go wrangling and angling along the boggy, curving shore of the bay for a mile or so, in the general form of the letter S, but without manifesting the slightest subordination to the points of the compass, or to building laws of any kind whatever. Stumps and logs block its two crowded streets, each stump and log, on account of the moist climate, moss-grown and grass-tufted on their tops, but muddy and decaying at the bottom and down their sides below the limit of the bog-line. The ground in general is a degraded bog, oozy and slimy, too thin to walk in, too thick to swim in. These picturesque obstructions, however, are not much in the way, for no wheels of wagon or carriage ever turns here.

° From "Notes of a Naturalist," *San Francisco Daily Evening Bulletin*, September 6, 1879.

There is not a horse on the island, and but one cow. The domestic animals are represented by a few hogs of a breed well calculated to deepen and complicate and complete the mud, and a sheep or two brought on the steamer for mutton.

Indians, mostly of the Stickeen tribe, occupy the two ends of the town; the whites, of whom there is perhaps about forty or fifty, the middle portion, opposite the wharf; but there is no determinate line of demarcation, the dwellings of the Indians being mostly as large and as solidly built of logs and planks as those of the whites.

The fort is a quadrangular stockade with a dozen block and frame buildings, located upon dry, rising ground just back of the business part of town. It was built shortly after the purchase of Alaska by our own government, and was abandoned in 1872—reoccupied by the military in 1875, and finally abandoned and sold to private parties in 1877.

In the Fort and about it, there are a few good, clean homes and people, golden nuggets of civilization which shine all the more brightly in their sombre surroundings. The ground occupied by the fort, by being drained around the outside, is dry and wholesome, though formerly a portion of the general swamp, showing how easily the whole town could be made clean, at least as far as the ground is concerned. Were it removed as it is to the sunshine of California, with all its miry squalor, it would become a reeking centre of pestilence, but here beneath shady clouds, and washed by cool rains and the fresh briny sea, it is ever safely salubrious.

Although seeming to rest uneasily among mire and stumps, the houses squirming at all angles, as if they had been tossed and twisted by earthquake shocks, leaving but little more geometry in their relations to one another than may be observed among the moraine blocks of a glacier, yet Wrangel is a tranquil place—tranquil as the lovely bay and the islands outspread in front of it, or the deep evergreen woods behind it. I have never yet heard a noisy brawl among the people, nor a stormy wind in the streets, nor a clap of thunder, or anything like a storm-sound in the waves along the beach.

At this summer season of the year, the abundant rain comes straight down into the lush vegetation, steamy and tepid. The clouds are usually united, filling all the sky, not racing along in threatening ranks, suggesting energy of an overbearing destructive kind, but rather in the form of a bland, muffling, smothering, universal poultice. The cloudless days, too, which, by the way, are not half so rare in Alaska as seems to be generally guessed, are intensely calm, gray and brooding in tone, and inclining to Turkish meditation. The islands seem to float and drowse on the glassy waters, and in the woods not a leaf stirs. The air has an Indian-summerish haze along the horizon, and the same kind of brooding stillness but is without the mellow autumn colors.

The very brightest of Wrangel days are not what Californians would call bright. The sunshine is always tempered in sifting down through the moist atmosphere, allowing no dazzling brilliancy—no dry, white glare. The town, like the wild landscape, rests beneath this hushing spell. On the longest days, the sun rises about three o'clock, but it is daybreak at midnight. The cocks crow when they wake, without much reference to the dawn, for it is never dark. Cock-crowing is the one certain, invariable sound peculiar to civilization, but there are only a few, half a dozen or so all told, of full-grown roosters in Wrangel to awaken the town to give it Christian character.

After sunrise, a few smoke columns may be seen rising languidly to tell the first stir of the people. Then an Indian or two may be noticed here and there at the doors of their big barn-like cabins, and a merchant getting ready for trade, but scarcely a sound is heard, only a muffled stir gradually deepening. There are only two white babies in town as far as I have seen, and as for the Indian babies, they wake and feed, and make no crying sign. Later you may hear the strokes of an ax on firewood and the croaking of a raven.

About 8 or 9 o'clock, the town is awake and on its legs and in its boats. Indians, mostly women and children, begin to gather in scores on the front platforms of the dozen stores, sitting carelessly in the blankets, every other face blackened hideously, a naked circle around the eyes, and perhaps a spot over each cheekbone and on the tip of the nose where the smut has been weathered off. Some of the little children are also blackened and none are over-clad, their light and airy costume consisting of a calico shirt reaching only to the waist, as if even this flimsy material were sorely scanty, the whole weighing, when dry, about as much as a paper collar. Boys eight or ten years old often have an additional garment—a pair of castaway miner's overalls. These also are wide enough and ragged enough for extravagant ventilation. The larger girls and young women are quite brightly and extensively calicoed and wear jaunty straw hats, gorgeously ribboned, which glow among the blackened and blanketed old crones like scarlet tanagers in a flock of blackbirds.

Most of the women who load the store fronts can hardly be called loafers, for they have berries to sell, basketfuls of huckleberries, red and black, and of the large yellow salmon berries and bog raspberries, all looking fresh and clean, relieved most strikingly amid the surrounding squalor. They sit and wait purchasers until hungry, when, if they cannot sell them, they eat them and go to the hillside back of the town to gather more.

Yonder you see a canoe gliding out from the shore containing perhaps a man, woman and a child or two, all paddling in easy, natural rhythm. They are going to catch a fish, no difficult matter, and, when this is done, their day's work is done. Another party puts out to capture bits of driftwood, for it is easier to procure fuel in this way than to drag it down from the woods through the bushes.

As the dozy day advances, there is quite a fleet of canoes seen along the shore, all fashioned after one pattern, high and long beak-like prows and sterns, and with lines as fine as those about the breast of a wild duck. What the mustang is to the Mexico vaquero, the canoe is to the Coast Indians. They skim along the glassy sheltered waters to fish and hunt and trade, or merely to visit their neighbors, for they have family pride remarkably developed and are extremely sociable, meeting often to inquire after each other's health, to hold potlatches and dances, and to gossip concerning coming marriages, deaths, births, or the last murder, and how many blankets will be demanded as blood-money, etc. Others seem to sail for the pure pleasure of the thing, their canoe decorated with handfuls of the large purple epilobium.

Yonder you may see a whole family, grandparents and all, making a direct course for some island or promontory five or six miles away. They are going to gather berries, as the baskets tell. I never before in all my travels, north or south, found so lavish an abundance of wild berries as here. The woods and meadows are full of them, both on the lowland and far up the mountains among the glaciers—huckleberries of many species, salmon berries, blackberries, raspberries, currants and gooseberries; with serviceberries in the opener places and cranberries in the bogs, sufficient for every bird, beast and human being in the Territory and thousands of tons to spare.

Most of the permanent residents are engaged in trade. Some little trade is carried on in fish and furs, but most of the business of the place, and its real life, is derived from the Cassiar gold mines, some two or three hundred miles inland, by way of the Stickeen River. Two stern-wheel steamers ply on the river between Wrangel and the head of navigation, 140 miles up, carrying freight and passengers and connecting with pack trains which make their way into the mining region over mountain trails.

These mines, placer diggings, were discovered in the year 1874. About 1,800 persons are said to have passed through Wrangel this season for the mines, about one-half being Chinamen. Nearly one-third of the whole number set out from here in the month of February, traveling on the Stickeen River, which usually remains safely frozen until towards the end of April. The main body of the miners go up on the steamers in May and June.

On account of the severity of the winter, all are compelled to leave the mines about the end of October. Perhaps two-thirds of all engaged pass the winter in Portland, Victoria and in the little towns on Puget Sound. The rest remain here, dozing away the long winter as best they can.

I want to say a line or two about the missionaries here, some of whom are devoting themselves to the Indians, while others seem to be devoting themselves to themselves. This letter, however, is already too long.

The steamer *California* arrived this morning, bringing the monthly mail and a large quantity of freight for the mines and building material for a Presbyterian church in course of erection here. I had intended leaving Alaska for the present on her return trip and spending the remainder of the season in Washington Territory and Oregon. But I have found so much to interest me in this noble wilderness, and so much kindness among the people, that I shall stay awhile longer and push back as far as I can into the mountains by any way that offers.

Muir explored southeastern Alaska on foot and by canoe until December of 1879. On his way home, he stopped in Portland and lectured about his time in the north. Reports of that event led to first local and then national reprints of his *Daily Evening Bulletin* articles. In time, Muir's effusive writings about Alaska would make up only a segment of a prolific lifework, much of that in celebration of other places.

Nonetheless, the significance of those 1879 and 1880 newspaper articles cannot be ignored. In spotlighting Alaska's natural beauty and scenic wonders, Muir had been the first to focus public interest on Alaska. Roderick Nash says that, at a time when the nation was unaware of the value of Alaska's wilderness, "Muir was the first to chip away at the iceberg image."[7]

Muir returned to Alaska in 1881 on the revenue cutter *Corwin* as it sailed through the Bering Sea and along the coast of Siberia. Although the ship was on a mission to assist whalers in distress, the journey provided Muir with an opportunity to study the glaciers of that region. He revisited southeastern Alaska in 1890, then returned to Alaska again in 1899 as one of the luminaries on the combination scientific and pleasure cruise sponsored by Edward H. Harriman, traveling on the *George W. Elder*, a former excursion vessel that Harriman had refitted into a luxurious yacht.

Of the eleven books Muir published during his lifetime, only *Stickeen: The Story of a Dog* (1909) was related to his Alaskan experiences. At the time of his final illness, Muir was reworking the journals he had kept in 1879 and 1880 and upon which he had based his *Daily Evening Bulletin* articles. The unfinished manuscript of what was to be his last book, *Travels in Alaska* (1915), was on his bedside table when he died. It was left to others to complete and publish the work after Muir's death.[8]

Notes

Epigraph: John Muir, "Alaska Land," *San Francisco Daily Evening Bulletin,* September 25, 1880, reprinted by Enberg and Merrell, eds., *Letters from Alaska by John Muir* (Madison: University of Wisconsin Press, 1993), 66.

1 Engberg and Merrell, *Letters from Alaska,* xvi.

2 Haycox, *Alaska: An American Colony*, 197.

3 Richard Nelson, introduction, John Muir, *Travels in Alaska* (1915; repr. New York: Penguin Putnam, 1997), ix. Nelson citations are to the reprint edition.

4 Sherwood, *Exploration of Alaska*, 74.

5 John Muir quoted in Sherwood, *Exploration of Alaska*, 73.

6 Roderick Nash, "Tourism, Parks, and the Wilderness Idea," 6.

7 Ibid., *Wilderness and the American Mind,* 3rd ed. (New Haven: Yale University Press, 1967), 281.

8 Nelson, in Muir, *Travels in Alaska*, xviii.

2

CHARLES HALLOCK

A Great Day in Sitka

> My thoughts were full of the unknown land.
> The outlook seemed without a horizon. I felt more than
> ever foot-loose—like a candidate blind-folded for a first degree
> or a novice after the preliminary toss of a blanket. . . .
> "Going to Alaska! Going to Alaska!"

Charles Hallock, magazine editor and founder of *Forest and Stream* (the magazine that became *Field and Stream*), was one of those readers whose curiosity about Alaska was piqued by John Muir's pieces in the *Daily Evening Bulletin*.

Known as the "Dean of American Sportsmen," Hallock was a conservationist who questioned wasteful hunting and fishing practices. He wondered whether "the record of great counts [of fish caught] establish one's title to superiority as an angler" or merely prove the existence of "a super abundance of fish." Among other achievements, he originated a code of uniform game laws that was endorsed by the US Biological Survey.[1]

Hallock was enthusiastic about Alaska's potential. He devoted a goodly portion of *Our New Alaska; or, the Seward Purchase Vindicated* to cataloguing the territory's undeveloped resources—its timber, minerals, commercial and sport fisheries, wild game, and furs. In support of his belief that the Alaskan climate would support agriculture, Hallock cited the eleven edible berries that ripened in August, the strawberries that grew near the glaciers, and the lettuce in the markets of Sitka. Although the interior was still unknown, tourists erred if they assumed that the snow-covered mountains and glacial fields of southeast Alaska were what filled the rest of the territory.

En route to Alaska, Hallock watched as "Vassar Girls" scribbled in their diaries, recording the dining room's daily menus and the captain's *sotto voce* confidences. The ship's crew had pets—a bear named Pete, a black setter, a terrier, and a tomcat. In a daily ritual, the Chinese cook selected a chicken from the coop on the hurricane deck. When only one old rooster remained, he managed to escape and ran around the deck, while the cook, cleaver in hand, gave chase. The fowl managed to evade the cleaver—and the soup pot—only by flying into the sea.

Hallock's excursion was typical but far from ordinary, for "surely there was never scenery more grand, or climate more delectable."[2] He had seen salmon before, but never packed so tightly that a man could stretch out a plank and cross the water on their backs. In Alaska, one perspired only upon exercising and was always cool without being cold. The fog burned off by ten a.m., rain seldom fell, and insects—at least along the Inside Passage where Hallock was—were of no concern.

In the passage that follows, Hallock describes a visit to the vestiges of Sitka's Russian occupation. At the "castle," the former residence of the Russian governors, he attended a dance where Sitka's hodgedpodged population mingled. White settlers, miners, Indian men (Siwashes) and their mates (Klootchmen), and Creoles of mixed Russian and Native parentage—all chose their partners indiscriminately.

Hallock doesn't say what year he visited Alaska, but it was sometime prior to 1886, for that was the date of publication of his book. Regardless of the date, the little town of Sitka was in something of a general decline.

CHARLES HALLOCK

*A Great Day in Sitka**

It is a "great day" for sleepy Sitka when the steamer comes up to her wharf and makes fast. The whole town rubs its eyes and turns out.

Ever since the previous sailing day, when the last box of freight was leisurely trundled into the warehouse, it has been supremely quiet. There has been absolutely nothing to do. The government vessels are off on duty; the miners away at the diggings; the fishing season over; half the tenements vacant; no entries nor clearance at the custom house; the governor is sticking type in his printing office; and the attorneys are matching kopecks to see who shall win the next case. Down at the Indian "ranch" the dogs are dozing in

*From *Our New Alaska* (1886), 178–86.

the sun; occasionally a Siwash will stroll to the beach, and straighten out the mats which cover his canoe; a few of the mission boys at the far end of the village come in to visit their low-down relations; groups of ravens are picking offal out of the land wash; a few cows graze on the parade; the black balls of the signal office anemometer scarcely turn in the wind.

Meanwhile, the melting snow from the mountains trickles unceasingly into the sea, and the process of decay eats into the solid timbers of the old houses vacated by the Russians; the rickety wharf, all deserted, steams in the humid atmosphere, and the teredos bore insidiously into the piles below the water line.

The last time the steamer made fast to the dock, her stern-line pulled off a section of the worm-eaten piling, and the splash woke up a couple of Siwashes who had been dozing against the side of the warehouse ever since the trip before.

But "steamer day is an event." Then everything is different. The stars and stripes are run up from the marine barracks and custom house; all the public offices are open; the marshal is on the *qui vive,* and the attorneys have two pens behind each ear; the war vessel comes into port; the governor shaves and cleans up to receive his guests; tawdry klootchmen open up their basket-work, berries and curios at eligible stands; and the distracted post-master is "just too busy for anything." Even the cows on the parade are too curious to graze for looking at the stir.

As soon as the brass gun of the expected vessel booms among the islands of the bay, the wharf is crowded. There are just 300 white people in town, and that is enough to make a crowd. If the wharf should give way, it would engulf the whole population—Siwashes excepted. There are no drays nor omnibuses nor wagons to be seen, for there are none in town, and only one horse to draw them; no hotel runners, for there are no hotels; no loud-voiced newsboys, for there is but one paper in the place, and the editor is too modest to have it hawked under his nose; no boot-blacks, no policemen, no peanut-vendors, no little flower-girls, no anything that one might expect to see at the chief commercial port of one of the biggest territories in the world.

A few impatient passengers get ashore before the gangplank is laid, and perhaps ten minutes later the entire compliment of sightseers is scattered about the town. Into the Graeco-Russian church with its green-painted minaret and dome; into the museum of the marine barracks where there is a collection of native curios which makes collectors envious; up the "castle" on an eminence, which was once the pretentious residence of the governors; out to the Indian "ranch" along the shore front, and to the Indian mission on the curve of the beach, in the opposite direction; up to the queer-looking cemeteries on the ridge, white and native; and to the old block-houses and the stockade, and trading stores, the public offices and the photograph galley.

Indeed, there is "lots" to see in Sitka, and one can remain over one steamer and spend a month most agreeably, extending his observations to the environs, and for miles around. Miners and toughs, who come by every steamer, camp out in gipsy fashion, or roll up in their blankets in some of the vacant rooms in the barn-like dilapidated government buildings, but fair boarding places can be found by sojourners after a little inquiry. At the stores one can buy almost anything which is to be found at Victoria or Portland. Washing is done by the Russian families. There is no physician in the place except the naval surgeon, and it occurs to the author that a fine opportunity is offered for a worthy disciple of Aesculapius to establish himself in a good business at Sitka, as the native Alaskans need the services of a physician to an alarming extent.

During the twenty-four hours which the steamer is required by contract to remain in port, although she frequently stays two days, all the elite of the town—the "leading ladies," the Creoles, the pure-blood Russians, and the better Klootchmen, crowd aboard to see their metropolitan sisters, and inspect the latest fashions; the merchants and officials obtain their mail matter and invoices; the naval officers 'see the boys' and receive their magazines and newspapers; if there is any fresh beef or fruit to spare, it is immediately bespoken. Meanwhile, the busy Siwashes on the dock are unremittingly trundling freight, and small knots of privileged rustics wander all over the ship and inspect her fittings and machinery. Sometimes there is opportunity to make side excursions to points of interest, in respect to which the blue jackets are of essential service, as they have a steam launch and light boats and are always hospitable.

Festivities, too, are in order, and invitations are issued for a "grand ball" at the castle, *sans ceremonie,* toilets at discretion. The invitations are general, for the shore community is not large enough to cut up into castes. If it were critically culled, there wouldn't be waltzers enough to go round, for the American population, all told, is but sixty. So the floor is sifted over with spermaceti shavings, and an old brass relic of a Russian chandelier is filled with candles and hung up, while a couple of marines or waiters from the mail steamer do excellent duty as musicians with banjo and accordion. Slips and mishaps never mar such an occasion—never; they embellish it.

"Select your Klootchmen" and "swing your Siwash!" fill up the measure of shuffling feet, and the ball succeeds until the antiquated dust of all the Romanoffs is stirred. 'Twas ever thus in the ancient days, I'm told; for even then, no crucial distinctions could be made if the necessary components of a ball would be forthcoming. But alas! Not a vestige of the old glory remains to illuminate the dark bare walls. Desolation reigns throughout the empty halls, and the wind whistles mournfully through dozens of broken panes. Not a tenant holds the venerable places in the castle except the US signal man aloft who keeps his lonely vigils in the cupola on the roof.

In Sitka and northward, revelers, owls and such, find small indulgence for orgies claimed for hours of darkness, for the sun is bright at 3 o'clock a.m. and he goes home early who goes "when daylight doth appear." In the longest days, there is no interval of night so dark that all the stars are seen. Only the brightest of the planets outvie the twilight. So, long before the "wee sma' hours do come" the candles have burned down in their sockets, and the dancers in the castle repair to the parade for an Indian performance on the grass; or sometimes there is a wedding in the church. Once in a while, the fire company turns out for review, 48 men strong, with hose-cart, fire engine, and tin buckets, improvised from oil cans.

Some ten miles from town is Silver Bay, with a trout stream and a superb waterfall, which is often visited by excursionists who go in boats towed by a steam launch, which tail out behind in a most exhilarating way. Indeed, a steam launch of light draft is indispensable to pleasure or business in these parts. Six miles north is Old Harbor, where the Russian Baronoff [Baranov] built the first fort in 1799, calling it Archangel. Three years later, its garrison was massacred by Sitka Indians, and the present site of Sitka was occupied instead, and named New Archangel.

The Hot Springs are ten or eleven miles south of town, on the main land, in a little bay which is protected by a break-water of pretty islands. There are three mineral springs—two of warm magnesia, and one of hot sulphur, the density of which is indicated by heavy incrustations in their basins. The temperature ranges from one hundred and twenty to one hundred and twenty-five degrees. Almost every visitor claims to have boiled an egg in them, but I have yet to learn where each contrives to get his egg. It might be well for future tourists who like positive tests to provide themselves with eggs in Boston,

New York, San Francisco or New Orleans, so as not to be disappointed when they finally reach the places.

The old Baronoffs lived high. They enriched themselves from the furs of the land, and subsisted on the appropriations of the crown. All they earned was clear profit, and whenever perchance a prince of the blood came over the Strait from Siberia, he was royally entertained; moreover, their spiritual welfare was zealously cared for by the church, which is able even now, so many years after the retirement of the Muscovites, to maintain gratuitously its several missions at Sitka, St. Paul, St. Michael's, Anvic, Oonalashka, and Andreavsky. And so it happens that Greek priests still officiate for penitents of the great Republic, and the three little brass bells that were cast in Russia ring out from the tower of the Sitka sanctuary a Slavic melody for all Americans who respect the Sabbath.

It has taken a good while for the country to adapt itself to the changed circumstances which followed its relinquishment by the Russians. The Muscovites left everything in good order when they evacuated Sitka. Indeed, they wisely let go by degrees, and not all at once; and they still retain some hold on the missions which they established. Had they not done so, nine years of utter neglect would have left the place a useless ruin. That there is a house still standing is largely due to the fact that they built [it] of great logs, both hewed and round, and often two feet square. The substantial structures which they have erected have not only withstood the high winds of winter, but the wearing tooth of time, very well for a climate whose rainfall is 55½ inches per year, soaking everything with moisture. The principal buildings which are now occupied by the territorial and naval officers as custom-house, court-house, barracks, and government warehouse have at some time been coated with a dull yellow paint which still sticks to a degree; some of the roofs are either of iron painted red, or they have grown rusty from rain.

Once they were pretentious structures all, large, spacious, two-storied, with hard wood doors elaborately carved, and some regard paid to ornament in the shape of stained-glass panes inserted in parts to be effective, but now the foundation timbers are eaten half through by rot, some of the 6-inch planking of the floors has been torn up for fuel; piles of rubbish fill one-half of the apartments; and, with exception of the marine barracks, there is not one of all the lot with its window-glass unbroken or the plastering intact. A fire once cleared out several of the rooms in the custom-house and there the charred débris still remains. Only three rooms in the entire great building are fit to be occupied and two of these are used by the judge and attorney. I believe the governor has to "rustle" for his quarters. The grand old castle which crowns a rocky eminence that overlooks the town, and was once the pride of all the Baronoffs and Romanoffs, is now the worst of all the Badly-offs; and although it looks imposing in the uncertain twilight, nothing but immediate relief will save it from the assaults of time and weather.

So it is throughout the town. With its population reduced two-thirds and its business nine-tenths, with half the shops and dwellings tenantless, there is not a building of any kind I venture to say without a window broken. Nevertheless and withal, the town has still a habitable and homelike look. There are gardens filled with vegetables and flowers, geraniums in window pots, cows quietly grazing along the street. Occasionally the thrum of a piano is heard, which is blessed music in the wilderness, though intolerable in town.

Although Hallock thought Alaska's future showed great promise for the nation, he also thought—given the challenges—that it might be centuries before the heart of "this strange country"[3] was explored. Nonetheless, once economic opportunities arose and homesteading laws were passed, he believed that Americans would, as they had done in other parts of the country, migrate to Alaska, develop the territory, and exploit its resources. In the long run, Hallock said, the purchase of Alaska would prove to have been not only a bargain but a sound investment.

Notes

Epigraph: Hallock, *Our New Alaska: or, the Seward Purchase Vindicated* (New York: Forest and Stream Publishing Co., 1886), 10.

1 "Dean of American Sportsmen," Conservation Minnesota, July 27, 2012, http://www.conservationminnesota.org/news/headlines/the-dean-of-american-sportsmen/.

2 Hallock, *Our New Alaska*, 36.

3 Ibid., iv.

3

C.C. HINE

The Patriarch and His Little Detective

Half a mile back from the edge of the precipice we found a "beacon" or tripod of slender timbers.... On one of the sticks, a box was nailed and in the box was a memorandum book and pencil. Everybody who visited this spot was expected to register his name with the date of his visit. Being followers of the fashion, we recorded ours for the future admiration of those who might be followers of us.

When the Fire Underwriters' Association of the Northwest met in Chicago in 1889, they asked the man their called their "patriarch," Charles Cole Hine, to tell them about his Alaskan trip of the previous summer. Hine accompanied his lecture with one hundred and thirty photographs he'd taken with his "little harmless-looking detective" camera,[1] and these were projected with the aid of a magic lantern—a stereopticon.

A Trip to Alaska: Being a Report of a Lecture Given with Stereopticon Illustrations is a stenographic record of Hine's two-hour talk. The audience was said to have been so raptly attentive they stopped Hine only to applaud when some particularly fine view flashed before them. As Hine explains, he had been determined to get good shots, no matter the subterfuge required.

C. C. HINE

The Patriarch and His Little Detective[*]

We shipped for Alaska at Seattle on the good steamer *Geo. W. Elder*, Capt. J. C. Hunter, on the 17th of July a year ago, a company of a hundred and fifteen

*From A *Trip to Alaska* (1889), 7–11, 14–16, and 18–19.

men, women and children, bent on enjoying the trip and getting out of it all that it would yield—and we succeeded. In a gathering of that size, it is not an uncommon thing to find a quota of grumblers and kickers and fault-finders, but we were exceptionally fortunate, for there did not seem to be a single conspirator against the public peace on board the vessel.

Our captain was kindness itself, and the weather was phenomenal for that rainy country. Out of seventeen days consumed on the trip, fifteen were fair and many of them were sunny. While we were at the Glaciers, we had some cold winds, but most of the time the weather was all that could be desired. The water was smooth, the air bracing, the wooded hills along the shore and the snow mountains inland were constantly in sight, and we sailed in a panorama of beauty all the time, and in one of grandeur much of the time, from the hour we left the Seattle wharf until the hour when we moored at it again seventeen days later.

We traveled, going and coming, 2,500 miles on the waters of the Pacific Ocean, and we never lost a meal or suffered a single qualm of sea-sickness. Oh! It was a landlubber's paradise in which to go to sea. If you are compelled to travel on the ocean, always take the inside route.

We sailed between these islands and the mainland going and coming, and, if there could be such a thing as a surfeit of the picturesque, we had ample opportunity to experience it. After touching at Loring and Kasaan, we stopped at Wrangel, where the totem posts are; at Juneau, where the Yukon miners start into the interior; at Douglass Island, where the great Treadwell gold mine is located; at Killesnoo, at New Metlakahtla, and at Tongas [Tongass]. We spent a day at the great Muir Glacier, we visited Sitka, went up to Pyramid Harbor in the Chilcat country, and then retraced our way, sometimes passing through the same waters, at other times seeing new beauties as we struck a different route.

Our stop at the Kasaan fishing village was brief but full of interest. It was the first native settlement that we had had an opportunity to inspect, and the passengers scattered in every direction looking for souvenirs, which were purchased from the natives in the form of carved horn spoons, bangles, baskets, furs, etc. There is a cannery here, which appeared to be doing a thriving business.

The true village of Kasaan is inland a few miles. We did not visit it, but it was the scene of the operations of a notable old Russian smuggler named Baronovich, of whom many stories are told, whose operations were conducted so secretly as to defy detection by the government officers, who would visit his place and be received with open hospitality and a free invitation to search to their heart's content. After they had scoured the whole region and found nothing, Baronovich would invite them to dinner and before they got through would set a bottle of smuggled wine or liquor in front of each man!

The visit to Juneau was interesting, as that town is a depot for the miners who enter the upper Yukon country, and contains a number of stores where furs can be purchased and other articles secured as souvenirs of an Alaskan visit. Great quantities of garnets are offered by the Indians, and a handful can be bought for a dime. Specimens embedded in the rock in which they are found were interesting, and a great many of these were secured by the passengers of the *Elder.*

Having experienced much difficulty in getting pictures of the faces of Alaska women, a little strategy was resorted to at this point. Wherever a steamer lands the women come out with their merchandise, baskets, bangles, furs, etc., and sit on the ground with their backs to the sun and their goods spread out in front of them for sale. They have already become familiar with the tourist's camera, and when anyone undertakes to set up a tripod in front of them they turn away, or run away, or pull their blankets over their heads. There appears to be an idea among them that, in having their pictures taken, they lose something of vitality, or of life, or of something else, nobody knows what, but an ill-defined, intangible notion of hurt or loss appears to be associated in their minds with the camera. However, the little harmless-looking detective which I carried resembled a satchel as much as anything else and excited no suspicion, and whenever I found a group facing the sun, I could manage to get a picture very readily.

On the wharf at Douglass Island, a great number of these women were seated but their faces were all away from the light. As I came along the wharf, I sat down on the railing at a proper distance, and after the instrument was focused and all ready for its instantaneous snap, I screamed at the top of my voice. Of course, everybody turned around to see what the matter was, bringing their faces to the sun, and, at the opportune instant, the little instrument clicked and a picture was secured with the faces of a dozen women plainly visible. At other points, more or less generalship had to be exercised to catch the faces of these native women, but I was fairly successful in a number of my experiments in that direction.

Chimneys are as yet an unknown luxury among the untutored natives. They build their fires in the middle of the floor on a place prepared for that purpose, and the smoke escapes through a hole in the roof. Dogs form a very important part of the Indian household; at some places they appeared to be in droves, and their daily experiences were not unmixed with those infelicities which are apt to accompany savage life; the biggest dog always got the best fish and the little fellow not unfrequently got nothing at all—except a shaking up.

At Tongas, we made a critical and detailed examination of the cannery which was in operation there, and the result is that we give our verdict in favor of Alaska salmon. We watched the operation from the time the fish was alive and flopping on the end of the wharf until he was sealed up in the cans ready for shipment within an hour after he left the water. The fishes were wheeled in barrow-loads to the place of execution, where a Chinaman at one end of a table whacked off the head, tail and back fins, and, disemboweling him, slid him across to where he fell into a tank of running water. Here he was washed, taken out, scraped and shoved along again into another tank, from the further end of which he was fished out and chopped into three or four pieces, and slid along a platform to the canning machine, whose claws drew him down into what in many respects looked like a large old-fashioned sausage-stuffer, to which the cans were rapidly fed on an inclined plane.

As each came opposite the proper place, it was stuffed full and shoved along to where a man put it under a press and forced hot water into it. From here it went onto a table around which a half-dozen Chinamen and Indians were engaged with little wooden mallets hammering on the tin tops. When covered, the cans were run through a trough of melted solder, rolling along at an angle so that only the rim of the top passed through the metal, and when a can came out at the further end, it was hermetically sealed.

A pin-hole was then made in the top and the cans were packed on an iron platform on wheels, about twelve dozen at a time, and rolled into an oven where they were kept until sufficiently cooked. As they were taken out of the oven, a drop of solder was put upon each pin-hole and the cans were then ready to be labeled and boxed. The whole process appeared to be clean, and it was so expeditious that the fish in the cans were certainly fresh, not having been out of their native element more than an hour or two when they were transformed into articles of commerce.

While Hine was walking along the shore at Muir Glacier, a huge chunk of ice—the size of the Grand Pacific Hotel in Chicago, site of the underwriters' annual meeting—calved into the ocean and threw water two hundred feet into the air. Hine escaped the resulting six-foot wave by running up a bank. His fellow passenger, a young woman on the beach, was not as lucky and was drenched in ice water to her waist. As was his wont, Hine seized the opportunity to snap two or three good shots of the event.

Some of the *George W. Elder's* excursionists were musicians who entertained in the evenings with tunes on the piano, banjo, and violin. After their visit to Wrangell, jolly young men gathered on deck and constructed totems, mounting higher and higher on each other's shoulders until the whole tower collapsed "into hilarious ruin."[2] Four clergymen could be counted on for "delightful" Sunday services, while the children onboard darted among the forty rocking chairs scattered about the decks—all of which were almost continuously occupied. At the conclusion of the voyage, the ship's passengers collected funds for a gift of silver for their captain.

Hine also wrote handbooks about insurance matters and a book-length poem entitled *Mrs. Leary's Cow: A Legend of Chicago.* That poem presents a cautionary tale about the risks of inadequate insurance coverage, is illustrated with cartoons of the Great Chicago Fire, and opens with these lines: "This is the cow, at the Leary back gate, / Where she stood on the night of October the 8th."[3]

Notes

Epigraph: Hine, *A Trip to Alaska: Being a Report of a Lecture Given with Stereopticon Illustrations* (Milwaukee: King, Fowle and Company, 1889), 21.

1 Hine, *Trip to Alaska*, 14.

2 Ibid., 25.

3 C. C. Hine, *Mrs. Leary's Cow: A Legend of Chicago* (New York: The Insurance Monitor, 1872), 3.

4

SEPTIMA M. COLLIS

The Alaska Barnum's Dancers

My sole object is to put on paper …
the impressions made upon me by the voyage, and to
explain how this delightful excursion can be enjoyed without
the slightest fatigue or discomfort, and at a trifling expense.…
The ship is a yacht, of which the Captain is the host, the
passengers his guests, and the object of the cruise
the pursuit of pleasure.

New Yorker Septima Collis was one of 5,007 excursionists who toured southeast Alaska in the summer of 1890.[1] Originally a native of Charleston, Collis had, as she said, "desert[ed] to the enemy" by marrying a northerner.[2] Having eagerly read everything she could about Alaska, she booked an excursion after her husband, Civil War general Charles Henry Tucky Collis, suggested that she "run up to Alaska"[3] rather than spend her usual summer at Saratoga.

A Woman's Trip to Alaska opens with a note of congratulation from an old friend, General William T. Sherman, and is illustrated with some of the author's own "Kodak'd" scenes. Collis dedicated the book to her daughter, Amelia, and, while she recommended the trip, she also advised Amelia and anyone else considering it to take along smoked glasses, a fur-lined cloak, a muff—preferably sealskin—and a pair of worn, low-heeled shoes with nails protruding from the soles to grip the surface of the glacial ice.

After setting out from her Fifth Avenue home, Collis traveled by rail to the West Coast, with stops in Chicago, Minneapolis, and Yellowstone Park. In Tacoma, she boarded the PCSC's *Queen,* where she found everything to her taste and "in apple-pie order."[4] The ship was brilliantly lit with electric lights from stem to stern and supplied with all of the comforts an exacting tourist might demand—outside rooms only, a promenade that ran the length of the ship, and a fresh coat of glossy white paint. Collis had only to whisper a word of complaint about her accommodations before she was speedily relocated to larger quarters with an adjoining room for her baggage.

The other passengers—some of them on a second Alaskan voyage—hailed from St. Louis, Philadelphia, New York, and London, the sort "whose good breeding naturally tends to a regard for the comfort of their companions. . . . scientists, savants, authors, and artists of renown from all parts of the world."[5] The ship plowed along at the rate of fifteen miles an hour through a "thousand islands of emerald and crimson"[6] on a sea as still as glass. The meals were "so excellent, so hot, and of such variety"[7] that Collis never slept late for fear of missing breakfast.

Her twelve-day excursion was filled with lovely weather, waterfalls, seals, porpoises, salmon, eagles, and Indian canoes. There were the confidences from her genial host, Captain Carroll—a character who once offered to buy Alaska as a publicity stunt. As the story goes, he also may have been a liquor smuggler, who, in an unlikely alliance with missionary Sheldon Jackson, attempted to secure liquor licensing in Alaska.[8]

Collis's condescending attitude toward the Tlingits Indians was characteristic of her day. By all accounts, the plight of Alaskan Natives in 1890—at least in the towns of southeastern Alaska—was pitiful. They were consigned to areas called "rancheries," where tourists felt free to roam about, poking their heads in houses to examine the Natives' living conditions. Thus, by the time of Collis's visit, the Natives of southeastern Alaska had been consigned to the status, as John Muir said, of "tamed eagles in barnyard corners."[9]

The arrival of the tour boats in southeast Alaska also had serious economic repercussions for the Indians. Genuine Native artifacts were quickly snatched up, and, by the time of Collis's visit, those remaining were priced beyond the reach of the ordinary tourist. Sales of original articles had given way to "curios"—baskets, jewelry, carvings, and other knickknacks—manufactured by Natives working overtime during the long winters and peddled to tourists during the summer season.[10]

In Juneau, Collis attended a Tlingit dance performance, which she describes here. The show was another entrepreneurial venture designed to generate revenue and, at least to Collis and her companions, a huge success.

SEPTIMA M. COLLIS

*The Alaska Barnum's Dancers**

Juneau, like Sitka, is nestled at the foot of a range of sheltering mountains. As I approached it, I wondered what would become of the adults if the small boys should take it into their heads to bombard them with snowballs from the tops of the mountains, which abruptly rise two thousand feet from the end of every street. I consider Juneau as prettily located as any city I have ever seen, and when the rich fields of gold which surround it are developed, it will very likely attain much commercial prominence.

From the bay, Juneau has the appearance of some systematic regularity of construction, but when you land it has quite the contrary; in fact, to quote the language of my companion, it "looked as if it had been built late on a Saturday night and never finished."

It is really a mining camp, founded by Joseph Juneau and Richard Harris just ten years ago this autumn, and yet it is to-day the most important commercial point upon the entire coast. This is owing to the existence of the gold placer mines of the Silver Bow Basin immediately back of the shore, many of them having been worked out, but leaving behind them the best evidences of the precious mineral awaiting the advent of capital. A serious embarrassment, however, exists as to the real ownership of the different properties, and these titles, I presume, will have to be adjusted before the risk is assumed of advancing the large sums necessary for intelligent exploration and experiment.

The streets of the town seem to follow the gulches or ravines, and the architecture is exceedingly primitive. There are three or four interesting shops at which may be purchased every known Esquimaux curio, and two or three where may be seen an excellent collection of sable, marten, lynx, silver-fox, and other furs. The signs indicate that the traders are not wedded to specialties, but keep a stock of varieties always on hand. One of them, of which I took a note, read as follows: "Whipsaws, potatoes, new onions, carrots, and wall-tents."

I spent a considerable portion of my time in the store of Messrs. Kohler & James, who, I believe, are the successors of the Northwest Trading Company. Here I had an opportunity of witnessing the system of barter and trade carried on between the Indian hunter and the white trader. Upon arriving in

*From *A Woman's Trip to Alaska* (1890), 164–74.

town with the skins, the red man visits every shop and trader before he parts with his supply, and he who is finally the highest bidder gets it. When the bargain is consummated, the Indian receives in payment a number of blue or red tickets, which are taken by the store-keeper in exchange for such commodities as he may require to carry back to his Innuit home, perhaps somewhere near the head-waters of the Yukon.

From this store, I carried off some beautiful furs at most reasonable rates and hoped to be the possessor of a much-coveted sable rug of thirty skins but failed to convince the trader that my valuation of it was a just one. In fact, the only regret I carried with me from Alaska was that I had not given what was asked for this rug, but my information then was to the effect that prices were specially prepared for tourists, which, I am now convinced, is not the case, certainly not at the store of which I speak. Just as the ship was leaving Juneau, I determined to hurry back and purchase it, but I was admonished by the Captain that "time and tide wait for no man," nor woman either, so I simply just gazed at that shop with a melancholy and rueful countenance, and the increasing distance, I assure you, lent the view no enchantment. (I ought to say here in a parenthetical whisper that the day I returned home to New York, I was surprised to find that dear coveted robe spread out upon the sofa in my library.)

Before leaving Tacoma, we had been handed a printed programme of a "native dance, by the renowned dancers of the Thlinkit tribe of Alaska Indians, under the management of D. Martini, the Barnum of Alaska, and the celebrated Taku Chief, Yash Noosh, head chief of one of the most warlike tribes of Alaska, but have succumbed to the influences of civilization. Admission $1. Children 50 cts. The performance will commence immediately after the arrival of the excursion steamer at Juneau, Alaska."

When we arrived, this Alaska Barnum, wearing a high stove-pipe hat, in company with Yash Noosh himself, not in the garb of a warlike Indian chief, but in that of a quiet guardian of the public peace, commonly called a policeman, met us at the dock and begged to inform us that the performance had been postponed until two o'clock, and they did this with an air of people who seemed to think we had come there simply to see their "greatest show on earth." While this ceremony was taking place, a savage noise of human voices and beating of drums came from a long tent on the beach, which, of course, we recognized as the place of performance. Very few of the passengers were willing to be humbugged by the man with the high hat and the policeman, yet our little party, which, by friendships created on the tour, might now number eight or ten persons, resolved to "take it in," as one of the gentlemen expressed it. We went; we were not "taken in." Those who failed to go were the only ones who were cheated and they cheated themselves.

It was a remarkable performance—picturesque, barbarous, unexplainable, and unique. The theatre itself was a long tent, with a platform curtained off by the commonest white muslin, rows of pine benches for seats, and a little dressing-room in the rear. The audience consisted of twenty-one persons who paid one dollar each, while the performers numbered about thirty men, women, and children in every imaginable garb, from the ultra-aboriginal to that of the present time. The tent was insufferably warm and smellful, the glare of sunlight through the thin canvas intense, so that the use of parasol and lavender salts was indispensable; the stray Indian squaws and their offspring sitting around the floors were repulsive. Nevertheless, with all its unattractive surroundings, I would not have missed it.

There was no humbug about the *dramatis personae*, the wardrobe, or the implements, and, therefore, I presume, none about the authenticity of the dances themselves. Two or three of the men, clad from neck to feet in skin-fitting white kid (much soiled), were most graceful specimens of perfect anatomy and agility; one or two of the women were quite attractive, but others were hideously painted, horribly shaped, and were either semi-idiotic or under the influence of *hoochinoo* (though I saw no evidence that any of them could procure liquor in the town).

I was specially moved to pity by a little girl about nine years old, evidently a half-breed, a truly pretty child, with beautiful eyes and fine features, a little gypsy creature who sat in a filthy calico dress, her only garment, and a bright red handkerchief across her black matted hair; the industry of her little fingers told the story of the lack of care of which this neglected bit of humanity was the victim; and in all her squalid loneliness, my mother instincts went out to her and I wished with all my heart that I could have saved her, body and soul.

I was so thoroughly unprepared for the scenes which the lifting of the curtain developed and paid so little attention to the explanations made by the Indian policeman, who was master of the ceremonies, or his interpreter, that I am unable to individualize the different dances. They all seemed alike, except one representing the incantations of the Shaman. As the cotton sheet was drawn aside by a pair of dusky hands, Indians of both sexes were discovered seated around the stage beating drums and singing a most discordant, monotonous, and dirge-like song; then from the little annex came a procession of dancers, male and female, dressed in buckskin and feathers, with horribly painted faces, each wearing on the head a hollow crown filled to the top with the down of the eagle's breast.

The dance commenced by a very slow forward movement of the body, the progress made being not more than an inch at each step, and while the whole anatomy was kept in constant motion, the principal feature of it was a jerky, forward movement of the head, a throwing out and drawing back of the chin, as it were, and a corresponding lifting of the shoulders; this, of course, agitated the eagle's down in the crowns, and in a few minutes the entire tent, stage and auditorium was a snow-storm. As the dancers became warmed to their work, which was manifested by the feathers completely covering their perspiring faces, giving them a Santa Claus expression that was very funny, their legs began to loosen, and tripped a cadence not unlike the old-fashioned Virginia break-down, while the totem-sticks, paddles, salmon-hooks, knives, and implements of warfare were flourished aloft in a most careless and hazardous fashion.

The peculiarity of the exhibition was that the dancing was palpably intended to give expression to some thought, and the looks of disdain, contempt, hate, rage, and tender love would have been appreciated even by Salvini. Some danced barefooted, others wore red socks; one or two women were robed in exquisite Thlinkit embroidered blankets, robes of fur graced the shoulders of others, and one wore an entire skirt of ermine.

The Shaman dance would not have been given but that we insisted upon the programme being carried out. It appeared that the Doctor was disgruntled about something—perhaps the "beggarly array of empty benches" disappointed him, and no wonder, for when he did finally play his part, it was so exhausting that he could hardly arise from the sitting posture which he assumed from the first. His was a dance of the arms, hands, shoulders, mouth, and eyes. It was a sorcerer's appeal, keeping time to the thumping of drums on the rear seats—the whites of his eyes were rolled upwards during the whole time, his head rocked from side to side, his fingers clawed the air, and his teeth fastened themselves in his lips during the fervor of his invocations. It was a weird spectacle, and if it didn't succeed in driving the worst evil spirit that ever lurked around a sick-chamber out of the window, it's a very great wonder.

We did not hesitate to express to the Alaska Barnum our commendation of his exhibition, and all voluntarily recorded our opinions of it in a book which, at our suggestion, he procured for our signatures, so that it might impress the tourists who followed us, Mr. Policeman Yash Noosh having informed the spectators that it was to be a permanent institution, and I hope it may prove so. It was my good fortune to be able to purchase the totem-pole which conspicuously figured in the evolutions, but I suppose it has since been replaced by another.

During the excursion season, daily life in the little towns of southeastern Alaska centered on the arrival of the cruise ships. One of the draws of the early Alaskan excursions was the opportunity for tourists to see Indians still living in something of an aboriginal state, and sales to tourists of Native-made trinkets allowed the indigenous people to acquire incomes and to improve their living conditions. The availability of ready spending money, however, resulted in the Indians' increased dependence on the tourist trade and the white traders' goods, and further chipped away at their cultural integrity.

In the summer of 1902, Collis was summering in Russia when she learned that General Collis had fallen ill. She set out to return to New York, and was in Paris when she learned that the general had died. The couple's two sons and daughter Amelia were at his bedside.[11] Collis herself lived abroad for the next fifteen years and died in 1917 at Aix-les-Bain, France.[12]

Notes

Epigraph: Collis, *A Woman's Trip to Alaska; Being an Account of a Voyage Through the Inland Seas of the Sitkan Archipelago in 1890* (New York: Cassell Publishing, 1890), preface.

1 Nash, "Tourism, Parks and the Wilderness Idea," 7.

2 Septima M. Collis, *A Woman's War Record* (New York: G. P. Putnam's Sons, 1889), 1–2.

3 Collis, *Woman's Trip to Alaska*, 1.

4 Ibid., 45.

5 Ibid., 193.

6 Ibid., 70.

7 Ibid., 71.

8 Hinckley, *Americanization of Alaska*, 208–9.

9 John Muir quoted in Nash, "Tourism, Parks and the Wilderness Idea," 7.

10 Campbell, *In Darkest Alaska*, 162.

11 "Gen. C. H. T. Collis Dead," *New York Times*, May 12, 1902.

12 "Mrs. S. M. Collis Dead in France," *New York Times*, July 29, 1917.

5

CHARLES M. TAYLOR, JR.

Riding the Rails through White Pass Canyon

We, sitting in our comfortable compartments,
know nothing of the experience of those days of close
communion with nature … the magnetism of continuous
contact with Mother Earth. It is true we have gained much
in these days of wonderful scientific knowledge,
but we have lost something as well.

In 1900, Philadelphian Charles Taylor travelled to Montreal, where he boarded the luxurious Imperial Limited for his cross-Canada train trip to Alaska. Taylor was a photographer as well as a travel writer, and he illustrated his *Touring Alaska and the Yellowstone* with photographs he took along the way.

After a stop for carriage rides at Banff, the train traversed the Selkirk Mountains, skirted the Kicking Horse River, and breezed by a place named Beaver Mouth Station. As the locomotive dashed along at twenty-five miles an hour, the engineers met sudden curves with "cool nerves and the utmost confidence."[1] Outside the window of his railcar, Taylor watched as squaws bent over their beadwork and pioneer women, surrounded by sunburned tots, stood in their doorways.

Passage from Seattle was on the PCSC's *Queen*, whose motto was "Safety, Speed and Comfort." While the ship sailed past a panorama of mountains, cascades, and forests, the captain's little terrier, Muggins, amused the passengers with his antics. After a daily two-mile constitutional around the deck, excursionists read and played cards in the ship's saloon as a piano tinkled in the background. Miners, reclining on coiled ropes, talked over their exploits, and Taylor enjoyed the company of one such fellow until he realized that the man wanted him to invest in some mining scheme.

At Ketchikan, the *Queen* tied up level with the dock, but then the tide fell and the dock was fifteen feet above the ship. The coming 4th of July celebration promised an Indian canoe race, a rock-drilling contest, and a tug-of-war—whites versus Indians. But once Taylor spotted a street crowd gathered around the body of a suicide, he concluded that the place held little attraction for the tourist.

When Taylor visited Wrangell in 1900, it was no less ramshackle than it had been when John Muir had visited twenty years earlier. The totems there were said to be the best in Alaska but were fast disappearing. Muir himself had watched an "archeological doctor" order one cut down and supervise removal of the finest section so he could take it home.[2]

After a visit to Juneau—where the 2,500 residents supported newspapers, breweries, a hospital, and an opera house—the *Queen* crossed Gastineau Channel for a tour of the Treadwell mines. There, the stamp mill ran every day except Christmas and the Fourth of July, smashing quartz to bits to recover a pea-sized lump of gold from a ton of crushed rock.[3] When Taylor visited, the Treadwell had been in operation less than ten years but had already produced seventeen million dollars worth of gold and created thousands of jobs.[4] At the tour's conclusion, the excursionists were invited to fill their pockets with gold dust. As the manager told them, "The company can well afford these small robberies by the tourists."[5]

The *Queen* sailed on to Skagway, a settlement that had mushroomed from a few tents a decade earlier to a town of between five and eight thousand residents. The place boasted wharves, landing facilities, electric lights, and drinking water piped in fresh from the glacier. A local newspaper claimed that half a million in gold had been brought in from the Klondike in one shipment and sent south.

Skagway's growth had been boosted by the building of a rail line that snaked up the mountains above Skagway and on into Canada. This new transportation route meant prospectors no longer had to engage in what had been for some a deadly proposition—crossing White Pass on foot. Later in this collection, gold-seeker Robert Kirk describes the perils of the trail before the advent of the railroad. But by 1900, when Charles Taylor arrived, anyone headed for the goldfields would have an easier time of it—at least on the part of his or her journey that led over White Pass.

Taylor had come to Skagway at just the right moment, for he would be one of the first passengers to travel on the newly constructed railway. As he describes here, he traveled alongside some of the men who had helped construct the line.

CHARLES M. TAYLOR, JR.

*Riding the Rails through White Pass Canyon**

We turn our attention to the trip over the White Pass to Lake Bennett and Bennett City. With little difficulty, we persuade our accommodating captain to hold his steamer in port until we have made this expedition. The distance is eighty-two miles, and a special rate of ten dollars each is made for our passengers. Freight costs sixty dollars a ton from Skagway to Lake Bennett.

The construction of the road was begun February, 1898, and finished February 22, 1899. The cost was $1,000,000 to the White Pass summit and another million thence to Lake Bennett.

This is a glorious day; the sun shining in all his splendor and the sky of purest blue give the keynote to the grand harmony about us. With light hearts and favorable prospects, we leave Skagway at nine o'clock in the morning. This is a narrow-gauge road, and the coaches are spacious and comfortable. Most of the passengers crowd into an observation car, which offers an unobstructed view of the scenery around us.

Our train consists of three observation cars, one drawing-room coach, and two freight cars. In our party are Captain Wallace of the Steamship Queen; Mr. John Hislop, constructing engineer; and Mr. M. J. Heney, contractor. We are running through acres of burnt forests and clearings, in which scores of small frame houses have been erected. On many of these are visible the signs "For sale" or "For Rent."

After passing the second station, we begin the ascent to the White Pass Summit, an altitude of 2,806 feet. The average grade is three and ninety-one hundredths. At Skagway River, we are stopped by the information that the trestle bridge, over which we are about to pass, has been reported as unsafe in consequence of high waters; and that passengers and baggage must be transferred to the inferior cars awaiting us on the opposite side of the river. The delay and the prospect of the second-class coaches rather dampen our ardor; but we accept the inevitable as gracefully as possible. As we mount higher and higher, our enthusiasm returns, and we enjoy the magnificent panorama before us. Lofty mountains tower above us giving the impression of massive strength and eternal endurance.

The ascent is continuous to Rocky Point, 500 feet above the plain; thence the road turns and we are carried over a wooden trestle, whose light and airy

*From *Touring Alaska and the Yellowstone* (1901), 201–18.

character awakens in our minds grave doubts as to its strength, and we contemplate gravely the fearful possibility of being suddenly precipitated from its height into the wild canyon beneath. As I gaze down into the dreadful abyss, and realize that an accident would mean a clear drop of six or seven hundred feet, I wonder still more at the genius and daring of the projectors of this railroad. This is the famous White Pass Canyon, once dreaded by all travelers in this region.

A great forest fire is raging on the opposite mountain-side, destroying acres of beautiful woodland. The flames are borne to a great height by the winds, and tossed hither and thither as though some gigantic demons were waving their crimson torches in every direction. The center of the conflagration appears like a vast cauldron, red and glowing with the intensity of the blaze. These fires are of frequent occurrence in this densely wooded section, originating, most probably, in the sparks from passing locomotives. They rage until they have completely exhausted their fuel, unless a heavy rain intervenes.

We mount higher and higher, drawn by two powerful engines, whose boilers seem ofttimes about to burst with their strenuous efforts. In the distance, the charming waters of Lynn Canal are visible, and the town of Skagway nestling picturesquely at the foot of her mountain. It is impossible to give an idea of the wild grandeur and beauty of the views above, below and around us. New visions of harmony, of peaceful loveliness, of rugged defiance, of sublime majesty constantly pass before our wondering eyes. We say at each point, "Surely nothing can surpass this!" And while we are yet speaking, a glory bursts upon us that transcends them all. It is utterly vain to attempt any description of these scenes. They are beyond all feeble efforts of tongue or pen.

An immense gateway, through which we pass, is cut in the solid rock called blue granite. Swiftly, we whirl under the canopy of the Hanging Rocks, whose huge boulders project ten to twelve feet over our heads, and weigh hundreds of tons. We are out of their shadows ere we have time for a passing thought of their enormous size and powers. Mr. Heney informs me that some of the cuttings through these granite rocks are seventy and eighty feet deep. They are made by blasts of Black Giant powder, of which from nine to ten thousand pounds are used for one explosion. In the largest of these, twelve thousand pounds of powder were used, and the recoil was so great that the mountains seemed to tremble at the concussion. Boulders, weighing thousands of tons, are scattered along our line of travel.

Still ascending; still awestruck, or mute with excess of delight! No point is without its majesty, no depth without its charm. Down in the picturesque valley is the gleam of half a score of tents, probably a little colony of travellers to or from the gold fields. Traces of many other campers are visible as we steam along. Here and there piles of tin cans may be seen, sometimes assuming the proportions of hills from fifty to sixty feet high, with a base from seventy five to one hundred feet in length. These must be the accumulation of years.

It has been stated that previous to the construction of this railroad, from twenty-five hundred to three thousand packhorses were killed or disabled while making the journey from Skagway to Dawson City during the winter and spring of 1898. A speculator, it is said as an experiment, bought twenty packhorses to hire out for transporting merchandise from Skagway to Dawson City and charged five dollars a day for each horse. On the first trip, but two horses out of the whole number reached Dawson City. The others perished on the way.

Here is the continuation of the old pack road over the White Pass, and I listen to another story in connection with this road. I will leave the reader to decide for himself how much truth there is in it. A miner one day plodded wearily over the trail, following closely in the footsteps of his horse, until they reached a pass at a great altitude, when suddenly the animal made a determined stand, and refused to proceed. His master urged him onward with all the means, both gentle and violent, at his command, but the beast moved neither forward nor backward—finally, with an almost human expression, he looked about him, shook his head, and deliberately jumped over the side of the precipice, choosing death, rather than the prospect before him. This incident has given the name Suicide Rock to the crag which stands out so prominently at this point.

In the valley, a thousand or more feet below, there is a little settlement, called White Pass City. It is of sudden growth, and consists of perhaps a score of frame houses, presumably the homes of foresters. It has been estimated that during the seasons of 1897 and '98, when the gold fever was at its height, at least ten thousand emigrants were encamped on this spot, on their way to the Klondike.

Many beautiful cascades and waterfalls may be seen, sparkling on the mountain-sides. Sometimes we pass almost through their silvery spray. One of the most striking of these makes a descent of fifteen hundred feet, but half-way down the mountain wall, it breaks into three lovely graceful cascades, from which it has received the name of Pitchfork Falls. Another, if possible, more picturesque still, is the North Fork Falls, which comes leaping and foaming from its lofty source, glistening in the sunlight and singing a glad song as it hastens away to the valley.

We are at an elevation of fifteen hundred feet, and seem so far removed from ordinary travel that we feel as though we are wandering among the clouds. A fellow-traveler entertains me with interesting tales of adventures experienced during the pioneer days, before the possibility of such a road as this was dreamed of. In those days, he travelled over the old "Tote Road," and paid as much as fifty cents a pound for the transportation of his goods to the Klondike or Dawson City.

As we ascend, more waterfalls appear and near the snowline the temperature is cooler, and the air fresher. As we whirl around the precipitous mountain-side at an altitude of 2,000 feet, one instinctively holds his breath, and feels his hair rise to an angle of forty-five degrees, especially if he is standing on the platform of the car, looking down into the wild canyon below. I certainly feel chills running down my back and wild phantoms flit across my brain.

We reach the Main Gorge, shoot by it, and quickly attain the Summit Gorge. Here great torrents make a mad rush over the rocks, and leap into the Skagway River at the foot of the mountain. The engine sounds its sonorous whistle, and I look ahead. Before us are large blasting operations, and rocks of every size and shape are scattered in all directions. In the distance, at the very edge of the precipice, is a tunnel. Before we enter this, we cross a rough wooden trestle, spanning a wild cascade, and follow the Glacier Gorge. As I look upon the scene before me, I am filled with admiration for the brains that conceived, the brave spirits that executed such a fine piece of engineering.

The tunnel is about three hundred feet long and fully two thousand feet from the surface of the earth. During its construction, I am told by the contractor, the workmen were let down by strong ropes, and held almost in mid-air, while drilling and blasting.

There is no fear regarding the durability of this road-bed, for it has existed since the beginning of the earth, and is composed of solid granite, whose natural foundation is two thousand feet in depth. Upon this immovable support, the railroad finds its perch. These wooden trestles spanning the gorge are to be replaced with structures of iron and steel.

At the tunnel, we are switched back, and train and engine are reversed. Our altitude now is 2,200 feet. As we stop to adjust the engine and train, I walk away from the track, about a hundred feet, and from a deep crevasse gather huge snowballs, with which I pelt the passengers to the amusement of all of us. Think of a genuine snowball fight on the twenty-ninth day of June, with the sun shining brightly down upon us!

During the winter months, severe gales rage through these gorges and the temperature falls to thirty-five degrees below zero. Much credit is due to the excellent management and system of this railroad company for the fact that during the whole winter season, there were only three weeks of impassable roads by reason of heavy snow-drifts. With the exception of these, the trains made their runs in all kinds of weather, forcing a passage through almost insurmountable obstacles. One of the snow cuts, I am told, through which engines and trains passed, was thirty feet in depth.

As the summit is reached, an expression of relief dawns upon every countenance. Within a few rods of the station is a beautiful lake, with clear cool waters, which, we are told, abound in mountain trout and white fish. This lake is at an elevation of 2,886 feet. The view from the summit fills us with delight, notwithstanding the many magnificent scenes through which we have passed. Groups of icy mountain crests surround us, glistening in the sun like great diadems of precious stones. Everything about us seems to gleam and scintillate.

I am invited by some of my companions to take a glass of beer in a small frame building close by, with the words Stage Saloon painted over the door. The beverage is cool and refreshing, and costs seventy cents a quart.

When the *Queen* departed Skagway, Captain Wallace sailed for a place that was a standard stop on the tourist itinerary, Glacier Bay. A severe earthquake in October of 1899 had caused significant damage to the face of Muir Glacier and, as a consequence, the bay was clogged with enormous bergs. Nevertheless, Wallace wanted to give his passengers a close-up view of the destruction and used the *Queen's* reinforced prow to repeatedly ram the ice pack. He was able to sail within four miles of the glacier, where passengers could see that the face of the glacier, formerly upright, had been sheared off and that the glacial ice sloped upward away from the water's edge for miles.

Before the captain realized what was happening, the *Queen* had become wedged in ice. With extraordinary effort on the part of captain and crew—and much anxiety on the part of the passengers—the ship was finally extricated and turned about. Wallace later admitted that he may have gone "a bit too far into the ice jam."[6] Because of the dangers posed to tour ships, Glacier Bay was soon removed from tourist itineraries and remained off-limits for decades.

Taylor wrote other travel books about Hawaii, Japan, and the British Isles. He also wrote a manual for early practitioners of the art of photography that was illustrated with examples of inferior work.

Notes

Epigraph: Charles M. Taylor, Jr., *Touring Alaska and the Yellowstone* (Philadelphia: George W. Jacobs & Co., 1901), 220–21.

1 Taylor, *Touring Alaska*, 67.

2 Muir, *Travels in Alaska*, 74.

3 Hinckley, *Americanization of Alaska*, 186–87.

4 Haycox, *Alaska: An American Colony*, 188–89.

5 Taylor, *Touring Alaska*, 184.

6 Ibid., 243.

“Bad Medicene [medicine] for bear,” n.d. Alaska State Library, P39-156. Case & Draper Photograph Collection.

PART II

UNTAMED ALASKA

Into the Vast Unknown

Herding horses one by one over miles of muck;
boiling beans, mixing bread, burning callous fingers
on the hot, collapsing reflector: never an hour to rest, to dry
off from the tortures of rheumatism, mend tattered boots
and clothes, forget the roar of icy water about your waist,
the crazing cloud of 'skeets. Do you wonder vacant
Alaska drives some men mad?

Robert Dunn,
The Shameless Diary of an Explorer, 1907

Contrary to what one might think, the idea of travel may not have originated in idyllic journeys spent in ease and pleasure, for according to the *Oxford English Dictionary*, "travel" means "labour, toil; suffering, trouble."[1] The French the verb *travailler*, which looks a whole lot like it has something to do with travel, means "work."

The concept would have been easily grasped by early adventurers who launched themselves onto the tabula rasa of interior Alaska. Of the area around Cook Inlet, the region that in the next century would be the site of Alaska's biggest city, Anchorage, and its exurbs, an 1880 census taker said this: "What [it] … is like, no civilized man can tell."[2] Indeed.

If a hypothetical nineteenth-century adventurer on Alaska's mainland had done the research, he would have known what to anticipate—mosquitoes, gnats, black flies; chilly, grey days of drizzling rain; muskeg swamps, icy rivers and streams; alders that could be penetrated only with an axe. That theoretical traveler was most likely a man, for few explorers in the day were women.

He would have had to learn to tromp through the wilderness in drenched clothing, to sleep on wet ground with a wet blanket under a wetter poncho, to look forward to the nightly pot of bayo beans bubbling on the fire. Once the supplies he was carrying on his back ran out, however, he would experience the delicacies afforded by the countryside—stewed moose nose, porcupine entrails, and beaver tail.[3]

Dealing with uncertainties was difficult for our traveler. Which was worse? To head into the wilds with no map or with a map that was incorrect? He might spend much of his time lost, coming back upon his own tracks, spending another fruitless day hacking a giant circle into the brush, and getting nowhere.

The rivers were especially confusing. One nineteenth-century group rafted up one stream and down another in search of a tributary of the Koyukuk. Three months later, they came out ten miles above the spot from whence they had set out. On the part of the Yukon River known as the "flats," the river separates into multiple braids with numerous sloughs, or side channels, that wander off for miles across the countryside and twist back to rejoin the river not far above or below the point of departure. Once a person got off into one of those, there was no way of knowing where or when he would come out.

Wilderness ventures—exploration, mountain climbing, and military expeditions—were generally confined (see Lieutenant Henry T. Allen's piece for the exception) to the short summer season, when daylight hours were long. In the summer in Alaska, the sun rises and sets each day at slightly different angle and a little more to the north or south of east or west. To confound the problem, the sun doesn't cross the sky overhead but instead traces a path farther down on the horizon. Those who lacked experience with this changing pattern, as the earth bent toward and then away from the sun, had little help from that source in gauging the direction they were heading.[4]

Moreover, the terrain in Alaska is liable to be different and yet sometimes dismally all the same. Robert Dunn, who drove half-wild pack horses across the tundra on his way to Mount McKinley in 1903, looked for the scabbed-over blazes of a trail broken the previous summer by an army expedition. In the absence of those, he looked to the far-off hills and mountains as guideposts. He called Alaska the "best lose-yourself-country ever."[5]

Englishman Harry de Windt was itching to get away from Cape Prince of Wales, but the surrounding countryside had been flooded by melting snows. At the village of Kingigamoot, he learned that the Eskimos had killed their missionary with a whale gun. If the sun emerged in that dismal place, de Windt said, it was accidental. "There is probably no place in the world where the weather is so persistently vile as on this cheerless portion of the earth's surface."[6]

Those who would be largely responsible for mapping much of Alaska, the members of the American military, may have had the worst of it. United States Army general Nelson Miles wanted to discover what lay beyond the mainland's coastline, and he used drummed-up fears of possible Indian hostility to enlist Congressional support for important military expeditions to the territory. The reality, as American troops learned when they were deployed to the Kenai Peninsula and to Kodiak in 1868, was that the Natives of Alaska were, for the most part, docile. The real menaces would turn out to be the cold and the wet, the icy rivers and murky swamps, and the constant rains and slushy snow. In spite of the difficulties, and with too little rations and inadequate footgear, the troops faced overwhelming odds—and marched on.

Most of the writers in this section, none of them faint-hearted, braved such hazards. Other than their shared qualities of fortitude and self-reliance, few generalizations about them can be made. In addition to the military men, there are mountain climbers, journalists, missionaries, an English aristocrat traveling with his manservant, a female big-game hunter. All were willing to confront the enigmas of Alaska, and the difficulties of their tasks were enormous.

In an 1899 report, the American Geographical Society said that, compared to what these early travelers faced, "the usual journey of the gold seeker of the Klondike was but a summer pleasure jaunt."[7]

Notes

Epigraph: Robert Dunn, *The Shameless Diary of an Explorer* (New York: The Outing Publishing Company, 1907), 105, 107.

1 J. A. Simpson and E. S. C. Weiner, eds., *Oxford English Dictionary*, 2nd ed. (Oxford: Clarendon Press, 1989), 28: 443. I am indebted to Roderick Nash for pointing out the etymology of "travel" in his essay, "Tourism, Parks and the Wilderness Idea in the History of Alaska," in *Alaska in Perspective*, ed. Sue E. Liljeblad (Anchorage: Alaska Historical Commission / Alaska Historical Society, 1981), 1.

2 Terris Moore, *Mt. McKinley: The Pioneer Climbs*, 2nd ed. (Seattle: The Mountaineers, 1981), 7.

3 Frederick Whymper, *Travel and Adventure in the Territory of Alaska* (London: John Murray, 1868), 215.

4 Richard F. Barnes, Alaskan sea captain, e-mails to the author dated July 26, July 30, and August 1, 2012.

5 Dunn, *Shameless Diary*, 65.

6 Harry de Windt, *From Paris to New York by Land* (London: Thomas Nelson & Sons, n.d.), 265.

7 American Geographical Society Bulletin, "Exploration of Central Alaska," *The Alaska and Northwest Quarterly* 1, no. 4 (January 1899): 66.

Baldwin and party from Bonanza Mine arriving at M. L. Heney Camp 18, Copper River Railway, September 29, 1908. Alaska State Library, P124-15. Eric A. Hegg Photograph Collection.

A summer on the *Thetis*, 1888. Alaska State Library, P27-009.
Mrs. Allen (Agnes Swineford) Shattuck Photograph Collection.

Milton Weil with his Malamute chorus, Nome, Alaska, ca. 1903–1907.
Alaska State Library, P12-064. B. B. Dobbs, Photograph Collection.

"Esquimaux familie [family] at Kotzebue Sound," Arctic Ocean, 1888. Alaska State Library, P27-021. Mrs. Allen (Agnes Swineford) Shattuck Photograph Collection.

Sitka Training School for Indian Children, ca. 1886–1887.
Alaska State Library, P88-12.
William H. Partridge Photograph Collection.

Athabaskan children, Copper River, ca. 1910.
Alaska State Library, P124-13. Eric A. Hegg Photographs.

Group of Alaska Natives and men from the *Thetis*, 1888.
Alaska State Library, P27-045. Mrs. Allen (Agnes Swineford)
Shattuck Photograph Collection.

6

CAROLINE WILLARD

Chilcat Mission, Haines, Alaska

> On Friday last the steam-launch of the United States ship Jamestown returned . . . with the word that there was war in Chilcat; that two men had been killed and several wounded, all on one side; that fighting would go on until they were even.

Missionaries Caroline Willard and her husband, Eugene, agreed to be the first whites to live among the Chilkats, a tribe said to be "the terror of all other Alaska tribes."[1] The Chilkat chiefs had asked Reverend Sheldon Jackson, a Presbyterian church organizer and missionary, to find a teacher for their people, and the young couple (Caroline was a mere twenty-eight when she arrived in Alaska) had responded to Jackson's call.

Sheldon Jackson, as Stephen Haycox says, left "his mark on Alaska."[2] In response to an Indian who wrote and asked for help with the drinking, gambling, and dissipation being brought into town by miners, Jackson went to Wrangell and established a church and a school in 1877. He went on to establish schools and churches all over Alaska, and, in the off season, traveled around the United States raising funds to maintain them. The story is undocumented, but Jackson may or may not have attended a meeting in New York where religious leaders agreed to carve Alaska into regions by their various denominations.[3] It is known that Jackson encouraged those with other religious affiliations to get involved in Alaska.

It was not until Caroline, Eugene, and their year-old baby, Carrie, reached Sitka in June of 1881 that they learned that the Chilkats were fighting among themselves. American soldiers had intervened, but the conflict had intensified, and the Willards were advised to stay in Sitka until the hostilities died down. The surrounding mountains were topped with snow, but berries, flowers, radishes, peas, cauliflowers, cabbages, and lettuce were abundant. Caroline sewed without lamplight until 11 p.m. and, just after she'd gone to bed, the sun dipped below the horizon, then rose again.

Eugene conducted the funeral of a Native woman who had drunk herself to death on gin. In retribution, the woman's family demanded an exorbitant number of blankets from Indian Charley, the man who had furnished the drink and who was thus held responsible for the death. Charley was unable to pay, threatened suicide, and was jailed for his own safety.

During Alaska's Russian tenure, the Natives had learned to make an intoxicating drink called "quass." When the Americans arrived, they introduced the Indians to "hoochinoo" or "hooch," a stronger home brew made up of various ingredients. The recipe was changeable and might include sugar, molasses, potatoes, or fermented whortleberries. A US Treasury agent, William Morris, gave it poor marks. He said of hooch that it was "the most infernal decoction ever invented, producing intoxication, debauchery, insanity, and death. The smell is abominable and the taste atrocious."[4]

The white population in Sitka—according to Morris, as "God-forsaken, desperate, and rascally a set of wretches as can be found on earth"[5]—manufactured hooch, consumed it, and sold it to the Natives. Someone named Billy the Bug was cited by the Sitka newspaper as authority for the fact that three-quarters of the residents of Sitka—white, Russian, Creole, and Native—were "on it."[6] Whether the figure was correct or not, it is known that hooch contributed to poverty and violence. It also exacerbated conditions in the poverty-ridden rancheries or, as they were also called, ranches, where the Natives lived.

In the late nineteenth century, American churches and missionaries augmented a new government policy of incorporating Natives into mainstream culture. In Alaska, Christian missionaries staffed schools and taught academic subjects, as well as the tenets of their religions. Among the values the missionaries wanted to inculcate were cleanliness and punctuality. Thus, they would hand out soap and clocks.[7] Caroline Willard gave away combs.

In his attempts to foster acculturation—"civilization of the Natives," as it was then termed[8]—US military commander Henry Glass required Indian children in Sitka to attend school. The houses in the rancherie were numbered, and each child was identified by a tag inscribed with his house number and his number in the family. If a child missed school without an excuse, the family was fined one blanket.

Prior to Glass's tenure, Caroline Willard wrote, the Sitka ranche had been "the scene of nightly horrors of almost every description … murder being of common occurrence and the town filled with cripples."[9] After Glass banned the purchase, sale, and consumption of liquor, the buildings in the ranche were cleaned up, gardens were grown, troublemakers were put to work, and the Indians had money to spend on calico and new blankets.

It was July when the conflict among the Chilkats finally settled down. The Willard family, with lumber and carpenters supplied by Sheldon Jackson, sailed to their new home. They settled near the head of Lynn Canal at a place they named Haines after a mission board officer. Although they spoke only a few words of Chilkat, the Willards would avail themselves of the translation services of a nearby trader's wife, Mrs. Dickinson, an Indian trained at the mission in Metlakatla. They also brought with them from Sitka a young Indian translator, a girl named Kittie.

Life in Alaska is a compilation of letters Caroline wrote to the folks at home. Until her marriage, Caroline had worked as an art teacher at a Presbyterian college, and she illustrated her letters with sketches of Native handcrafts—wooden utensils, baskets, and woolen shawls. The recipients of the letters sent back items the Willards needed—a church bell, yeast, fabric, and hymnbooks.

Initially, the Chilkats welcomed the missionaries, giving them seats of honor and Indian names, but the Willards' efforts to substitute Western values for traditional beliefs and customs met with resistance and led to friction. In the winter of 1881, Caroline and Eugene's first at Haines, some of the Chilkats fell ill with a smallpox-like illness and died. Caroline's efforts to nurse the sick were resented by the shamans, and considered suspect by others. One conflict, as seen in the following passage, stemmed from the Willards' encouragement of Christian burials. The Chilkats practiced cremation and believed it would protect the deceased from suffering eternally from the cold.

The following excerpts, written during that first winter at Haines, begin just after a visit by Captain Glass and the naval man-of-war. Glass told the Chilkats that, if necessary, he would use the man-of-war's guns to quell disturbances.

CAROLINE WILLARD

*Chilkat Mission, Haines, Alaska**

December 13, 1881

My Dear Friends: I did not tell you in my last letter what had been done by the man-of-war. This time the *Wachusette* was commanded by Captain Henry Glass. He called for the headmen to come to him; only two of the higher chiefs

*From *Life in Alaska* (1884), 127–30, 137–41, 165–73, 177–78, and 180.

he invited into the cabin. He gave them nothing but a sound and forcible exposition of the law: 1. That he would punish anyone who made, sold or introduced any intoxicating drink, or anything to make it of. 2. That if they had any fighting, if anyone was killed, he would be here immediately; the murderer would be seized, taken below in irons, and tried; if proved guilty, he would be hanged as any white man would be. 3. If they harmed the whites who came among them, he would storm their village and blockade their river. He then showed them what the big guns were made of by firing quite a number of balls and bomb-shells, which shook our house, although sent in an opposite direction; and the big braves didn't laugh any more.

Another little child has been called away from our village—one who had been sick for a year or more—and this morning its body was burned; this was the second cremation since our coming.

While we were at breakfast, Esther, the mother of the little boy of whom I wrote you as having been buried by the church, came in looking very sad and saying that her heart was sick; that ever since her little boy had been put in the ground, the Indians had troubled her so that she could neither eat nor sleep, taunting her in every way, saying, "Ah! You are the minister's friends. Oh yes! You are white people. Why do you live here? Why do you eat Indian food? Yes, a minister you are."

Then they had tried in every way to induce her to have the body disinterred and burned. This morning, before they started … the burning, the people crowded into her house and besieged her with new force. At last Esther's mother (and this is so remarkable, because, as a rule, the old people are obstinate and tied to their old superstitions, and therefore very hard to bring to accept new ways) said to them,

"No, we will not do it. As for me, I have only just begun to learn about God, but I want to believe in him with all my heart. I want to go to him and to my grandchild when I die. And I want to tell you all now that when I die I don't want you to burn my body; I want to be buried."

January 23 and 30, 1882

Dear Friends:

Mr. Willard returned a few days ago from a tour among the villages. Two weeks ago he started by canoe for Chilcoot, but, getting caught in the floating ice from the large glaciers on the way, in which he and the man with him worked for their lives for an hour or two, he was obliged to give up the journey; and, turning into the fishing village of Te-nany, he came home the same evening. But on the Chilcat [Chilkat] River, he was gone a little over a week, holding school in the upper villages. He went on snow-shoes and skates. In the meantime, I stayed here at home with just my baby Carrie and the little Indian girl Kittie for company, holding daily court, and the service on Sabbath. It occurred to me that to home-friends it would seem a little startling if they knew that I sat night after night in a sense alone, the large windows of the sitting room—without blinds—frequently revealing the dusky faces of those who wished to come in; but then, as at all times here, there was a sweet and peculiar assurance of safety—no dread, no fear of evil. God is our keeper.

The greatest burden which falls upon me in my husband's absence is the care of the people—the responsibility of deciding, alone, matters which might among white people be trivial enough; but with this people, where there are so many complications of the family and tribal relations, together with ancient customs and superstitions, a very small matter often becomes very great in its consequences. We need more than man's wisdom; and please let this be among your petitions to God for us—that he will give such wisdom as we need for his glory in this place.

We were besieged, as usual, for medicine and comforts for the sick. An old woman died and was cremated.

February 17, 1882

My Dear Friends: We held a regular council of war yesterday. Jack had brought charges against one of the Chilcats for having killed, in Juneau, last fall, his own wife, who was of Jack's tribe, and the latter, being short of funds, was determined to have payment, and was more than ready to fight for it. On the other hand, the accused denied the charge and demanded the proof, which Jack could not give. We knew nothing of the trouble until about fifty of the strongest men of both tribes filed into our house with their faces painted black and red and their heads tied up. They arranged themselves—one tribe in a close row on one side of the room, the other tribe on the opposite side—and called for the minister. I had dinner just ready to put on the table, but I set it back and called Mr. Willard from the study, and that was the last of dinner till about eight o'clock that evening. We had no interpreter but Kittie. The poor child did grandly in all the circumstances, which were of a trying nature to all. Hour after hour the loud, violent charges were made, and the refutation as loudly and angrily given, until we were all tired out.

Mr. Willard, after getting the run of the trouble, took paper and pencil, and, charging the men to tell the whole truth, and nothing else, he proceeded to write down their words for the man-of-war, to which he referred the whole matter. Several times they seemed on the very point of breaking over into cutting and shooting. Twice in particular I thought it was come to that, but, while I held Baby tight in my arms, Mr. Willard had sprung into the middle of the floor, and with a tremendous setting down of his feet and bringing down of his fist, and with a voice that almost made me quail, he brought them back to something like order. Then he stood up and talked to them until you could almost have heard a pin drop, except for the often-repeated "Yug-geh" ("Good"). Old Jack left with angry threats before the good feeling came, when he found that he could gain nothing unjustly through us.

Last week, Mr. Willard probed another of their deepest cancers.

The Stick Indians of the interior, from whom these people get all their furs and their wealth, are a simple, and, so far as we can judge by those who have dared to come here, an honest tribe—much more than these superiors, who consider them beasts, just as some of the whites esteem these Chilcats. The Chilcats have lied to the Sticks and cheated them, and to prevent their coming to the coast to trade have told them horrid stories of the whites, and that they would be killed if they came. The few who have ventured here have been dogged about by the Chilcats and look like haunted things. We have, however, gotten hold of every one and told them of Christ.

One of the Sticks brought a nice squirrel-robe to Mr. Willard last week, and, as he wanted one, he bought it from him at just the same price that he would pay either our own people or the trader; he paid him in flour, shot, and powder. You can scarcely imagine the hornets' nest that was stirred up; the people were ready to mob us. Early next morning, before we could get our breakfast, we were set upon by some of the headmen, of whom Cla-not was spokesman. Many and many a time, he had asked prices of goods, and we had told him; but he wanted us to tell him the truth and everybody else a lie. He charged us with having robbed them; for, said he, "the Sticks are our money; we and our fathers before us have gotten rich from them. They are only wild: they are not men; and now you have told them these things and taken away our riches."

Mr. Willard told him that he spoke the truth to all men, nor would he lie for any. He told him that a certain advance on prices here was just and right when they carried their goods into the interior, but that it was wrong to hinder the Sticks from coming here, and that when they brought their skins here it was only right that they should buy and sell at the same prices which the Chilcats did. He asked, too, what they brought into this world and what they expected to take out of it, and tried to show them that they were heaping up wrath against the day of wrath. That one question as to his natural prestige, although Mr. Willard has used it many times in church to check their pride, seemed altogether new to Cla-not, and touched him more than anything else that was said. He reminded us of his high class and that his father and grandfather had had wealth before him; told us that it had offended him, that he had come to this place expecting us to build him a nice house, as they did in Port Simpson; there the people prayed, then told the missionary, and he gave them the things they asked for. The people here could not believe what we preached to them when we gave them nothing, and now we had taken away what they had. He would not stay in this place any longer. He has not allowed his wife to come to church since we talked to him here about polygamy. He says if he lets her hear she will give him shame—leave him, I suppose he means. He has three wives.

Monday, February 20—On Saturday we came home from our usual visiting of the village with sick hearts, having been confronted with the charge that we had brought on this "terrible" winter of storm and snow. In the first place, it was because those children had been buried instead of burned. Then Mr. Willard had put on his snow-shoes in the house; and lastly, we had allowed the children that night in their play to imitate the noise of a wild goose. We had very few at church yesterday, and those mostly children. Two women came to us in great trouble. One, the mother of the first child that was buried, had been the subject of persecution for some time, and now, since Jack had gone below and Cla-not was away seal-fishing, the people declared that should the storm continue and the canoes be lost they would kill her without mercy.

All day Sabbath the people had been ready to kill her, and themselves too. She had slept none that night. The people were out of food, and were unable, on account of the snow, to go to their village storehouses for more, and they were desperate. If she did not get the minister to show her where the grave was and build a fire over it, they would kill her, anyway. Mr. Willard told them that neither the burial nor the place had been any secret; it had been done in daylight; all had the opportunity of knowing all about it. Then we talked with them for a long time, trying to show them the foolishness and sin of their superstitions; and they listened so well that they went away saying the people might do what they liked; they would build no fire. They said the people had built great fires over the other little graves, and had brought two days of beautiful weather.

Monday, February 27—We had only about sixty at church yesterday. The women were out in a body, working nearly all day at the snow with their canoe-paddles, trying to find the little grave, but with no success. Late last evening, they came again to get Mr. Willard to go with them; of course he would not go. This morning, before breakfast, our kitchen was about filled with them again. He told them that he knew no more about it than they did. If he did, he would not show them; and he wished them to come to him no more for such a purpose. Of course in all these talks, we tell them why it is wrong and what is right.

Last evening we saw the sun set gloriously after so long, and this morning it rose with equal splendor. About noon, we heard the report that the woman had at last been successful in finding the grave some time during the forenoon.

In the spring of 1882, baby Carrie came down with smallpox, Eugene developed fever and grew delirious, and the family was running out of food. The winter had been so severe that Eugene had been able to kill no game, and the tinned foods that could be purchased from the trader were expensive and of poor quality. Ordinarily, the Willards' supplies came from a dealer on the West Coast who sent the order to Juneau, where the goods were transferred and transported to Haines. Due to a mix-up, the shipment for the summer of 1882 never made it to Haines, and instead sat rotting in a Juneau warehouse.

Then more illness befell the family. Kittie and baby Carrie contracted scarlet fever, and Carrie was so debilitated that Caroline thought she would die. Caroline and Eugene came down with a mysterious sickness that made their hands swollen and useless and that deprived Eugene of the use of his legs. When Caroline wrote to a fellow female missionary and asked her to care for Carrie if she and Eugene did not live, the woman realized that the situation was serious and sent a rescue party. The Willards were taken to Sitka in a state of near-starvation where, shortly after their arrival, Caroline delivered a healthy nine-pound baby she named Fred.

Despite these difficulties, Caroline never wavered in her commitment to her work among the Chilcats, and, as soon as feasible, the family returned to Haines. During their nine-month absence, salmon canneries had been built on the Lynn Canal and hundreds of whites were working in the area. Caroline knew that the intrusion would not bode well for the Natives, but the increase in population and commerce did ensure that the Willards would receive more frequent and reliable delivery of mail and supplies.

Sometime after the fall of 1883—which is when *Life in Alaska* ends—the Willards gave medicine to a sick child who subsequently died. Thereafter, the general Native hostility toward them increased to the point that they were forced to leave Haines. They relocated to Juneau, where they continued to serve as missionaries.[10]

In 1949, daughter Carrie donated to the Alaska State Museum the surgical kit—with its forceps, tweezers, lancet, and inoculation needle—which her mother had used to treat the Chilkats.[11] Carrie was then known as Kotzie, a shortened form of Kling-get Sawye K-Cotz-e,[12] a name she had been given by the Chilkats as a year-old baby. Although Kotzie had been so ill during her first year in Haines that she had nearly died, she lived to be one hundred and seventeen and is buried in Roswell, New Mexico.[13]

Notes

Epigraph: Mrs. Eugene S. Willard, *Life in Alaska: Letters of Mrs. Eugene S. Willard*, ed. Eva McClintock (Philadelphia: Presbyterian Board of Publication, 1884), 14.

1 Willard, *Life in Alaska*, 19.

2 Stephen Haycox, *Alaska: An American Colony* (Seattle: University of Washington Press, 2002), 185.

3 Ibid.

4 Morris quoted by Morgan Sherwood in "Ardent Spirits: Hooch and the *Osprey* Affair at Sitka," *Journal of the West* (July 1965): 321.

5 Morris quoted by Ted Hinckley, *Americanization of Alaska, 1867–1897* (Palo Alto, CA: Pacific Books, 1972), 159.

6 Sherwoood, "Ardent Spirits," 321.

7 Haycox, *Alaska: An American Colony*, 186.

8 Ibid., 185. See also, Haycox, "Sheldon Jackson in Historical Perspective: Alaska Native Schools and Mission Contracts, 1885–1894," *The Pacific Historian* 28, no. 1:18–28.

9 Willard, *Life in Alaska*, 31.

10 Eliza Ruhamah Scidmore, *Appletons' Guide-Book to Alaska and the Northwest Coast* (New York: D. Appleton and Company, 1893), 93.

11 "Sheldon Jackson Museum, Sitka: May Artifact of the Month," Alaska State Museum, July 21, 2012, http://www.museums.state.ak.us/documents/sjm/artifacts/may_2006.pdf.

12 Willard, *Life in Alaska*, 84–85.

13 "Memory Lawn Memorial Park Cemetery, Roswell, New Mexico," July 21, 2012, http://www.nmchaves.net/nmchaves/memorylawncomplete.html.

7

LIEUTENANT HENRY T. ALLEN

Living Upon the Country

From Fickett's journal:
Indian gave us a dinner of boiled meat,
from which we scraped the maggots by handfuls
before cutting it up. It tasted good, maggots and all.

Lieutenant Henry Allen was a ladies' man—tall, pleasant, good-looking, neither blunt nor sharp-spoken. Consequently, some thought he was unsuitable officer material.[1] However, Allen was smart, driven, and had a goal. He believed that he could achieve something in Alaska that a fellow officer had told him was impossible.

In 1885, the Copper River basin had never been penetrated, and the region was largely unexplored. The Russians who had tried to ascend the river had failed, and at least one of their expeditions had been massacred by Indians. In 1884, General Nelson Miles had sent then Lieutenant William Abercrombie on a large-scale operation to explore the Copper River. After several difficult months on the river, Abercrombie had turned back, concluding that glaciers, rapids, and other obstacles made the task impossible.

Into the breach stepped Allen. He had researched the question and decided that if he got an early start, he could get up the river and into the interior of Alaska before the ice went out. He persuaded General Miles to let him try and asked to take along only two men, Private Fred Fickett and Sergeant Cady Robertson. When Allen and his two companions struck out into the country in the winter of 1885, they had so few rations that they were to spend much of their time looking for something to eat. At times, the party was so debilitated by hunger that they didn't have the strength to march.

Little was known about the Copper River tribes, but they were rumored to be fierce defenders of their territory. Allen was charged with impressing the

Natives with the government's "friendly disposition" toward them,[2] and he took the task to heart. The success of Allen's mission was due to many things, including his innate abilities and determination, but one key factor was his ability to secure the cooperation and assistance of the Natives he met along the way.

Part of that cooperation resulted from a fortunate event, which, at first blush, had been a setback. When Allen, Fickett, and Robertson reached Sitka, they discovered that the schooner that was to carry them on the next leg of their trip had already sailed. Their only option was to wait in Sitka for the navy to grant permission for the man-of-war to take them farther north. This delayed the start of the mission, but the arrival of the three soldiers in Indian country on the man-of-war worked to their advantage. The inland Natives had never laid eyes on the naval vessel, but had heard about it, and, the farther upriver Allen went, in the Indians' telling, the larger the ship and its guns became. One man told Allen that the man-of-war's length was half a mile and the bore of its guns as wide as his outstretched arms.

The ship left Allen and his men on Hinchinbrook Island, where they engaged Indian boats to carry them across fifty miles of open sea to the mouth of the Copper River. Although it was then late March, snow was still on the ground, and the men were sometimes so numbed by cold that they were unable to strike matches. "These days were severe," Allen said, "but an excellent discipline for the even more trying work that was soon to follow."[3]

At the mouth of the Copper River, they loaded supplies onto sleds and set out on thin river ice that was sometimes flooded with water. Continuous rains made the snows so soft that the sleds sank into it. Unable to manage, the men abandoned their tent and much of their ammunition, food, and clothing. The three then slept under ponchos in rain-saturated clothing and hunted for their meals. Game was scarce, and they survived by eating whatever they came across. This led to some interesting meals, Allen noting that his first porcupine entrails were "not relished then as they were at a later stage."[4]

The expedition was joined by prospector Pete Johnson, who was searching for his partner, John Bremner. At the native village of Taral, the party of four hungry men hoped to find food. Instead, they found a starving Bremner. Allen knew that prospectors were a good source of information about the country, so he took Bremner and Johnson along when he left Taral.

Allen's "skillies," his packers and guides, were known to him as Midnooskies, Russian for "people of the Copper River." In reality, they were members of the Ahtna and Eyak tribes. Many of Allen's spellings, such as "Tarál" and "Chittyná," are Russian.

In this selection from *Report of an Expedition to the Copper, Tananá, and Kóyukuk Rivers in the Territory of Alaska in the Year 1885*, Allen describes his exploration of the Chittyná (Chitina), a Copper River tributary. While looking for Chief Nicolai—a man who Allen hoped would lead him to a rumored copper site—he would explore the Chittystone (Chitistone) River.

LIEUTENANT HENRY ALLEN

Living Upon the Country[°]

The party now consisted of five white men and one native. The packs were divided so that each man should carry an equal portion of baggage that was for the general welfare. An allowance of one blanket per man, a sleeping bag, or its equivalent, and a change of underwear was agreed upon for each. Carbines, pistols, ammunition, and cooking utensils were no small part of the weight. Any of the party was at liberty to carry articles of "luxury," provided he had also his allowance. One carried an extra blanket, another a coat or shirt.

From this time, we began to realize the true meaning of the much-used expression "living upon the country." The provisions with which we started could easily have been consumed by us in four days, but they were held as a reserve. Our main dependence was on rabbits, the broth of which was thickened with a handful of flour.

The snow had nearly all disappeared on the river-bed and lowlands, and much of the journey was now over granitic bowlders and pebbles. Our feet were encased in native boots, and to persons unaccustomed to such footgear, the use is a severe trial.

On April 13, we came up with Skilly, the Midnóosky, who would not wait and start with us from Tarál. He had parts of a moose that the wolves had killed during the winter.

The following is from [Pvt.] Fickett's journal:

> They had left a few scraps lying around, and these, that neither they nor their dogs would eat, we were forced by hunger to gather up and make a meal on. This is Lieutenant Allen's birthday, and he celebrated it by eating rotten moose meat.

If we had been so fortunate as to obtain even rotten moose meat a few days later, there would have been none of the party too dainty to enjoy it. There

°From *Report of an Expedition to the Copper, Tananá, and Kóyukuk Rivers* (1887), 50–54.

were both snow and sunshine on the day of the 13th; on the night of the same day, ice froze two-thirds of an inch in thickness. This cold was greeted with joy, because it enabled us to pursue a more direct course and permitted us to walk on the ice rather than the pebbles, a boon to our much swollen feet.

About noon of the 14th, we passed three deserted houses on the south bank of the Chittyná, much concealed by a growth of cottonwoods and alders. Our camp was at the mouth of a small stream, reported to flow from a lake about twenty miles to the north of the Chittyná. This spot had been chosen as a camping-ground, and had a bath-house erected near the spruce-bough tepee. From here one of Skilly's subordinates started to the lake, where we were informed his mother lived. The name Skilly, by which we had known our native friend, I found to be a term applied to the near relatives of a chief. Our Skilly was a brother of Nicolai, whom we hoped to soon find, and upon whom great dependence for future assistance whilst on the Copper River was placed.

On the 15th, we obtained observations for both latitude and longitude. To our camp, 30 miles from Tarál, the general direction was east southeast. The sun during the day had again loosened the ice in the river, and crossing it became very perilous. In an ordinary river, such frequent crossings would not have been necessary, but in rivers similar to the Copper or Chittyná, to follow a channel, if it were possible, would be to add from 30 to 40 per cent to the distance. The beds of these rivers and their tributaries are frequently one mile wide, with several channels.

Near the end of the day's march found us with deep, impassable water to our front and right, and a very high, rugged point to our front and left. To climb this when in good physical condition, without packs or guns, would have been a difficult task. To cross it under the circumstances severely tested both the courage and strength of the party. The most difficult of all our endeavors, however, was the necessity of hunting supper at the expiration of such a day's march. Sometimes a halt was made during midday to hunt food for supper.

On the 17th, we started at 7 a.m. from the mouth of the Chittyná, which bore no signs of breaking up, and having marched 5 miles, went into camp. The following is from Fickett's journal:

> Rotten moose meat would be a delicacy now. So weak from hunger that we had to stop at noon to hunt. All so weak that we were dizzy, and would stagger like drunken men.

Fortunately, an old woman brought into camp a small piece of meat and a moose's nose, which, with the rabbits we killed, considerably strengthened us.

The old woman was [guide] Wahnie's mother, who was in camp a few miles from the river. The latter, while out hunting, had gone to her brush house and told her to bring over the meat. She reluctantly obeyed, crying in a plaintive voice, "Skunkái descháne keelán" ("My children are very hungry").

The hunting party, for such it was we were near, consisted of two men, two women, and a number of children. They had been very unsuccessful in hunting, and were accordingly in reduced circumstances; yet we obtained of them a little meat. Our importunities for more were silenced by the verification of the old woman's sentence.

One of the men of the party was a "skilly," the other unfitted by age for carrying a pack. From them I learned that Nicolai was on the headwaters of the Chittystone, near the mouth of which we had camped the previous day. At one time, they would tell us that Nicolai had "Tenáyga keelán" ("Moose plenty"), at another that "Nicolai descháne keelán" ("Nicolai is very hungry").

In making short marches, the Midnoóskies, as do most of the natives of the Tananá, travel with remarkable speed, but they never load themselves with weight to exceed 20 pounds. Generally they carry, besides a very light gun, only a skin blanket, with dimensions of 4 by 5 feet. I do not refer to the men slaves, who bear packs equal to those of the women. A day's march with them is so very variable that we had no definite mode of arriving at the distances to the sources of the tributaries except by reduction of the time it required us to reach Nicolai's home; and using this as a standard, I have traced in dotted lines the supposed courses of the tributaries. Had I considered it prudent to attempt the source of Central Fork, subsisting on rabbits alone, with no prospects of any other food, the chart would not show dotted lines. The party was daily growing weaker on account of an insufficient quantity of food.

The skilly of this camp, after much persuasion and rewards, was induced to go with us to Nicolai's, but would carry nothing except the "white tyone's" pack (mine). I was much degraded in his eyes by carrying a pack of any description, and yet more so when I shouldered the moose meat we had obtained from him.

On April 18, we started overland for Nicolai's. For an hour, our course lay along the south bank of the Chittyná, then across it, over the treacherous ice, to the north bank, into a wood of dwarf spruces and deep moss. After an hour's marching through this, we unexpectedly found ourselves on a high bank of the Chittyná, from which with the field glasses we could see the locality pointed out to us as the junction of the central and southern forks.

There was no trail and nothing to indicate the way save the blazing of the trees, which had evidently been done only a few weeks previous. When we halted for our noon meal, a considerable quantity of the moose meat and two or three blue grouse were eaten, yet our hunger was not appeased. The skilly, soon after the halt, had fainted away, and remained in this condition during most of the meal. Wahnie felt much uneasiness concerning him, but most of the party seemed to realize the old maxim: "All is for the best." Certainly the portion of the meal intended for him was relished by us.

We left camp the following morning at 6 o'clock, and after marching about seven miles found the strength of the entire party nearly exhausted. All of us now realized that a diet of meat alone should be very abundant to produce the necessary working strength. After consuming all the food on hand, we started off with the hopes that Nicolai would have something for us, and we were not disappointed.

The last 5 miles of our march was either on the ice of the Chittystone or very near the river. Many rounds of ammunition were fired by us in answer to Nicolai's salute. On occasions of this kind, a Midnoósky will fire his last charge of powder, though hunger stare him in the face. It is courtesy that each shot be answered, and the number of shots with them, as with more civilized people, indicates the rank of the tyone. On one occasion, on the north side of the Alaskan Mountains, probably one hundred and fifty shots were fired to welcome us. Long before we had reached the source of Copper River, I was compelled to limit the number of shots, lest our supply of ammunition be too much reduced. We were always so delighted to arrive at a settlement that a celebration of some sort seemed very appropriate; moreover, it was claimed the greater the demonstration we made, the more food we would obtain.

It is also *en regle* among the natives to provide some kind of refreshments on the arrival of a guest, and we early learned to expect it as a matter of course. After having been once so entertained, any subsequent meal must be purchased, and that at a very dear price. They realized our necessity and made the most of it.

To reach Nicolai's house, we had marched a distance of 30 miles, and on finding on the fire a kettle with capacity of about 5 gallons, filled with meat, we were happy. The allowance of this per man, exclusive of the broth, of which we drank large quantities, could not have been less than 5 pounds. Much of it was fat or tallow run into the small intestines of the moose. All immediately fell asleep after eating, and on awakening were nearly as hungry as before. The donation of such a quantity of meat was frequently cited by Nicolai to show how great a tyone he was.

We soon examined the contents of the surrounding *caches*, and, from our inspection of them, concluded our guns must be largely depended upon to win us our food. The 20th being stormy, the party rested and gorged itself on moose, beaver, lynx, and rabbits, cooked entirely in native style, which does not reject in their preparation the entrails *in toto*.

Chief Nicolai did lead Allen to a secret outcropping of copper, and Allen's inclusion of the information in his report directed prospectors to the spot. The operation that was later established there, the Kennecott, is said by some mining engineers to have been the highest-grade copper mine in the world. It began production in 1911 and, by the time it closed in 1938, had produced copper with a value of somewhere between $200 and $300 million.[5]

In spite of the severe obstacles Allen faced, he managed to ascend the Copper River and cross the divide into the interior. When he reached the foot of the Alaska Range, local Indians told him that it would take thirty days to cross the 4,500-foot summit. However, after many *wahwahs*—the Alaskan equivalent of a powwow—the Natives concluded that if Allen and his men marched long days, they could do it in a week. Three days later, at one thirty in the morning, Allen had reached the summit—Mentasta Pass. The sun was rising not in the east but two points east of north. Allen forgot his hunger and fatigue as he gazed on the country behind him, "the promised land" before him, and the "grand sight which no visitor save an Atnatána or Tananátana [Indian] have ever seen."[6]

The party spent the summer exploring the Tanana River, feasting on salmon and, when the fish played out, eating the tallow they had saved to fry fish in. This put them into a state that, according to Allen, was "not conducive to cheerfulness of mind."[7] Descending the unexplored Tanana, the men encountered Native children who had been taught the alphabet by an English missionary and others who had never seen whites. At the settlement of Nuklukyet, Allen and his men were eating fish fried in machine oil when they met a storekeeper named Joe Ladue, later famous as the founder of Dawson. Ladue gave them a gift that fed them for four days—a fifty-pound sack of flour.

Allen's mission had been exploration of the Copper and Tanana Rivers. After completing the task ahead of schedule, he set out to map a third major river, the Koyukuk. He sent Robertson on to St. Michael by steamer while he and Fickett, equipped with only their instruments, weapons, and tattered sleeping bags, went up the river with Koyukon Indian guides. As autumn approached, the men ate ducks and geese they shot from their canoes. In September, Allen and Fickett joined Robertson at St. Michael and sailed for San Francisco.

Because Allen started his expedition while it was still winter, he stretched the summer exploration season into nearly seven months. He proved that Americans had no reason to fear the starving Athabaskans along the Copper River or the Natives along the Yukon, a fact later confirmed by other explorers who reported the hospitality of other Alaskan Natives.

In the end, Allen's three-man expedition had covered 2,500 miles, charted three major unmapped rivers, and explored 1,500 miles of what previously had been unknown territory. In addition to rarely having enough to eat, Allen marched for ten days on the Tanana without footgear of any kind. According to historian Morgan Sherwood, the expedition "was an incredible achievement that deserves to be ranked with the great explorations of North America."[8] Another early explorer, Alfred Hulse Brooks of the US Geological Survey, said no one added more to the knowledge of Alaska than did Henry T. Allen.[9]

Allen went on to teach at West Point and to lead US Army forces in Germany during World War I. Although some predicted he'd never make it as an officer, he retired as major general in 1923 and was buried at Arlington National Cemetery.

Notes

Epigraph: Private Fred Fickett quoted by Lieutenant Henry Allen in *Report of an Expedition to the Copper, Tananá, and Kóyukuk Rivers in the Territory of Alaska in the Year 1885* (Washington, DC: Government Printing Office, 1887), 65.

1 Sherwood, *Exploration of Alaska, 1865–1900* (New Haven: Yale University Press, 1965), 107.

2 Letter of Instruction from Asst. Adjutant-General H. Clay Wood to Second Lieut. Henry T. Allen, January 27, 1885, *Report of an Expedition to the Copper, Tananá, and Kóyukuk Rivers*, 11.

3 Allen, *Report of an Expedition*, 39.

4 Ibid., 46.

5 Melody Webb Grauman, "Kennecott: Alaskan Origins of a Copper Empire, 1900–1938," *Western Historical Quarterly* 9, no. 2 (April 1978): 200, 207.

6 Allen, *Report of an Expedition*, 73.

7 Ibid., 85.

8 Sherwood, *Exploration of Alaska*, 115.

9 Ibid., 115–16.

8

H. W. SETON KARR

Escape from Icy Bay

The mountains are covered with snow and glaciers from sea-level to summit. The air of early morning in latitude 60° N. is exceedingly transparent, while … these mountains … impress the beholder … with the sensation of their being too ethereal to have any actual existence.

Englishman Heywood Walter Seton Karr set out alone for Alaska, hoping to be the first to climb Mount St. Elias. A veteran of the Swiss Alps, he hoped that further achievement in Alaska would qualify him for membership in an exclusive English Alpine club. In 1886, when Seton Karr went to Alaska, two things about St. Elias remained unknown: its location—whether in Canada or Alaska—and its height—12,672 feet, 19,000 feet, or something in between.[1]

For his part, Seton Karr thought that the mountain was 20,000 feet and wholly on Canadian soil. He was later proven wrong on both counts, since St. Elias straddles the boundary between Alaska and Canada and is only a little over 18,000 feet. As Seton Karr noted in *Shores and Alps of Alaska*, the territory surrounding St. Elias was then still unexplored.

When the *Ancon* sailed from Victoria, one of Seton Karr's fellow passengers was Frederick Schwatka, a former US Army lieutenant who had recently resigned from the military. Schwatka was already famous for his exploration of the Yukon River and for his efforts to locate the remains of Sir John Franklin's Northwest Passage expedition. By coincidence, Schwatka and his companion, Princeton geology professor William Libbey, were headed for Alaska with the same goal as Seton Karr—to be first to climb St. Elias.

Although neither Schwatka nor Libbey had ever climbed a mountain, their attempt at St. Elias was being sponsored by the *New York Times*. Schwatka later said that he quickly sized up Seton Karr and found him "physically … in very good trim."[2] Once Schwatka learned of Seton Karr's climbing experience, he invited him to join the expedition.

In Juneau, Schwatka hired three helpers, an interpreter named Kersunk—who preferred to be called Fred—and two men named Dalton and Woods who would act as cook and helper. As the party sailed northward on the navy's *Pinta*, Seton Karr first sighted St. Elias at Yakutat Bay. The mountain stood on its broad base, rising like a Pyramid, "straight, regular, and massive, from an icy plateau of enormously extensive glaciers."[3]

The man-of-war's arrival at Yakutat checked a conflict that was brewing between white traders and some local Indians who were distilling liquor. The Indians' fear of the *Pinta*'s machine guns and brass howitzers soon restored order.

The *Pinta*'s captain, Nicholls, had intended only to take the Schwatka-Seton Karr group as far as Port Mulgrave, where they could obtain guides and canoes to take them on to Icy Bay on the coast below St. Elias. However, when the party reached that place, they learned that all of the canoes had been taken away on a hunt. No ship as large as the *Pinta* had ever been into Icy Bay, but Nicholls nonetheless agreed to go. When the man-of-war entered the bay, massive swells were breaking against the shore "with a threatening aspect very disturbing to landsmen,"[4] said Seton Karr.

The intense surf did not portend a successful landing, but Schwatka's Indian guides insisted that they could reach the shore. Nicholls volunteered the use of one of the *Pinta's* whaleboats, and that, along with Professor Libbey's dug-out canoe, would have to serve for landing supplies and men. The two craft were launched into breakers so high that those standing on the *Pinta*'s deck could see neither the boats nor the men in them. The trip was treacherous and harrowing, and all were thoroughly drenched in the process, yet the men and their outfit were safely put ashore.

Quoting *Rime of the Ancient Mariner*, Seton Karr said that the party was 'the first that ever burst' on the wild shores of Icy Bay."[5] First or not, they were definitely alone. It was mid-July when the *Pinta* sailed away, and it would not return until September.

Ominously, the sand on the beach was laced with eight-by-fourteen-inch bear tracks. Between the party and Mt. St. Elias lay miles of wilderness, rivers, and glaciers. When they started toward the mountain, the men found the woods so thick that it was impossible to travel with their packs. They turned to the riverbeds, waded through icy waters that reached their chests, and floundered through mud and quicksand.

The group crossed mucky ground and glacial moraine, following bear trails.

"Bruin is the great road-maker of Alaska,"[6] Seton Karr wrote. When three of the party—Schwatka, Seton Karr, and the expedition's helper, Woods—reached the foot of Mt. St. Elias, they roped together and began climbing. At "fourteen stone"—more than 250 pounds—it soon became clear that Schwatka was too heavy for Alpine climbing. Besides that, he developed chills and fever and had to drop by the wayside. Seton Karr and Woods reached 6,800 feet, and the Englishman sent Woods back to check on Schwatka while he continued on alone. At 7,200 feet, the ground fell away before him, and Seton Karr realized that he, too, would have to turn back.

With neither enough food nor time to make another attempt, the group had no option other than to return to Icy Bay. They had landed a mere ten days before, and it would be another month before the *Pinta* was scheduled to return. The nine men—the three members of the expedition; their cook, helper, and interpreter; and three guides—had a choice: they could remain on the beach and face possible starvation or they could attempt to get away. To succeed at the latter, they would have to launch their boats into that pounding surf.

In the selection that follows, Seton Karr describes how he and his companions decided to risk the loss of everything, including their lives.

H. W. SETON KARR

Escape from Icy Bay[°]

July 30, Midday

All day yesterday we rested, watched the surf, listened to the roar of the ocean, and wondered how we were going to get away. We determined to try to get away by that night's tide. It was high water at about 11:30 p.m. We packed the things, leaving most of the remaining provisions, and other things that were not indispensable. Towards sundown, everything had been carried across the sand dunes to the side of the whale-boat. Oars and mast were made ready and everything prepared. *Breakers* were filled and *rollers* laid, the very names conveying unpleasant reminders. The anchor had been thrown out as far as possible by Woods wading out at five that afternoon at low water, when the Indian canoes are said to be able to make a landing.

Still the length of cable we had to haul on to get through the breakers looked miserably short and insufficient, and threatened that we should be unable to take quick advantage of the calm moment on account of the difficulty of raising the anchor, which, as well as the chain, sinks in a few minutes

°From *Shores and Alps of Alaska* (1887), 113–22.

to a great depth in the sand. How deep would it sink in six hours? The last twenty yards are of chain, and this, as well as the anchor, was very heavy, making it slow and hard work moving it. I advised not using them. The pile of *impedimenta* looked formidable and was packed into the boat to occupy the smallest space. As midnight approached, we made ready. We took off our boots and coats, and stood round the boat to hold firm as the foam rushed by. It was icy cold to legs and feet; and uniting our strength, we moved her down upon the underwash of each succeeding wave.

We had suspected that the boat was too heavily loaded for nine men to manage, and too low to give her the necessary chance of rising over the foaming breakers, comparatively small though they were when contrasted with those of winter.

But most of the scientific instruments were the private property of one of the members of the party and were valuable. We were therefore unwilling to abandon them to their fate. To make the situation more unpleasant, it was nearly midnight and the darkness was increasing. Our legs were numbed, for the many glacial rivers and the glaciers along the shore made the water bitterly cold. The waves seemed getting larger. It was spring-tide. Soon an enormous breaker came on like a wall, and broke with a roar like thunder. The foam rushed up the beach towards us. Now was the time. We gasped for breath in the icy water, and held firm to the boat till the wave began to retreat again.

"All together now," someone shouted, and, exerting our full strength, we rushed her down a few yards on the retiring flood.

We were now nearer to danger than ever. Some water had entered the boat over the gunwales already. The sand seemed to hold her sucked down. The canoe had been tied behind with twenty yards of rope. We had seen it rush past us, caught by the back sweep of the water, and next moment become broken into small pieces which floated uncomfortably round about, like an entanglement, till someone cut the rope adrift.

We were watching the next opportunity—a retreating underwash followed by calm water for a moment. The Indians strained their eyes seawards. Everything was obscured by the darkness, for it was past midnight. We had calculated on its being lighter. Now—now was the time, and a yell arose from the whole party. Next minute we were completely enveloped in foam, as we struggled to keep a footing, gasping from the cold. The rush of water was terrific. It seemed like a nightmare enacted by madmen. Wave succeeded wave till she was filled and immovable.

Everything became confusion. Behind was a desert, in front the roaring sea in which our effects were at the point of destruction, while the surf breaking upon us chilled us through and through. We were between the devil and the deep sea, and the devil received the vote, for "back" was now the cry. We were defeated and cast once more upon an inhospitable shore. Four held the boat, while the rest carried package after package above the reach of the waves.

Shouts for assistance were heard as the waves got the better of the four, and "slewed her broad-side," till bailed out and dragged up she was made fast for the present out of reach of the tide. So ended our first attempt to leave Icy Bay.

Here we are still. We have still some provisions left and must make one last desperate effort if the surf remains moderate. The matches were dry, and a hot fire and coffee were cheering, as were also the few blankets that remained dry.

The roaring of the surf kept every one awake till the sun was high in the heavens, reminding us as it did that calmer weather was the only alternative to capsizing or semi-starvation, while the brightest star in the mental atmosphere is the return of the man-of-war in a month.

To-day the weather is clear and cloudless, the mirage along the shore rising and falling as the wind drifts the spray from the breaking surf inland. The beach is strewed with things laid out to dry. Luckily, it is a fine warm day.

August 2, 1886

Fresh preparations for departure were begun. The anchor and chain were extracted from the sand and laid thirty yards farther out at low water, favored by the spring-tide, by Woods and Dalton, after a violent struggle with the waves. It grew gradually calmer; our expectations rose. The scientific instruments were heavy; must the Professor leave them? No, they must be taken in the cause of science. If we were destined to swamp, we should swamp without them as easily as with them. The Indians were consulted. They would start at daybreak on the ebbing tide. It grew calmer still. If it should only keep so for eight hours longer! At all hazards, we must break through the bounds of our prison-house.

The surf broke in long straight lines, every portion simultaneously. The sound of it was louder, but the sea in reality calmer. Each roller was clearly defined from each succeeding one. We could pick out the moment for the last rush with certainty. It was 7 o'clock in the evening. We lay down and each one feigned sleep, but no one slept. We were face-to-face with a danger, but we talked of other things. The Indians watched the sea by turns all night, and roused Dalton to prepare breakfast as the first light of morning lit the sky behind the vast ranges of alps. Almost everything was abandoned this time. The boat was therefore nearly empty.

The air was thick with sea fog, but the sea was still in good condition. It grew lighter and lighter. Everything is ready, and away we go down the beach. Now she touches the wash. We haul in the slack of the anchor rope and bide our time. Determination is imprinted on every face. The undemonstrative Indians get really excited and show it. We leave it to them to give the word. The glaciers make the sea almost icy cold, and we shudder as each surge breaks and rushes under us. The moment arrives when we see a calm stretch.

"All together!" and she moves seaward. Now she floats. Pull on the anchor rope for life or death.

"Jump in, boys!" "Row, for God's sake, row!" The chain is caught in the sand and refuses to come up. Someone cuts the rope. All is confusion. The oars are entangled and refuse to enter the rowlocks.

"Row, for God's sake, row!" At last I get one in, and a wave strikes it out again. (I found afterwards this rowlock was bent.) She surges to and fro. Nothing at this moment could take my attention from the rowlock, though it were to rain "chained thunderbolts and hail of iron globes." I wrestle with my oar, and everything beside passes unheeded except the cry dinning in one's ears, "Row, for God's sake, row!" A small wave passes under her and breaks just under the keel; she turns broadside. Has no one got an oar out? Ten yards more and we shall be safe. I seize another oar; someone is sitting upon it. I try another, and the stay catches. At last one oar is got to work; then another. Every one shouts at once.

Never was seen such confusion or heard such pandemonium. Hades must have broken loose. The importance of the next few seconds is immense. At last she moves—faster and faster—no heavy sea yet. We are safe. No! Look out—yes, safe at last. An immense roller arrives. She rises to it, and it passes under and breaks just beyond us. The shore recedes. We are soaked through and through but safe. We are exhausted and can afford to rest. We bail the boat, and change into dry things which we have taken care to place in rubber bags. The fog lifts. Never did Mount St. Elias look so grand, so magnificent. Our deserted tent stands lonely on the shore. It shows white against the dark narrow belt of forest, which in its turn shows up blackly against the glittering sea of glaciers beyond.

Once safely beyond the line of breakers, the men rowed sixty miles across open sea, with seals bobbing in the water around them. At Yakutat, they were welcomed by an Indian chief dressed in a uniform given him by the crew of the USS *Adams.*

Schwatka and Libbey decided to await the return of the *Pinta,* but Seton Karr departed on the trader's schooner. As he sailed past Icy Bay, Seton Karr saw the expedition's deserted tent on the beach, "a shining, square, white speck upon that grand and awful coast."[7] At the Native village of Nuchek, he found the abandoned journal of prospector John Bremner, the man who had been rescued the year before by Henry Allen. From Nuchek, Seton Karr traveled to Kodiak Island, and from there sailed on the *St. Paul* to San Francisco.

The 1886 expedition members were the first non-Natives to set foot on St. Elias, but achieved little else of note. Schwatka's earlier journey down the Yukon River had similarly contributed little to the annals of Alaskan exploration, but he wrote prolifically about Alaska and provided the territory with much publicity. He told his *New York Times* readers that he hadn't realized until well into the St. Elias venture that he was too heavy for mountain climbing. Nonetheless, he assured them, he had never attained his "full capacity of endurance and muscles."[8] The *Times* itself proclaimed, somewhat hyperbolically, that the St. Elias venture had "done more to realize the expectation which Mr. Seward founded upon his purchase of Alaska than any other event."[9]

As for Seton Karr, he was not only an explorer and a writer but an artist. *Shores and Alps of Alaska* is illustrated with watercolors and sketches he made en route. He returned to Alaska in 1890 to further explore the St. Elias region, and during his lifetime made a number of big-game hunts—nineteen of them in Africa, twenty in India, and twenty in the Arctic. By the time of his death at age seventy-eight, his collections of prehistoric implements from Somaliland, Egypt, and India were housed in over two hundred museums. His artwork was displayed at the Imperial War Museum in London.[10]

Notes

Epigraph: H. W. Seton Karr, *Shores and Alps of Alaska* (London: Sampson Low, Marston, Searle & Rivington, 1887), 48.

1 Sherwood, *Exploration of Alaska,* 81.

2 "Nearing Mount St. Elias: Progress of the *Times*'s Alaskan Expedition," *New York Times,* August 9, 1886.

3 Seton Karr, *Shores and Alps of Alaska*, 49.

4 Ibid., 65.

5 Ibid., 67.

6 Ibid., 77.

7 Ibid., 137.

8 Frederick Schwatka, "King of the Continent," *New York Times*, October 19, 1886.

9 Editorial, *New York Times*, September 20, 1886, quoted by Sherwood, *Exploration of Alaska*, 79.

10 "Capt. H. W. Seton Karr: 200 Museums Had Trophies of Explorer and Artist," *New York Times*, January 1, 1938.

9

JOHN BREMNER

Living Off the Enemy

> Oct. 26. Clear but verey cold the floor of my cabin is frose two foot from the fire and I thought I had made it almost air tight so you see I am in no danger of melting with the heat.

Other than a few footnotes here and there, not much record of John Bremner survives. He may have forsaken a wife and children on a farm in Iowa for a life of adventure, may have spent time in Africa and Australia, and may have been a sailor.[1] What is known is that he wound up in Alaska, where he prospected along the Copper and Koyukuk Rivers. The story he left behind, however, is not about his mining ventures but instead about a lonely winter he spent at Taral, a place that was just a couple of shacks at the confluence of the Chitina and Copper Rivers.

In the spring of 1885, Indians had told Lieutenant Henry Allen that Bremner had been at Taral but might be dead. When Allen reached the site, he fired several rounds, which Bremner answered with the last shot he had. Then, on the bluff above, appeared what Allen described as "a picture of wretchedness, destitution, and despair, suddenly rendered happy."[2]

Bremner told Allen that he had ascended the Copper River the previous summer with some Indians and 300 pounds of provisions, most of which he said the Indians had taken. Of the two houses at Taral, one was occupied by Bremner and the other was empty. His nearest neighbors were Ahtna Indians two miles away, and he claimed to have so little food that he was tightening his belt a notch every other day.

Allen's report included only an outline of Bremner's story, but, in the following year, Englishman H. W. Seton Karr was on his way home from Mt. St. Elias when he found the dirty canvas bag holding Bremner's handwritten account of his winter at Taral. When Seton Karr wrote *Shores and Alps of Alaska,* he had the journal transcribed and included it.

Seton Karr described Bremner as an "intrepid prospector and plucky Yankee" whose story was told "in the language of his class."[3] Suffice it to say, the journal is replete with poor grammar, poorer spelling, and erratic punctuation. Bremner's references are sometimes obscure, but one thing the document makes clear is that the winter of 1884–85 was—at least for Bremner—a long, hard slog.

The story begins as the Ahtna Indians, whom Bremner called Ma Nuskas, from the Russian "Midnoosky"—which, according to Lieutenant Henry Allen, means "People of the Copper River"—are leading him upriver to Taral. Bremner had other visitors that winter, members of a tribe he knew as Col Chinas. The first entry provides a taste of what lies ahead, for when Bremner writes that the Indians were eating "Mouse," they were actually eating moose. As Seton Karr said, the work is one that is "unencumbered by redundant verbiage."

The diary entries reproduced here are excerpted from the version reproduced in *Shores and Alps of Alaska.*

JOHN BREMNER

Living Off the Enemy[*]

Sept. 4. After georgeing themselvs with Mouse meat till about four o'clock the d—— rascals wanted to leave all my grub except one sack of flour and they would come back in the wenter and get it I told them no if they left my grub they hade to leave me to I did not prepose to trust my suplies out of my sight then they undertook to force me along but they found that uphill woark when they looked in the muszel of my revolver so they left me and said they would be back in ten days how I wish I had a few of the boys in blue here to teach them a lesson.

Sept. 6. Remained in camp rained hard all day repaired some of my cloths and saw a pair of woodcock I don't know how thay make out to live here in winter.

Sept. 7. Went about ten miles to see that stream that I mencentioned comeing in on the East side it is about two hundred yards wide and not fordeable killed four ducks and am cooking one of them for my supper so you see I am liveing of the enemes contrey.

[*]Bremner's diary reproduced in Seton Karr, *Shores and Alps of Alaska* (1887), 202–21.

Sept. 9. Staid in camp all day a bear came prowling about camp last night could not get a shot at him it was so dark.

Sept. 10. Nothing to record only that I am tormented with misquiters thar name is legion.

Sept. 11. A drove of Mouse passed close to camp in the night I shot at them by guess could not tell if I hit one or not this morning I went ant looked and saw whear one had bleed freely so I am going to track him up and see if I cant get him.

Sept. 12. I did not get my Mouse he had streangth enough to cross the river though he is dead enough by this I am sorry to lose so much meat but better luck next time.

Sept. 18. Rained hard all day I have given up looking for the Ma Nuska the d—— liers I will get even with them yet and dount you forget it.

Sept. 19. The Ma Nuska came last night so thay are better than I thought we will make another start for Tarrel to-day in the meantime they are stuffing themselves with beaver.

Sept. 21. Rained hard till about one o'clock when we started and did not camp till after dark made about ten miles the river verey rapid and shalow have to use the rope all the time a few scatring spruce but mostly cottonwood.

Sept. 24. Got started about six o'clock and worked hard till after dark and made about ten miles the river verey bad the mountains getting lower as get nearer the canyon the Ma Nuska say we will get to Tarral to-day I hope so for I am about wore out.

Sept. 25.... We are camped on the west side of the river whear theare is three houses we stoped hear to see the Tayon.

Sept. 25. He is a large stout-looking man but ston blind he was verey pertacler to find out what I wanted up hear but was satessfied that I wont going to take his throne away from him.

Sept. 26. Well I have got to the great city of Tarrall at last forty-seven days from Nu Chuck it is a h—— of river to navigate no good as a route to transport troops I went through the canyon again to-day and from whear the river first begines to narrow to the mouth is as near as I can estimate about two miles the city consistes of two houses and about forty-five or fifty inhabitants men wemen and children....

Sept. 28. Wourking hard fixing a place to winter in it froze water in the house.

Sept. 30. The river is full of floating ice this morning as cold as it is in November in God's contrey and the princeple food of the inhabitants is rabbets they apear to be a cross betwen the jack rabbit of the plains and comen cotentayl thar are lotes of them around here.

Oct. 2. I am liveing alone not a native withen two miles I went out about sundown and killed five rabbits I am beginning to live like the natives.

Oct. 14. Snowing hard been at it all day and I have been with the negroes in Africa and the natives of Australa and among the Indians of the plains but of all the dirty divels I ever was with the Ma Nuska can beat them two to one. They take the hide of the rabbit and then boil him guts and all … thar clothes are never taken of till they fall of or ruther rot of the wemen all take snuf and I have never seen one of them wash her hands or face since I have been hear so you can judge how thay look and still the men watch them like a cat would a mouse.…

Oct. 15. A pleasant day so I can go out without an overcoat. Three of the Ma Nuska dogs got in a air hole and went to the dog heaven or h—— more likely and they are making as much fuse about it as if it was three of theare young ones.

Oct. 17. Bright cold day the Ma Nuska have just killed a bear on the other side of the river you would think h—— had broke loose if you heard the infearnel noise thay make.

Oct. 20. Had a veiset from the Cheif's son a verey good-looking man for a Ma Nuska he lives about five milles up the river it is verey cold the natives all dress in fur I think I can stand the cold better than they can.

Oct. 22. Thur is mourning in the camp No-til-nes passed in his checks this morning him and two others wear crossing the river at a place whear it is open and the raft capsized and he went under the ice I dont think thay make hordly so much fuss as thay did over the three dogs thay lost. It is not quite so cold to-day.

Oct. 24. Pleasent for this place. Two Col Chins came in from the headwaters of the Chitanah to-day one of them came to my hut and gave me a peace of native copper it is about one inch thick with rock atached to each side he says thar is mountins of it whear he got it I hope thar is I will find out how much thar is of it if I live.

Oct. 25. Clear but very cold my daley woark is to get wood to burn and kill rabbits to eat thar is no large game aurund here at preasent the natives say thar will be plenty of dear by un by thay say thar plenty of foxs but I have not seen a track so I don't think they are verey plenty.

Oct. 26.… I saw the Volcano smoking for the first time to-day it is the mountin laid down on the chart as Mount Wrangle it dont look more than twenty-five or thirtey milles from here but the natives say it will take me three days to go thar I cant get one of them to go near it so I will have to go alone I sholl go as soon as the river is safe.

Nov. 16. I have not writen aneything for some time it was the soame thing over and over every day. I made the atempt to get to the Volcano and failed I got within about one mile of the crater when one of my snow shoes broke and I came verey near passing in my checks before I could get back to the timber I froze several of my toes and my ears you ought to see them thay would match a goverment mules I don't think it is possible to make the ascent in the wenter but I think it would be easey in the summer I could not get aney of the natives to go with me thay are all afraid to go aney whear near it.... I wish you would inform the proper athortys that the traders at Chilcat are selling stricnyen to the Col China thay are no more fit to have poisen then a five year old child. The Ma Nuska are mostly armed with light double barrel guns or old Hudson Bay flent locks thay are very good marksmen considring the guns they have and in case of trouble with them thar powder would soon be spent and they could not get aney except at Newchuck or Chilcat and thay can't live away from the rivers one hundred white men could clean them out without much trouble....

Nov. 28. This is a quire contry October was verey cold November has been quit pleasent a man could go around in his shirt sleaves and not feel cold....

Dec. 4.... It is looking bad for me the Ma Nuska have killed three Col China and the Ma Nuska are nearly scared out of wits thay just brought me a report that the Col China have murdered the store keeper that keeps the Co. store on the Uycon somewhear near the mouth of the Tinenah the Ma Nuska say it was Tinenah cuses that done it but they are such d—— liars I dont know wheather to beleave them ore not.

Dec. 7. Rain poured down all day water a foot deep in my house it hase raised the river seven fut the river don't look so much like freasing over as it did two months ago.

Dec. 8. Clear and freasing a little the Ma Nuska and the Col China are going to have a grand pow wow about one hundred miles up the river I want to go and see the plaver but the Ma Nuska say the Col China will kill me and then the Americans would come and kill them I shall go if I can.

Dec. 18.... Things is looking bad the Col China have come to the Ma Nuska frontier and say thay are going to clean the Ma Nuska out a runner came in last night from the front he made the hundred milles in twenty-four hours the Tyon was at my cabin when he came and he came rushing in as if the divil was after him in less than an hour every man and boy old enough to handle a gun wear on the march up the river thay wouldnt let me go thay swor thay would tie me up if I tried to go the Tyon told me he did not think thar would be aney fighting he thought it would all end in talk but he promissed if thar was aney fighting to send for me so I am left the onley man in Taryel with all the wemen and children a fine dirty lot thay are.

Dec. 25. I wish you all a merey Christmass I had rabbet for my diner insted of turkey the weather has moderated and it is quit pleasent no news from the seat of war.

Jan. 1, 1885. I wish you all a happey new year it is quit pleasent weather hear somewhear about zero but I do not fell it cold thar is not a breath of wind thar has been no stormey weather since the seventh of Dec. nor wind enough to stir a leaf the war is over it all ended in talk and a big dance and I expect to start for the copper mines the midle of the month the natives say the ice will be good then I dont write much for the simple reason that thar is nothing to write about.

Jan. 4.... I have been haveing a little fun to breake the monotoney of life at Tarrell the Ma Nuska have got it into thar heads that I am a big medicen and one of them came to my cabin earley yesterday to get me to go and see his wife he said she was going to die if I did not go and cure her I went with him about three miles through the snow and found that the most that alled the slut was dirt.... I gave her eaght of Haynes piles and then made them strip her clothes of and scrub her from head to foot when they had got through scrubing her I made a mustard plaster ... her husband has been to my cabin to-day he says she is all right now he thinks me the boss medicen man I want the doctor when he writes to tell me if I treated the case properly.

Jan. 6. Verey cold this morning when I went to get up I found my whisker froze fast too my pelow and still I had slept warm and comfertable all night I wish I had some means of telling how cold it is and not a breath of wind.

Jan. 8. Not quit so cold I had a vesit from a Col China to-day he told me thar was a hundred white men on the Youcon somewhear near the mouth of the Tanenah as near as I could make out he says they have gone into camp thar I expect that Sheglen found good diggings thar and a porty have gone in to be ready in when spring opens I don't know what else would enduce white men to winter thar.

Jan 11. I had to go about four mils to-day to see a sick young one the fools think I can raise the dead.... There was an old woman in the house in the last stage of consumption and the fools wanted me to cure her I told them that the Big Tyon up aloft said no that she must die and that I could not do aneything for her.

Jan. 14. Verey cold froze water three feet from the fire I went yesterday to see how the Ma Nuska performed at a funral thay told me a young woman had died and thay weare going to burey her soon after I got thare one of the wemen began to chant a sort of tune in a low tone and preasently all hands joined in and thay kept geting louder and louder till I had to stuf my ears thay made such a noise after a while I thought I would have a look at the corpse I puled the cloth of her face and while I was looking she opned her eyes she want near as dead as thay had thought it apears she must have had some sort of a fit aneyway it bursted up the fun she lookes to be as likeley to live as aney of them when I left thay wear feeding her the soup from a rabbit's gutes.

Jan. 16. The cold is instense five feet above the fire the chemley is white weth frost.

Jan. 18. Still verey cold it would be all most imposable for troops to make a winter campaign the cold is so intense thay would all frease to death.

Jan. 29. Quit warm and pleasent the natives are cursing the warm weather it weats thar fur boots.

Feb. 2. The weather is still mild and pleasant the natives are scatring of from this place they squat here till they have eat all thar dried fish and stole nearley all my grub never hunted at all and now thay are half starved serves them right I wish thay weare more starved.

Feb. 5. Cloudy and colder light wind from the north the Ma Nuska have been promsing too start for Nuchuk for the two weeaks and thay hant started yet thay havent the least ideah of the value of time.

Feb. 7. The natives have promised to start to-day I am lookeing for them every menuit so I will seal up the book.

P.S.... The countrey here is intierley difrent from the coast it is a dry climat verey cold in winter and verey hot in summer not a bad contrey to live in if it want for the rascals that live in it if the divil is the father of liars he has got a fine lot of children up here and as for stealing I defy the worald to produce a more expert lot of theives thay have stole nearley all my grub thay broke in to my cabin while I was away up the river and stole all my tea and sugar and two sacks of flour and worst of all nearly all my tobacco I have onley one sack of flour left no tea or sugar I have been liveing on rabbet strat for the last month. I wish if you can get it you would send me a small flag I would like too have the honour of raiseing the old Flag whar a white man has never been before at the Coper mine.

JOHN BREMNER

When Allen left Taral, Bremner went along, traveling up the Chitina and Copper Rivers and then across the Alaska Range. By the time the party reached the Yukon River, Bremner was suffering from scurvy and a swollen sprained ankle. He stayed at the Yukon when Allen went on and said he would spend only one more season in Alaska and then head outside. That didn't happen, for he was later one of the first prospectors on the Koyukuk River. Then he and his partner Pete Johnson worked the Tramway Bar where, after Bremner was gone, gold would be found in the 1890s.

One day in 1888, Bremner offered to share his dinner with a young Indian and an older shaman. When the meal was concluded, the younger man took Bremner's gun and shot him. The two men threw Bremner's body in the river and stole his supplies and boat. When Fortymile miners learned of the killing, they hunted down the boy and hung him. The boy's family later killed the shaman.[4]

Although the only thing Bremner left in Alaska was his journal, two rivers bear his name. Henry Allen named a tributary of the Copper River the Bremner, and his fellow prospectors named a tributary of the Koyukuk the John.

Notes

Epigraph: John Bremner, quoted by Seton Karr, *Shores and Alps of Alaska* (London: Sampson Low, Marston, Searle, & Rivington, 1887), 210.

1 "History of the Bremner family," July 22, 2012, http://www.bremnerhistory.com/C_3.html.

2 Allen, *Report of an Expedition*, 48.

3 Seton Karr, *Shores and Alps of Alaska*, 200.

4 James Wickersham, *Old Yukon: Tales—Trails—and Trials* (Washington, DC: Washington Law Book Co., 1938), 127–28.

10

HERBERT L. ALDRICH

Whaling with the Fleet of 1887

I found a most interesting field of study in the whaling industry. Its records spread out before me a series of marvelous adventures and what seemed like foolhardy attempts to outdo human possibilities.

Although he was only twenty-five, Herbert Aldrich had already been managing editor of newspapers in Cleveland and Jacksonville. A graduate of Cornell, Aldrich was working as a journalist in New Bedford, Massachusetts, the world's preeminent whaling port, when he became interested in the subject of whaling.

By the 1880s, much had been written about whaling and whalers, but no one had documented Arctic whaling, and Aldrich decided to be first. In order to do that, he would have to sail with the fleet. This was a dicey proposition, given the serious risks involved, but Aldrich's case was even more complicated, because he had been diagnosed with tuberculosis and told that he might not survive the year.

Nevertheless, packing along his notebook and Scoville detective camera, in 1887 Aldrich traveled for eight months with the Arctic whaling fleet. He moved from one ship to another as whaling crews and their captains confronted whales and ice. As he explained in *Arctic Alaska and Siberia; or, Eight Months with the Arctic Whalemen*, whale hunters of the day no longer depended on old-fashioned harpoons and spears but on more modern methods—lethal blows delivered by bombs loaded with gunpowder. These were shot into whales and exploded. Aldrich said that what had "once" been a royal sport had become a mere "butchering operation,"[1] albeit a dangerous one. In the pages of *Outing Magazine*, he described an incident in which a badly wounded whale had balanced a boat on its back, risen in the air, and, sweeping its flukes, "smash[ed] the stern off the boat with almost the neatness that a buzz saw could cut it off."[2]

At the whaling industry's high point, in the mid-1840s, New Englanders were the primary whale hunters in Russian-American waters, with nearly 300 ships in the fleet. With the discovery of petroleum and kerosene, the reliance on whale oil decreased. Demand for whalebone continued, however, as it was still needed for corset stays, parasol ribs, brushes, and whips.

The Civil War delivered further blows to the industry. The fleet was depleted when the Union loaded forty whaling ships with stone and sank them to blockade southern ports, and when Confederate raiders captured and burned forty-six of the North's boats.

The industry suffered a series of mishaps beginning in 1871, when thirty-four ships chased whales into an open stretch of water between the ice pack and the far northern coast of Alaska. The winds shifted, the ice closed in, and the ships were crushed. The crewmen survived, but the ships were lost. A few years thereafter, twelve more ships were crushed in ice. The sailors who abandoned ship were rescued by Natives, while those who had refused to leave the ships—for fear of the Natives—all died.

It was a squally day in March when Aldrich left San Francisco on the *Young Phoenix.* He was bound for a region where three hundred lives and millions of dollars in property had been lost in the preceding thirty years. The Arctic was a place "beset with danger,"[3] with frequent gales, fogs, and ice, and Aldrich knew there was a one-in-fifteen chance that the ship he was traveling on would be wrecked.

Whales followed the melting ice pack north, and the fleet, in turn, followed the whales as they migrated past St. Lawrence Island, through the Bering Strait into the Chukchi Sea, then east toward Point Barrow and the Beaufort Sea. Hugging the edge of the ice, the whales surfaced now and again as the crewmen watched for their spouts.

The most dangerous waters in Alaska were those off the North Slope, for there the ice appeared without warning. The waters were shallow, and there was neither a place to which a ship could retreat nor a means of communication with the outside world. Besides the possibilities of death by freezing or drowning, there was the potential for conflict with Eskimos intoxicated on hooch.

With sailors standing poised on deck calling commands to the steersmen, Arctic whalers took great care to avoid the ice. Winds could shift suddenly and enclose ships, and even the strongest vessels were as fragile as eggshells in a confrontation with an ice floe. There were some steamships in the fleet, but many were sailing ships and were difficult to steer. Collisions with ice and other ships were inevitable. When gales blew, ships were bumped from one cake of ice to another, sometimes with disaster averted only by an intervening block of ice.

At the time of the following passage, Aldrich was sailing on the steamer *Lucretia* in the hazardous waters off Point Barrow. The ship had passed the scene of the 1871 disaster, where the hulls of the wrecked ships stood coated in ice. The *Lucretia*'s crew pushed on, moving slowly in a heavy fog and dodging ice. It was in those far northern waters that Aldrich would witness his first kill.

HERBERT L. ALDRICH

Whaling with the Fleet of 1887[*]

Though many whales were caught by the ships in Behring Sea, I did not happen to be near enough to enjoy the sport, and it was not until we anchored under East Cape that I saw my first whale caught. Everything had been so interesting, however, that I had not been disappointed, and after I had seen the first one, I rejoiced that it was the first, everything was so favorable. The day was beautiful, and the captain and I embraced the opportunity to make the round of the nine ships at anchor and relate the story of the wrecked man [who had been rescued] at Cape Navarin. When, on the extreme northern ship, a whale was "raised," or seen, coming leisurely along up the edge of the shore-ice, the news spread like wild-fire, and in a few minutes thirty or more whale-boats were flitting about, each endeavoring to get as near as possible to the spot where the whale would next rise to spout.

When he rose, a boat darted an iron but it did not hold. At the next rising, another boat attempted to hit him, but also failed; but the third boat made fast to him. It was a grand sight to see the whale make a lunge and start seaward, towing the boat after him at a terrific pace. He went a mile or two, then wheeled about and made a straight line for the shore-ice. Another boat was soon alongside to bend on more line to the nearly exhausted tubs of the fast boat.

All the captains became so excited and interested in the chase that they longed for some of the fun, so four of them took the *Hunter's* steam-launch, I accompanying them. As soon as we reached the shore ice, I saw the whale

[*]From *Arctic Alaska and Siberia* (1889), 90–98.

spout behind a long point of ice. It would have taken a boat considerable time to sail there, but we steamed around it, and, before I could comprehend the situation, were alongside the monster. It seemed incredible that such a powerful creature could be killed. With Captain Cogan at the helm, Captain Sherman with a darting-gun, Captain Kelley with a shoulder-gun, and Captain Winslow and me as ballast, we bore down on him, fired two bombs into him and rushed past, just in time to escape a sweeping blow from his powerful tail.

It is disappointing to see a whale, for most pictures represent him as standing up like a buoy or posing on his tail on top of the water. The real fact is that only the top of the head about the spout-hole and a small piece of the back are seen, and perhaps the "flukes," or in common English, the tail, may take an occasional sweep in the air. As near as we were, we could look down into the water upon the creature, [and] his great size could be partially comprehended.

It seems to be the duty of every man in the boat, when the whale is struck, to yell at the top of his voice. Even where there is dignity to be kept up, a certain amount of this has to be done. In the midst of the shouting was heard the muffled "boom," "boom" of the two bombs, and the whale rolled over, dead, without a struggle. I stayed aboard the *Lucretia* that night to see the whale cut in.

As soon as a whale is killed, the vessel gets under way and sails to him, taking him on the starboard side, in front of the gangway. With a steamer, as in this instance, this is very easily done, but a sailing vessel may find it necessary to maneuver some time before getting the conditions right for work. First a strong chain, or hawser, is secured around the flukes. This runs through the hawse-pipe and is firmly fastened to the forward bit near the windlass. Then another chain is secured to one fin, and it is with this second chain that the whale is managed.

The carcass runs fore-and-aft, the head being aft, and the fin in front of the gangway. With sharp cutting spades, a man cuts through the blubber, circling around the whale from the extremity of the mouth toward the tail, corkscrew like. He cuts down to the "lean." By hauling on the fin-chain the carcass rolls, and the "blanket-piece" of blubber tears itself off, aided by the cutting spades. When the whale is rolled quarter over, one lip comes uppermost. A tackle is fastened to this; then it is cut off, hoisted on deck and dropped into the "blubber room," as the space between decks, from the mainmast to the forecastle, is called. All hoisting is done by the windlass, and in most of the vessels power comes from a donkey-engine. The blanket-piece is started again and the whale rolled half-way over. The throat is then uppermost. This in turn is cut off, and deposited in the blubber room, then the other lip is rolled up and removed. By this time, the blanket-piece becomes unwieldy in its length, so another hold is secured close down to the carcass, and the strip of blubber, perhaps fifteen feet long and six feet wide, cut off and dropped into the blubber room.

The most difficult part of the whole operation is now at hand, and that is to cut off the "head," or upper jaw, which contains all the whalebone. A false or careless move might destroy hundreds of dollars worth of bone or, possibly, cause the loss of the whole head. A chain is carefully drawn through a hole cut between the scalp bone and the tough blubber about the spout-hole. The backbone is chopped nearly through, near where the blanket-piece was started, then by a jerk of the tackle the weight breaks the remainder and the head is hauled on deck. There was once a whaling captain who disjointed the head instead of chopping it off. This whale's head contained about twenty-five hundred pounds of whalebone, and as the price of bone was three dollars and fifty cents a pound at that time, it can readily be seen how anxious a whaleman must be, when cutting-in, until he gets the head on deck. Heads contain over six hundred slabs of bone, and in a large whale like this, the pieces range in length from twelve feet, or a little over, down to a few inches. For convenience in working, each ship has a "cutting stage" of planks that hangs over the water in front of the gangway, so that the men can stand nearly over the whale. It is from this that the work is done, and it was here that I stood to see the whole operation.

With the head cut off, the rest of the cutting-in is easy and simple. The blanket piece is peeled off in strips about fifteen feet long, until a point near the flukes is reached. There the backbone is disjointed. The final haul brings on deck the flukes with the blanket-piece. The carcass either floats off or sinks. These blanket-pieces of blubber are cut and torn off the whale in the same manner that the peel is cut and torn off an orange when paring it. Frequently, the natives are aboard, and work is done slowly in order that they may have an opportunity to cut off as much as possible of the lean meat. The cutting-in was a novelty to me but the work of the natives was more entertaining. They had six canoes crowded in near the whale, and the instant there was a lull in the proceedings, a man from each would clamber on to the carcass, splash about in the blood and water, and slash away at the meat with villainous looking knives. They worked like heroes and yelled like fiends. Some worked with their hands under water, and most of them were knee-deep in it all the time. One fellow lay almost flat on his stomach and burrowed in under the blubber in advance of the cutters. His feet were flying about dangerously near keen-edged knives, but he did not get cut.

Whalemen still observe the old sperm-whaling custom of lustily shouting, "Hurrah for five and forty more" when the head or last piece of blubber is landed on deck. But this shout is not because the work is all done. Early the next morning, the try-pots were set to working. First, the blubber was cut into "horse pieces" about a foot square and two feet long, then "minced," that is cut into thin slices to facilitate the trying-out of the oil. The blubber then goes into the pots, and after the oil is boiled out, the remains of the blubber have become hard and brittle, but are pressed to get the last dregs of oil; then these "scraps" are used for fuel, and they make a hot fire.

This night the sun barely dipped below the horizon at midnight, but when darkness does interfere with the cutting-in, or the trying-out, a lot of scraps are put into a wire basket and lighted, making a "bug light" which is equal to a pitch pine torch. The oil is slowly bailed from the try-pots into a cooler, and, after running through two or three, is pumped into casks and stowed down in the hold. This whale made one hundred and twenty barrels of oil.

Such a feast as the natives had after their work was finished! They scattered all over the ship, and in their canoes, eating blubber. Each one was gnawing away on a big chunk, sometimes of several pounds. He would surround one corner with his mouth, grasp it in his teeth, then saw it off with his knife. Why the lips were not sawed off was a mystery. The bigger the mouthful, the more happy he appeared.

When no whales were in sight, the winds were becalmed, or ice floes blocked further passage, the seamen passed the time "gamming." Crews of neighboring ships would be invited aboard for communal meals and storytelling. There were tales of attempted mutinies and criminals who evaded the law by joining whaling crews. There was also the story about a crew who survived thirty-six days of Arctic weather in an open boat by eating raw seal. Their captain said, "I aroused the men only to find that one had died."[4]

During these gatherings, good food was provided—fried oysters, lobster salad, sugar cookies, and pear preserves. Aldrich sampled meatballs made of whale meat ground with pork and spices and found them "surprisingly toothsome," if a little gamey.[5]

After the conclusion of his Arctic venture, Aldrich continued to write about whaling. He also established a publishing company and a successful magazine, *Marine Engineering*. His 1887 photographs of North Slope Inupiaq Eskimos and of Arctic whalers at sea were the first ever taken of those subjects. Some of his pictures, including one of heavily bundled whaling captains, can be viewed online at the website of the New Bedford Whaling Museum. Aldrich's work has been exhibited there, as well as at Barrow, on Alaska's North Slope.

Despite the doctors' prediction that Aldrich might not survive his twenty-fifth year, he was a mere six weeks shy of his eighty-eighth birthday at the time of his death. He was then living with his wife in the Dakota apartments on New York's Upper West Side.[6]

Notes

Epigraph: Herbert L. Aldrich, *Arctic Alaska and Siberia; or, Eight Months with the Arctic Whalemen* (Chicago: Rand, McNally and Company, 1889), ix.

1 Aldrich, *Arctic Alaska*, 103.

2 Herbert L. Aldrich, "Eskimo Whaling," *Outing Magazine* 18, no. 1 (1891): 13.

3 Aldrich, *Arctic Alaska*, 87.

4 Ibid., 190.

5 Ibid., 25.

6 "Herbert Aldrich, Ex-Publisher, Dies," *New York Times*, March 28, 1948.

11

HARRY DE WINDT

Perilous Crawl Up the Chilkoot

Everything had to be thought of—provisions, arms, and ammunition, especially the first-named, for Alaska produces absolutely nothing in the way of food.

English explorer and travel writer Harry de Windt went to Alaska twice, accompanied both times by his companion and aide, manservant George Harding.

De Windt had been born in Paris and was educated at Cambridge. Before his first Alaskan venture, he had traveled from Peking to France and from Russia to India via Persia. Among other things, he inspected prisons in Siberia and served as aide-de-camp to his brother-in-law, Rajah of Sarawak; he would eventually publish a number of books about his adventures.

Both of the Alaskan trips had the same goal: to prove that it was possible to build a railroad between New York and Paris by traveling overland through Alaska, across the Bering Strait, and through Siberia. Never mind that a goodly portion of the journey—namely the sailing through the Inside Passage—would perforce be over water. To de Windt, the trip was strictly overland.

It took nearly a year to complete the plans for the first trip. As de Windt explained in *Through the Gold-Fields of Alaska to Bering Straits,* his route entailed travel by rail from New York to Vancouver, by tourist boat from Vancouver to Juneau, by private craft from Juneau to Dyea. Having reached the head of Lynn Canal, he would cross Chilkoot Pass on foot, sail the Canadian lakes and rivers to the Yukon's headwaters, and then continue downriver to the Yukon's mouth on the Bering Sea. He hoped to mush across the Bering Strait by dogsled and, having gained the coast of Siberia, to continue by sled to the terminus of the Russian railroad. He would complete the trip by rail to Paris. At least, that was the plan.

With this ambitious agenda, de Windt and Harding set out from New York in May of 1896. In June, under cloudless blue skies, they reached Juneau and found it full of gaily dressed tourists. These persons, de Windt said, would go home satisfied they had "done" Alaska, "unmindful of the fact that their Alaska bears about as much relation to the entire country as the county of Kent to the rest of England."[1]

Juneau boasted two hotels, numerous drinking establishments, and a blaze of electric lights from dusk until dawn. Roaming the streets were prospectors getting outfitted for the goldfields, ladies of "doubtful reputation" hanging about in their bloomers, and sharks waiting to fleece the unwary. The tourists explored the streets, knee-deep in mud from the constant rain, while a local photographer did a brisk trade taking their pictures and Indians hawked them curios at outrageous prices.

De Windt engaged Joe Cooper, an experienced miner headed back to the Yukon, to guide him and Harding over Chilkoot Pass and on to Forty Mile City on the Yukon. The three sailed from Juneau on the *Rustler*, a forty-five-foot-long craft. The boat had a capacity of twenty-five, but, on this occasion, was carrying sixty-seven, and many of them were inebriated. As the boat pulled away from the dock, the passengers crossed to port side to wave goodbye, and, with water pouring in over the gunwale, the *Rustler* was nearly swamped.

The pilot, whose most recent experience had been as a milkman in San Francisco, shared his whiskey with de Windt, then went aft to refresh himself, leaving de Windt at the helm. By midnight, drunks lay sprawled about the deck like a "Texan saloon after a free fight."[2]

Also onboard the *Rustler* was Josiah Spurr, whose account of his geological survey of the goldfields appears later in this collection. Spurr and de Windt had met at a hotel in Juneau, and, although Spurr enjoyed the Englishman's tales of his travels in Borneo and Afghanistan, he thought there was "a hint of recklessness or carelessness in his face."[3]

When the *Rustler* reached Dyea, the landing was in waters so shallow that passengers had to wade ashore half a mile in water up to their knees, "occasionally," de Windt said, falling in up to their waists. "Alaska is no place for the fastidious," he wrote. "If you want a thing done, you must do it yourself, or 'get left.'"[4] Apparently de Windt did not consider himself bound too strictly by that maxim, since he had made arrangements for Indian packers to carry his goods over Chilkoot Pass.

De Windt reached Dyea in June of 1896, only two months ahead of the great gold strike at Dawson. There were a few prospectors headed for the goldfields, but their numbers were insignificant compared to the masses that were to come.

In the following passage, de Windt describes his climb up and over the 3,500-foot Chilkoot Pass, providing a taste of the hardships in store for the tens of thousands who were soon to follow him over the mountain.

HARRY DE WINDT

Perilous Crawl Up the Chilkoot[*]

Glorious weather favored our departure from Dyea. About 7 a.m., Heron and the Indians appeared, leading the three sorry-looking screws that were to carry our outfit as far as Sheep Camp, twelve miles distant, beyond which there is no foothold for horses. Flapjacks and coffee were discussed while the packs were adjusted, and by nine o'clock all was ready for a start, my party consisting of our three selves and the four Indians who were to accompany us as guides and packers as far as Lake Lindemann [Lindeman].

The first part of the trail after leaving Dyea follows the bed of the Dyea River, which in springtime is a roaring torrent, but which dwindles down in summer to a narrow stream, partly concealed by huge boulders. There is no path of any kind, and the rough, rocky ground made walking so laborious that frequent halts were necessary, and we travelled barely two miles an hour. The horses slipped and slithered painfully over the smooth, worn rocks, and often fell heavily, which entailed further tedious delays while their burdens were set straight. I did not regret having refused [local trader] Heron's kind offer of a mount!

Three hours of this work brought us to a spot where the trail turns off abruptly to the right, and where the actual ascent, through a dense forest, commences. The path here was very bad, and in many places almost impassable—partly on account of roots and tree-stumps, but chiefly because it is laid across a succession of deep morasses, which cannot be avoided without making a détour of several miles. In one of these bogs, where the mire was quite waist deep, a horse lost his footing and fell. More than an hour was occupied in extricating him, and, indeed, it looked at one time as though he would dis-

[*]From *Through the Gold-Fields of Alaska to Bering Straits* (1898), 24–38.

appear altogether, packs and all. Two swift mountain torrents, several yards across, fed by a large glacier this side of the Chilkoot, were then forded.

This was only accomplished with difficulty, for the poor, jaded nags were exhausted by their struggles in the swamps, and the swift rush of the icy cold water nearly carried them off their legs. At some seasons of the year, these fords constitute a very dangerous feature of this portion of the journey, and several men have been drowned while crossing them. Near one of these streams we found a party of gold-seekers camped, who were returning to Juneau, having failed (owing to lack of provisions) to reach the lakes.

Towards mid-day the heat became intense, and I drank more than once from the clear brooklets that, fringed with cool green ferns and wild flowers, came rippling down the mountainside. But I paid dearly for my rashness by suffering for many hours after from the raging thirst that snow and glacier water invariably create. Joe Cooper informed me that this is one of the chief discomforts of Alaskan travel, especially in winter. A small pebble kept in the mouth will afford relief, while cold tea is the best thirst-quencher that exists. Water (in Alaska) only increases the evil.[*]

Sheep Camp was reached about 6 p.m., both men and horses being pretty well done up after the trudge over what Joe Cooper described as "a pretty easy trail." The place was deserted, though a smoldering camp-fire showed that a party had only recently left for the summit. The camp is a circular clearing in the forest, where trees have been felled for perhaps fifty yards around. We encamped on the banks of a swift, shallow stream that bisects the circle. It is a sheltered, picturesque spot, and the bright sunshine, fragrant grass and flowers, and brawling brook would have reminded one of a bit of Devonshire scenery had it not been for a range of rocky, precipitous mountains that barred the way a few miles ahead. From here can be seen the huge Sheep Camp Glacier, suspended so insecurely between two granite peaks that it looks as though a child's touch would send it crashing into the valley below. The face of this glacier is about 300 feet high. Loud reports, like the distant roar of heavy guns, are continually heard issuing from it, and these were at times so deafening that on one occasion we rushed out of the tent expecting to find that the whole mass had fallen from its precarious perch. (I am informed that a portion of this glacier became detached in the summer of 1897 and flooded Sheep Camp, killing a number of people.)

[*]According to "Dehydration in Extreme Environments," Oklahoma State Department of Education, July 22, 2012, at http://ok.gov/sde/sites/ok.gov.sde/files/PE-Fluids.pdf, glacial water may have a deyhydrating effect.

The ever-changing effects of light and shade that passed over this glacier were indescribably beautiful. In dull weather, the surface would be a turquoise blue, and its crevasses the color of a sapphire; on sunny days the entire expanse would be white, bright, and dazzling as a huge diamond; while during the twilight hours the most delicate shades of pink, mauve, and tender green would sweep like a movable rainbow over the icy wilderness, that seemed so near and yet was unapproachable.

One could stand for hours and watch this natural kaleidoscope. And, indeed, there were plenty of opportunities for studying the beauties of nature, for a delay of four days occurred here. Some Indians returning from the summit came into camp about 4 a.m. the day after our arrival. They looked worn out and exhausted, and, after some food, told us that no outfits could be got over for a couple of days at least. The trail beyond Stonehouse (the tree limit) was in a shocking condition, and the snow in many parts waist-deep. It was therefore decided that Cooper should push on alone, if possible, to Lake Lindemann the next morning, and commence building our boat. Harding and I were to follow with the Indians and outfit on the first favorable opportunity; but as travelers are sometimes detained here for a fortnight, waiting for fair weather, the date of our departure seemed rather uncertain.

It was weary work waiting, for there was absolutely nothing to do. Books do not form part of an Alaskan traveller's kit, for, owing to the barren nature of the country, every ounce must be sacrificed to the food supply. On the second day, two parties arrived from Dyea and encamped on the other side of the stream. We recognized some of our *Rustler* friends, who greeted us cordially, and were not in the least surprised to find that we had come to a full stop so early in the journey.

A letter was brought in by one Daniel, an Indian, early on the third morning, from Joe Cooper. Joe had safely reached Lake Lindemann and had begun to build the boat. He had been overtaken by a heavy snow-storm on the summit, which made the trail on the downward side very bad, and more risky than usual. Joe begged us to send food at once, having finished the bag of biscuits with which he started. Several parties were camped on the lake, boat-building, but provisions were very scarce.

The weather being favorable, I resolved to move on that night with the outfit, and dispatched Daniel in the meantime with a small quantity of flour and some bacon. Hearing of my intention, our Dyea Indians slouched into the tent and obstinately refused to pack one ounce to the lake unless they were paid $12 for every 100 pounds. They had agreed at Dyea to take $9, but the scoundrels knew, as we did, how helpless we were up here. Our *Rustler* friends had foolishly promised to pay $11, so there was nothing for it but to do likewise. Besides, another day's delay might have meant another week's bad weather.

The passage of the Chilkoot is generally made by night, as the soft, deep snow is then in firmer condition. The outfit was dispatched at 3 p.m., to await us at Stonehouse, about 2,000 feet below the summit, where a halt is made to gather strength for the real struggle. I must admit that when I saw the crushing weights carried by the Indians, and the perilous trail over which they were borne, I ceased to wonder that the Dyea men had struck for higher wages. A Thlinkit Indian will pack 120 pounds with ease up places where an unencumbered white man would be toiling on his hands and knees. One of the Chilkat tribe has even packed a piano-organ, weighing 220 pounds, over to the lakes, alone and unassisted. And yet these natives subsist almost entirely on dried fish. They are terrible drunkards, but, as a severe penalty awaits those found selling them whiskey, they can seldom indulge in their favorite vice.

By 10 p.m., all is ready for a start. We have no mountaineering paraphernalia, and are armed simply with three stout wooden staffs, cut that afternoon; but these are discarded long before the summit is reached. Passing the silent white tents of our sleeping companions, we enter a dark and narrow defile that becomes steeper and steeper as the pass is approached. The trail is rough and stony and intersected by numberless streams, while tree-stumps, gnarled roots, and tangled brushwood occasionally bring us down headlong. Presently, the forest becomes less dense, and patches of snow appear on either hand. An hour later, we take our first rest, drenched with perspiration, at Stonehouse, a rocky ledge overhanging the first of seven or eight snowy "plateaus" that must be crossed to reach the foot of the actual peak, which is itself nearly 1,000 feet high. The Chilkoot cannot really be called a pass. It would be considered a dangerous mountain in Switzerland, and a question of guides, ropes, and ice-axes.

Stonehouse is the limit of trees. A huge granite rock, shaped something like a human dwelling, suggested the name. We found our Indians huddled up under this, sheltered from an icy wind that whistled through my fur jacket as though it were muslin. After a brief halt, we pushed on, descending a steep ridge until we stood on the first ice "plateau." The travelling here was much easier, and we went cautiously ahead in Indian file, two Siwashes (the Alaskan term for Indians) in front, two in the rear, and ourselves in the center. And yet this portion of the ascent is, perhaps, the most perilous.

This "plateau," like all the others, was broken away by numerous water-courses, and was simply a kind of crust, suspended 15 to 20 feet above the ground. Had there been fir-trees below, we should have been standing on the upper branches! There was absolutely no path or trail to guide one, and huge crevasses, where the snow had fallen in upon some foaming torrent, appeared at frequent intervals. We progressed but slowly, for our guides probed the snow carefully at every step. They knew that a breakthrough would mean certain death.

These "plateaus" increased in steepness until midway up the last we had thrown away our sticks and were scrambling painfully on hands and knees. It was necessary to scratch holes in the snow with our fingers to gain any ground. The Indians, with their heavy packs, used short knives for this purpose, but stopped every few moments to regain their breath, for which I was not sorry. It was impossible to rest for more than a few moments, for to let go would have meant a fall of perhaps a couple of hundred feet to the foot of the slope. The Bishop of Alaska has described this portion of the ascent as "hair-raising" work, and he does not exaggerate. To make matters worse, a thin, drizzling rain now fell, which chilled us to the bone and made the going even worse than before.

These plateaus appeared to be oval in shape. Each terminates in a kind of narrow antechamber formed by enormous boulders. These gloomy portals, which were passed with some difficulty, recalled [nineteenth-century French illustrator Gustave] Doré's pictures of the "Inferno," and the outlook, when we emerged from them on to another almost perpendicular wall of ice, was not a cheerful one. The scene was one of utter desolation. Here and there, below us, masses of black rock dotted the white expanse, like islands in a sea of snow; while overhead towered the grim, spectral peak of the Chilkoot, rendered still more vague and terrible by a rapidly rising mist. This presently grew so dense that further progress became impossible.

Scaling the rocky ridge that encloses the last "plateau," we descended into a kind of cavern, which, though open to the rain, afforded some protection from the cutting blast. Here we managed to light a smoky, spluttering fire, over which we shivered until the gray dawn partly dispelled the fog and enabled us to resume our journey.

We soon reached the actual base of the Chilkoot, and here hard work commenced in grim earnest up the granite face of the mountain. The distance from our camping-ground to the summit is barely 1,000 feet, but the ascent occupied nearly two hours. There is, of course, no path, nor would it be possible to make one; for the rocks are loose and insecure, and the passage of a man will often send a boulder crashing down, to the deadly peril of those below. In some places, it was necessary to squeeze round the wall of the precipice on narrow ledges of rock that trembled underfoot and threatened to dislodge and send one whirling through space into eternity. The last 300 feet was like scaling the walls of a house. With ropes and proper appliances, the passage of this mountain could be made far easier; but it was, under the circumstances, such exhausting, heart-breaking work that I more than once had serious thoughts of turning back. Finally, however, at about 4 a.m., we stood on the summit, breathless, bleeding, and ragged, but safe.

At Lake Lindeman, every man, whether "millionaire or miner," was compelled to "turn to,"[5] fell timber, saw it into planks, and build a craft—apparently de Windt was the exception, since he had turned the task over to guide Cooper—and when de Windt arrived, Cooper was, in fact, hard at work on a craft that looked "as crank as a Thames canoe."[6] He was building a boat for a party of three, not knowing that on the way over the Chilkoot, de Windt had invited a wandering Catholic priest to join his party.

Among those de Windt encountered at Lindeman were the Ashes, a traveling impresario and his wife—"a massive golden-haired lady of pleasing presence in bloomer costume."[7] The couple was headed to Circle City with such a great quantity of belongings that they were building a scow capable of hauling ten or fifteen tons. One of their possessions was a roulette board, leading de Windt to conclude that the Ashes had more in mind than theatrical presentations.

While some of the boats built at Lindeman sank upon launch, de Windt's party floated off in Cooper's little "*chef-d'oeuvre*," as de Windt called it. The priest, Father Barnum, seated himself "with mathematical precision" in the center of a pile of baggage. The boat was so heavily loaded that freeboard was a mere two inches, and the slightest movement, even the dipping of an oar, brought water over the gunwale. At the head of Lake Bennett, de Windt purchased a second larger boat. The party then loaded the gear into Cooper's boat, named the *Slug*, and towed it along behind as they rode in the larger *Marjorie*.

As things developed, de Windt was not able to mush across the Bering Strait, for it never froze over in winter. Falling back on his alternate plan, previously arranged through diplomatic channels, he caught a ride on the revenue cutter *Bear.* He and Harding were landed at a settlement in Siberia with the unpromising name of Oumwaidjik. At first it appeared the Natives there would help de Windt along the next stage of his journey. Instead, they took the Englishmen captive and robbed them of their stores.

When they learned there was a plan afoot to kill them, the resourceful and desperate Harding tied a Union Jack to a whale rib on the beach. A passing ship spotted the flag and rescued de Windt and Harding. In the six weeks they had been ashore, the Englishmen had been so debilitated—Harding was suffering from a mysterious illness, and de Windt's body was covered with scabies—that the *Bear's* crew didn't recognize them.

Seven years later, de Windt and Harding were back in Alaska on their second attempt to make the overland trek between Paris and New York. This time, they achieved their goal, and de Windt recorded the journey in *From Paris to New York by Land.* He attributed the success of the second trip to the lessons he had learned on that first failed venture, and acknowledged that one such lesson was to avoid Oumwaidjik at all costs.

Notes

Epigraph: Harry de Windt, *Through the Gold-Fields of Alaska to Bering Straits* (New York and London: Harper Brothers, 1898), 3.

1 De Windt, *Through the Gold-Fields*, 2.

2 Ibid., 7.

3 Josiah Edward Spurr, *Through the Yukon Gold Diggings: A Narrative of Personal Travel* (Boston: Eastern Publishing Company, 1900), 24.

4 De Windt, *Through the Gold-Fields,* 13.

5 Ibid., 42.

6 Ibid., 43.

7 Ibid., 43.

12

CAPTAIN WILLIAM ABERCROMBIE

One Night on Valdez Glacier

The thermometer registered 8° below zero. . . .
at daylight the next morning some of the men were beating
their frozen boots on the crust of the snow so as to get
them in condition to pull on their feet.

In 1884, William Abercrombie went to Alaska at the behest of General Nelson Miles, the officer Morgan Sherwood called the "champion of old-style Army exploration in Alaska."[1] Congress was unwilling, in the 1880s, to spend money on military expeditions to a region largely unsettled by whites. Miles, who wanted to know more about the unmapped interior, used the unfounded threat of potential Indian trouble to obtain the financial means needed to fund the exploring parties that he would send into various regions of Alaska.[2]

On his 1884 expedition, then Lieutenant Abercrombie had two goals: to reconnoiter the Copper River region and to locate a route from the coast into the heartland. He was supported by a large, well-equipped party, but the task he faced was formidable. Along the coast near the Copper, mountains and a series of glaciers block access to the interior. Abercrombie and his men tried to ascend the river, but the water was so cold that they could pull their boats upstream for only fifteen or twenty minutes before having to release the towlines and run along the bank to get warm.[3] The waters were high, the snow was soft, the river was filled with massive floating chunks of ice—and his Indian guides deserted. Abercrombie was a veteran of Indian wars in the West and no ninny, but, at the end of the season, he judged his mission a failure.

Back home, Abercrombie announced that ascension of the Copper River was impossible and confided in a fellow officer that he would never go back to Alaska. He would be proven wrong on both counts. The fellow officer was Henry T. Allen, who the following year would show that it was indeed possible to ascend the Copper River. And Abercrombie would return to Alaska—although it would be fourteen years before he did so.

When Abercrombie returned in 1898, the number of prospectors in Alaska had grown, thus increasing political interest in the territory. Abercrombie, by then a captain, was in charge of one of three army expeditions sent to Alaska that year. His assignment was to find a route leading from Valdez on the coast to the goldfields—the "all-American route"—so that prospectors no longer had to pass through Canada to get to the interior of Alaska. This operation brought Abercrombie back to the Copper River, the very region that had defeated him years earlier.

Abercrombie, his three officers, and twenty men got off to a rocky start. On the voyage north from Puget Sound, their ship was beset by a continuous driving snowfall. When they reached Haines, Abercrombie discovered that the reindeer allotted for the group's transportation needs were unfit. At Valdez, he learned that his supplies had been commingled with those of two other expeditions, as well as with six hundred tons of prospectors' freight. The goods were divided equitably, but Abercrombie found that no provision had been made for off-loading them. His men waded in with rubber boots and carried the supplies ashore on their backs.

It was mid-April in Valdez. Seven feet of snow covered the ground, with more falling. Abercrombie sent out scouting parties, and they met with disaster. One man was drowned while trying to cross the Tonsina River; other soldiers and stock were caught in a snow slide and nearly lost their lives. A private on a glacial summit was diagnosed with typhoid fever. When told that the man would die if he had to travel the twenty-five miles back to camp on a sled, Abercrombie responded that the trip could hardly be more deleterious to the man's health than if he were left lying in a sleeping bag in the snow, and ordered the man be brought down.

To reach the interior, Abercrombie needed animals, and, despite his efforts to obtain them, none were forthcoming. When the mail boat arrived near the end of May with no stock onboard and no letter promising the future delivery of any, Abercrombie decided to sail back to Seattle to locate pack animals. Once there, he realized that all trained pack animals had been sent to Cuba, where the nation was engaged in war, so he shipped wild horses north.

When Abercrombie got back to Valdez, it was July. There, he learned that he had lost two officers—one had been ordered to rejoin his regiment, the other had been sent home suffering from snow blindness and exposure. He now had only Lieutenant P. G. Lowe under his command, but Lowe was a man who could "be killed but not conquered."[4] So long as Lowe's health held up, Abercrombie wasn't worried.

There were two potential routes to the interior: one led up the Lowe River and through Keystone Pass; the other crossed Valdez Glacier. Lowe and Abercrombie decided that the glacial route was more feasible, and that Lowe and some of the men would go first, while Abercrombie and others would follow.

But once on the glacier, Lowe sent back a report saying that the snow was too soft and that the route would not be safe until the snow hardened up. Given that, Abercrombie decided to try the alternate route that went up the Lowe River. Not long after he started, he reached a glacial stream that had been turned into a torrent by steady rains. Having forded a number of "ugly-looking" streams, Abercrombie plunged in anyway. He was midstream when he heard the boulders being washed along the river bottom and realized that he was in trouble.

His horse, in water up to its shoulders, was knocked over and rolled a hundred and fifty yards or so downstream while Abercrombie clung to its mane. The horse was then pinned against a rock, with his legs in the air and Abercrombie caught underneath. The animal finally regained footing and scrambled from the river with his rider hanging on by the tail. In the mayhem, one of Abercrombie's hands had been smashed, and, after exposure to the thirty-five-degree water, he was unable to stand.

In spite of Lowe's warning that it was too late in the year to cross Valdez Glacier, and despite the drubbing he had received the day before, Abercrombie set out with his wild horses the very next morning, determined to follow Lowe. Here, he describes the journey.

CAPTAIN WILLIAM ABERCROMBIE

One Night on Valdez Glacier[*]

The following morning I found my entire left side to be black and blue and my left hand swollen to twice its normal size from the pounding I had received in trying to ford the Valdez glacial stream. Nevertheless, with Corporal Koehler and Private Bence, I started for the camp established at the foot of the glacier by Lieutenant Lowe and began laying off a trail through the crevasses between the terminal moraine at the foot of the glacier and the top of the third bench.

[*]From *Reports of Explorations in the Territory of Alaska, 1898* (1899), 304–9.

Private Bence was found to be particularly adapted to this work, and he was therefore appointed guide of the expedition over the glacier, with instructions to patrol the trail from the foot of the glacier to the third bench, building small stone monuments and noting from day to day the changes in the crevasses and snow arches. In the meantime Packer Lynch, who had formerly been a farrier in Troop B, Second Cavalry, was set at work sharp-shoeing pack animals. This was an extremely difficult job, owing to the fact that it was constantly raining, leaving the sod saturated and the ground in the vicinity of the field forge a series of miniature lakes. The ponies, having never been shod, fought desperately. Each horse in being shod had to be thrown.

Everything being in readiness July 27, the fog set in so dense it was decided not to attempt to cross the glacier until landmarks could be discerned. July 31, Private Garrett was sent up on the third bench of Valdez Glacier to bring in eight prospectors who had lost their way in attempting to cross Bates Pass. Some of these men had been on the glacier for five days, and during that interval had abandoned everything—guns, clothing, and food. There was rain and fog August 1, 2, 3, and 4, and the humidity was so pronounced and so continuous that bacon and ham became one mass of mold, while, the water of crystallization in the sugar being liberated, the sugar wasted away in the form of a sirup.

August 5, notwithstanding the foggy, rainy weather, the expedition was ordered to proceed at once for the interior. Camp was broken at 5 a.m. At the foot of the glacier, Private Bence was found, and when asked what he thought of the prospect of getting over the summit, replied that if the wind shifted and the pass was missed, that the stock and outfit stood a chance of being a total loss. On the arrival of the train at the foot of the glacier, each section of it was inspected. Each section consisted of five horses, each horse being led by a man, and there was also an extra man and extra rope to each section. The instructions to the men were to proceed over the glacier at given intervals as a unit, and whenever a horse broke through a snow arch over a crevasse they were all to join at once in roping and pulling him out without unpacking. After seeing that everything was in its place, the train started, with Private Bence, with pickax and alpenstock, in the lead. I followed, leading my horse, on which I had packed a 5-gallon keg of whisky to use as a stimulant during the night and the following day.

Passing onto the glacier, the animals seemed to know instinctively that there was danger ahead, as they would tremble and keep their noses close up to the backs of the men who were leading them. Whenever they broke through a snow arch, as they often did, they would lie perfectly still until roped. This applied equally to those which had been extremely shy and hard to approach prior to leaving the camp on the beach. As the expedition passed up through one crevasse, and turned to make an ascent of some 50 or 60 feet up a grade of not less than 45 degrees onto the cone of a hogback that was obscured in the thick fog, some of the civilian employees were inclined to be a little weak-kneed, as it looked very much like climbing up the fog into space. But by a judicious use of the stimulant referred to, this was overcome, and, placing them along in the niches cut by Private Bence, we roped the entire train up with but few accidents.

Now and then a horse would lose his footing and go down to the bottom with a rush. But as the trail was constructed so that all the attendants and packers were on the upper side of the horses, nothing worse than bruises and cuts to the animals was the result of their falls. Never once did one of them refuse to climb out of an ice gulch when called upon, although many times they left a trail of blood behind them when the disintegrated rock of the moraine had cut them in their falls.

Arriving on top of the first bench, the fog was so dense that it was impossible to see more than five or six animals of a train at any one time. It was like a man groping his way in the dark, and, at the end of two hours' traveling, the expedition was completely lost. Every once in a while it was found that the melting ice had caused one of the stone monuments which had marked the trail to slide from its position. Then a halt would be called and Bence sent forward in the fog, just far enough to keep within hail. Having found the continuation of the line of monuments, he would call back and the train would move forward again. These were trying moments.

In this way the train was kept moving during the day and well into the night, until 12 miles had been covered up the glacier. Here a bivouac was made for the night, as it was becoming so dark that one could not see to go farther in the rain that had been falling in torrents the greater part of the day. The picket line was stretched from one ice hummock to another, the pack animals tethered, and the cargoes removed from the pack saddles. As the rain was extremely cold, the saddles and blankets were left on the animals to protect them as much as possible. Their grain was portioned out on the ice.

To each man in the party a small tin cupful of whisky was issued, some canned meat, cheese, and hard-tack. Some of the men pitched their shelter tents on the glacier and attempted to sleep, but in a few minutes they joined their comrades who kept up a steady tramp all night backward and forward in rear of the picket line. I here take occasion to remark in this part of my narrative that during my twenty-two years of service on the frontier, I never experienced a more desolate and miserable night.

Not only was the night black, but the rain was continuous. Occasionally, the mighty glacier would crack as it settled in its passage to the valley below, with a vibration that would cause the men to stop in their tramp and the horses to nicker with apprehension, if not fear. Then would follow a deafening roar as some thousands of tons of ice was detached from one of the hundreds of glaciers that fringed the mountain sides. As these high fields of ice and snow would come crashing down onto the main glacier, they would bound from wall to wall of the canyon, and the echo would die out finally down the valley many thousands of feet below. Like all other nights, this one came to an end. At daybreak another allowance of whisky was issued to the outfit, and the animals were packed and the party proceeded on its way toward the summit.

Four or five miles were covered, when a section of the glacier was encountered that was so bisected with crevasses of such width that for a while it was a question of getting through. But taking the train down a long narrow peninsula of badly crevassed ice, an outlet was found which could be doubled back on. The expedition was now in a position where it was as dangerous to go back as it was to go ahead. The mental strain on all at this stage of the journey was terrific. Progress was very slow; not more than a quarter of a mile an hour for the next three or four hours was made. Working in and out of this mass of crevasses we finally crossed what was known as the fourth bench, and found ourselves on better footing. Up to this point the glacier had been free from snow. A zone was now reached where the snow and slush were about knee deep, through which we plodded. Looking up toward the summit of the pass, the eye could not define where the sky line began and the snow ceased.

In the middle of this zone, which was limited only by the range of vision, was a beautiful stream of clear water, with a deep blue bottom. It seemed in perspective, being so rapidly foreshortened by the fog, to be a blue column ascending into the sky. Following up the banks of the stream there suddenly flashed out through the fog the panorama of the fifth bench, which was composed of huge ice cliffs, through which the wind shrieked and moaned in a most weird and unearthly manner at an extremely high rate of speed.

During all this time, the march had been confined to the center of the glacier. A course to the right was now chosen, and we struck off for the mountain on the right of the pass, with a view of avoiding the fifth bench and striking the snow-slides on the right-hand side of the pass. This is the point where so much stock was lost early in the season from avalanches. A number of snow-slides were reached which were packed as hard as ice and over which the expedition traveled a number of miles, until the foot of the summit was reached.

This summit is where the glacier comes off the top of the mountain and is an abrupt descent of about 1,100 feet in the mile, or about one in five. The effort required to climb this pitch can be realized, in a measure, when it is understood that to make twenty yards of the ascent at once taxed the wind and energy of the strongest mountain climber. The four animals and five men ahead on the trail resembled small birds following each other as one looked at them far above in the fog. Halting at intervals of 5 or 10 yards, the summit was finally reached.

The wind was blowing a hurricane through the pass into the interior, accompanied by gusts of sleet and snow, which, freezing as fast as they struck, coated men and beasts with an armor of ice. At this point, having a lighter load than the others, I found myself in the lead. I halted to wait for the rest of the party but soon found that if I did not keep moving, I would freeze. My horse also suffered severely from the cold. The wind was terrific. In vain I tried to catch some landmark to guide me in laying my course through the pass. If I made a mistake and left the pass by one of the feeders that came in from the higher peaks on each side, the remark of Private Bence of the day previous would be verified.

To stand still was impossible. The only thing left to do was to simply drift with the blizzard, and this I did. Fortunately for the expedition, the point at which the summit was reached was exactly in the middle of the pass, and whenever an attempt was made to veer either to the right or left from the true course of following through the pass, the sleet cut the faces of the men so they would turn their backs to the storm and proceed in the proper direction. Had the wind blown into the pass from the right or left, the expedition would have simply drifted out onto the great glacial fields. As the storm continued for several days, the men would have been snowed in, and probably the entire outfit frozen to death, as no living man could face the gale. But as luck was on the side of the expedition, it drifted through the pass and down toward the Klutena Valley.

After some five or six hours' travel in the howling storm where it was impossible to hear or see a comrade, a high and rocky cliff was finally rounded and the expedition beheld the most beautiful sight I ever witnessed. The change was almost magical. Two yards after passing behind the shelter of this rocky cliff, there was a perfect haven of rest and sunshine, while out of the pass rushed the howling storm like the water out of the nozzle of a fire hose. Throwing ourselves on the snow in the sunshine, we stretched ourselves at full length and enjoyed that rest which only men can who have been battling for their existence. As if understanding the situation, the poor, miserable-looking pack ponies, their manes and tails all clotted with ice, lay down in the soft snow and grunted with satisfaction as the rays of the sun peeled the coating of ice off their bodies. After resting here a short time and eating lunch, the expedition proceeded down the glacier to the timber line.

Here camp was made for the night in a grove of stunted cottonwoods and willows. I had now successfully crossed the Valdez Glacier at a season of the year when it was universally conceded to be impassable for man, making the journey in twenty-nine consecutive hours of practically continuous work, without sleep, rest, or shelter. The command was, however, in bad shape. The men were more or less frost-bitten about the ears and hands, and the pack animals bruised and lacerated to such an extent as to render some of them unfit for service. After enjoying the luxury of the camp fire, and relating to each other our various narrow escapes, we rolled up in our sleeping bags and soon forgot the past in the sound and pleasant sleep that comes to the weary man in the field.

Given its hardships, that 1898 expedition may not have been justified, but the venture gave Abercrombie a chance to have a "good look" at the country between the coast and the Tanana River.[5] He had learned that the way into the interior was not across Valdez Glacier but up the Lowe River and through Keystone Canyon. Making that route usable would require significant manpower, but Abercrombie was convinced it would work and recommended continuation of the operation the following year.

In the spring of 1899, Abercrombie returned to Valdez, his goal to survey and begin construction of a military road that would run from the coast up to Copper Center and then to Eagle City on the Yukon. During that winter, a significant number of prospectors had gone to Valdez, having heard rumors that a route to the interior existed. To their dismay, they arrived only to find the rumors were untrue.

When he landed, Abercrombie was met by a "motley-looking" crowd of ragged, demoralized, and drunken prospectors who were living like sardines, crowded fifteen and twenty into filthy cabins reeking of damp footwear and filthy clothes, the stench of frozen limbs, and the bad breath of those with scurvy. Those who had fallen into crevasses, frozen to death, or died of scurvy were being put to rest in a newly constructed graveyard, and hundreds more were said to be dying in the Copper River valley.

"My God, Captain," Abercrombie's quartermaster reported, "it has been clear Hell! I tell you the early days of Montana were not a marker to what I have gone through this winter."[6]

Abercrombie concluded that many of those stranded in Valdez were mentally deranged, some of them convinced that a demon had killed those who had tried to cross the glacier. Seventy-five percent of the prospectors who had set out to cross the glacier since the previous summer had returned to Valdez, most of them having never been "out of sight of the smoke from a factory chimney"[7] and ill-equipped for the task they had undertaken.

The day after his arrival, Abercrombie started work at four in the morning as a blinding snowstorm dropped flakes as big as half-dollar pieces. He put idle and destitute prospectors to work on construction of the trail. To those too debilitated to work, he provided government relief funds, withholding enough from their payments to transport them south on ships headed home. By the end of the season, in addition to those to whom he had paid wages, Abercrombie had provided relief to four hundred and eighty others "of all nationalities, professions, and classes, both white and black"[8]—most of them so embarrassed at having to accept government aid that they asked that their names not be released.

By October of 1899, Abercrombie had overseen construction of twenty-six bridges, ninety-three miles of pack-horse trails, and a hundred and twelve miles of foot trail, with other parts of the trail in various stages of construction.[9] This trail, the Trans-Alaskan Military Road, was the first direct land route into Alaska's interior and, when completed, was used to transport passengers and freight by wagon in summer and by sled in winter. With the onset of motorized vehicles, it became the route of the Richardson Highway.

In his more than thirty years of military service, Abercrombie was said to have spent ten of them living in a tent. His final post was as commander of a fort in Washington State, where he got into a dispute with a superior officer and was relieved from duty. After his retirement, he owned gold and silver properties and was involved with mining interests in Oregon. Until his death in 1943, he and his family resided in Spokane, where his home is listed on a registry of local historic buildings.[10]

Notes

Epigraph: William Abercrombie, "Report of Captain W. R. Abercrombie," *Reports of Explorations in the Territory of Alaska (Cooks Inlet, Sushitna, Copper, and Tanana Rivers), 1898* (Washington, DC: Government Printing Office, 1899), 299.

1 Sherwood, *Exploration of Alaska*, 98.

2 Ibid.

3 Abercrombie, "Supplementary Expedition into the Copper River Valley, Alaska," US Congress, Senate, Committee on Military Affairs, *Compilation of Narratives of Explorations in Alaska* (Washington, DC: Government Printing Office, 1900), 387.

4 Abercrombie, "Report of Captain W. R. Abercrombie," *Reports of Explorations, 1898*, 301.

5 Sherwood, *Exploration of Alaska*, 159.

6 Abercrombie, "Report of Captain W. R. Abercrombie," *Copper River Exploring Expedition, 1899* (Washington, DC: Government Printing Office, 1900), 15.

7 Ibid., 18.

8 Ibid., 19.

9 Walter Babcock, "Report of First Lieutenant Walter C. Babcock," *Copper River Exploring Expedition*, 62.

10 "Historic Properties of Spokane," July 22, 2012, http://properties.historicspokane.org/property/?PropertyID=1713.

13

ROBERT DUNN

From Nowhere to Nowhere

> I had traveled over tundra in Alaska and knew its hateful yellow moss bordered by white skeleton spruces, its treacherous ponds sprinkled with white flowers, its willow thickets concealing abysses of red muck.

Born at Newport, Rhode Island, into a family so snooty they asked to be removed from the social registry because it included "upstarts" like the Vanderbilts,[1] Robert Dunn spent summers mountain climbing in New Hampshire and winters trekking through the woods. When he was a boy, he ran ahead of other campers and a counselor so that he could be alone on the top of a mountain, "the sole being on earth, as alive as its woods and ridges."[2] He attended Harvard and was editor of the *Monthly*, then, at twenty-one, traveled 1,500 miles overland from Boston to the Klondike goldfields.

Two years later, in 1900, Dunn went to Alaska and discovered that Mount Wrangell was an active volcano. Captain Billy Richardson, a military man who Dunn ran into at Copper Center, told Dunn that he should notify the folks in Washington of the discovery.

"They don't know a damn about anything here,"[3] Richardson supposedly said.

On that trip, Dunn traveled through Copper River country, crossed the Alaska Range, and went down the Yukon River to Forty Mile country, where he visited the gold mining operations. For much of that journey, Dunn was alone except for a white husky he had gotten from an Indian for $7.00—and a razor. The dog, Qui-ner-atl, "All-Over-Snow Dog," was nicknamed Qui—with a long *i*. Dunn and Qui became separated on the trail, and, after hunting for him for a while, Dunn gave up the dog as lost. That autumn in Dawson, Qui ran up and jumped into his arms.

“Will you sell the dog to me?” Dunn asked the Dutchman who then had custody of the husky.

“You take him,” the man replied. “I see he is your dog.”[4]

Back in New York, Dunn worked as a journalist, writing “potboilers” for magazines and newspaper stories about crime and politics, and working for muckraker Lincoln Steffens. Steffens introduced Dunn to Frederick Cook, a medical doctor planning an expedition to climb Mount McKinley. “The Professor,” as Dunn called Cook in *The Shameless Diary of an Explorer*, was tall, blond, Germanic, and uninteresting. Even though he had never climbed a mountain in his life, Cook said that he could ascend McKinley at the rate of 5,000 feet a day.

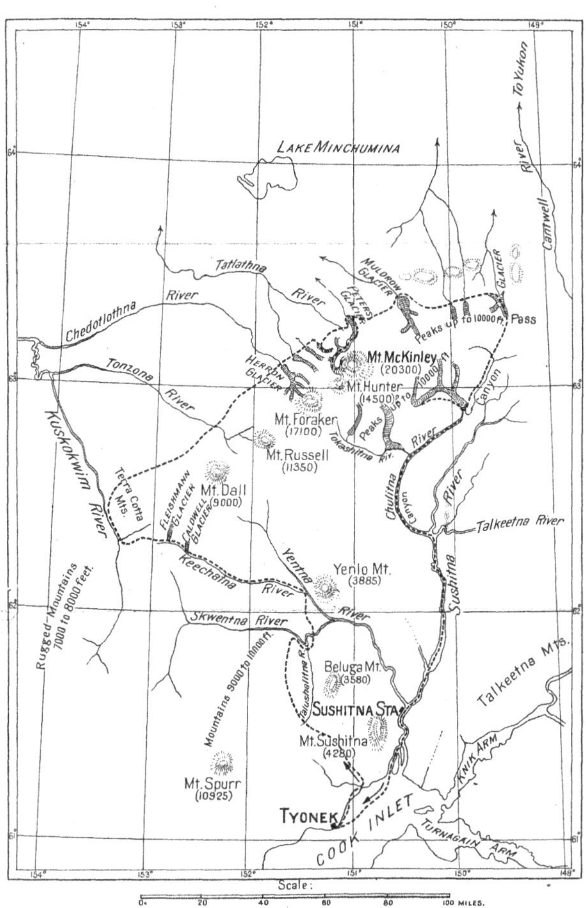

Map of author’s route from Cook Inlet to Mt. McKinley and return. From Robert Dunn, *The Shameless Diary of an Explorer* (1907).

Dunn's friends told him, "You'll get killed, of course." But Alfred Brooks, who had led a US Geological Survey in the area the previous summer, was encouraging. Brooks said that Cook had a "fighting chance"[5] of reaching the top of the mountain. As for Dunn, he would have returned to Alaska at any price, since he loved what he called its "hard freedom."[6] Armed with a soupçon of knowledge and a rock hammer, twenty-six-year-old Dunn signed up as Cook's geologist.

To act as the group's botanist, Cook enlisted "Simon," a twenty-one-year-old scion and heir to a fortune with no wilderness experience and even less common sense. The assignment was a hapless one, said Dunn, for Simon didn't know the difference between a pistil and a stamen. The group's wrangler, "Fred King," in his mid-thirties and unmarried, was a plain-spoken Montanan who had acted as horse packer on Brooks's expedition the summer before. The two final expedition members were Miller, a young office worker invited to act as photographer because a more likely candidate hadn't appeared, and Jack, a bad-tempered Scotch Irishman who planned to pan for gold along the trail.

The party of six, with fifteen unbroken Cayuse horses and a ton of goods, sailed from Seattle for Cook Inlet. From the trading station at Tyonek, they would set out overland on foot. Their route would take them northwest, up tributaries of the Susitna River, across the Alaska Range, and toward the Kuskokwim River. Once near McKinley, they would turn to the northeast and travel along the north face of the mountain. That had been Brooks's route in 1902 and was part of the route pioneered by Lieutenant Joseph Herron on his 1901 military mapping expedition.

By the time Cook's party reached Tyonek, it was June—well into summer—and the group had already traveled 4,000 miles. One horse, Bosco, bolted into the wilderness upon landing and had to be given up for lost. The men were a mere hundred and fifty miles from Mount McKinley as the crow flies, but their route would take them four hundred and fifty miles overland in another direction. To get to McKinley, they had to cross miles of boggy tundra and wade icy, raging rivers, herding those wild pack horses all the way. However, wrangler King was fairly confident he'd be able to find the trail Brooks had blazed.

In the passage that follows, Dunn was dreading the tundra, for he had heard of men who had left Tyonek and been so crazed by the mosquitoes, they'd turned back. Nonetheless, there was no time to waste. By the time the expedition reached McKinley, most of the summer would be gone.

ROBERT DUNN

Headed from Nowhere to Nowhere[*]

June 25—Here we're camped under the sea-terrace, in long sand grass, vetches, and driftwood, eight miles above Tyonek. We gave up Bosco to be bitten to death, for revenge. Packing took only four hours and we had no circus at the get-a-way. Not a beast bucked; the train only broke through a log-pile; the Professor, who led with the Big Bay on a long rope, was stood on his head, and Jack was tumbled for a foot-long hole in his overalls. We straggled north up the beach, Jack and I falling behind to smell for oil seepage in the sandy cliffs. At a ruined cannery, the horses waded to their packs, and staggered out through quicksands.

Sure it's the first night on the long trail! I hear the first pot of Bayo beans a-bubbling, and the first dose of dried peaches is cold and porridgy by the lignite fire. Jack has burnt the beans, for coal fire is hotter than you think. The Professor is taking a bath. Simon is mussing around, doing amusing, superfluous things with smudge fires, a whetstone and a brand-new knife, asking geometrical conundrums and whittling a puzzle. Jack, stretched flat on his stomach, a red handkerchief over his head, is deep in my geology book. King is biting off chewing plug—in quarts. The fourteen horses are slowly back-trailing down the beach, stretching their necks for bunch grass on the terrace.

Miller left Tyonek tonight on the rising tide with a third of the outfit in [Tyonek trader] Holt's long, dory-like river boat. He is to follow up the shore and meet us tomorrow at the mouth of Beluga River; thence with Simon or the Professor to pole and cordelle up Sushitna [Susitna] River, its west fork, the Skwentna, and that river's tributary, the Yentna. Roughly, the boat is to travel two sides of a right triangle, while we, hitting inland northwest, follow its hundred-mile hypotenuse, for the first fifty miles by a half-effaced winter trail. The land stretch, according to King, is too soft for horses packed with more than a hundred pounds each, and we must have a boat to ferry the grub at the Yentna and Skwentna fords.

Far across the Inlet, the snow-blue mountains, where Knick Arm breaks the range, open like mighty jaws. South rages the muddy tide out of the Inlet, bearing derelict cottonwoods on its bosom, which now and then we start up to gaze at, for their black roots seem to be swimming moose or bear.

Jack and I have lost our pipes. Wonderful, isn't it? The aesthetic new oaths this country can inspire.

[*]From *The Shameless Diary of an Explorer* (1907), 32–43.

June 26—An hour to herd the horses over beach and terrace; another to make corrals with cinch ropes, noose their necks, tie each to a willow bush, unsnarl ropes and twigs, coax them one by one to the saddle and grub pile; more hours to blanket, saddle, sling packs and cinch. I'm up first about five, cooking. Jack and King hunt the beasts while I wash dishes and pack the white grub horse with the two panniers that hold the pots and food we're using. Jack and I saddle and cinch seven horses; King and Simon seven. The Professor fusses about. He's very funny and energetic trying to catch the beasts.

Miller arrived unexpectedly on the tide at dawn and took Simon into the boat for the mouth of Beluga River, which we hit for overland, trailing inland from the beach.

Right by camp, the wild Dark Buckskin rolled down the bench, and chawed blood from my fingers when I dragged him up. Twice he fell into a crick, wedged on his back between logs, waving his legs, so we had to cut the tie-rope. The Professor looked on with a queer, quiet look. This is his first dose of cayusing in the North. Fred led the train with the Big Bay, we driving all in line, each behind four or five beasts. Even had we enough horses, it would be impossible for anyone to ride. Too much doing.

We cursed and stumbled through snags and muck; staggered across open tundra; hacked the dense alders of treacherous cricks; halted to re-cinch one horse, while thirteen stampeded, wedging packs between the spruces. It was the familiar old game. Off bucks the Light Buckskin, his fifty-pound flour sacks spraying half an acre. Chase him, catch him, hunt the sacks, lug them up, re-saddle, re-cinch—while again the train wanders away, scraping off its load.

The Professor took things stolidly. I think he would face death and disaster without a word, but through the insensitiveness of age and too much experience, rather than by true courage. I cannot believe he has imagination; of a leader's qualities he has shown not one. He seems our sympathetic servant. I suspect no iron hand behind his innocence. He doesn't smoke, and that makes me uncomfortable....

At two o'clock, we reached this grassy alder swamp, each in his 'skeet cloud-of-witnesses, where the terrace dips down to the melancholy tide-flats of the Beluga, strewn with wrecked spruces. Belugas, which are white whales, were plunging shoulders in the river, as should be. A white fan emerges from water the color of cafe au lait, with a "tsschussk," as if it belched steam. And an old brown bear, pawing for candle-fish, looked at us in a lazy, human way, and galumphed off into the cottonwoods across the sticky silt.

Simon and Miller came in with the boat at eight o'clock. I doubted if they'd make it. If they hadn't, they couldn't take the boat to the Skwentna ford, and have no business on this trip. That's all.

Jack and I unloaded the boat, and ferried everything that the pack train is to carry to the north side of the river. Again and again, we crossed the brown swirl, till even when we looked at them from shore the very woods still swam inland. We pulled off our arms, bucking the current straight, hitting land half a mile below our aim and cordelling up. The thirty-foot tide was rising, but under the current, which it simply lifts without slacking. Then, like nigger coal-heavers in the tropics, we hustled the sacks on our backs from shore into the bear's cottonwoods, wallowing ankle-deep in the glacial muck. The 'skeets, as always in such desperate work, enraged us.

Jack and I are alone on the far side of the river. It is raining; we have no tent, and I am trying to make the small sleeping-bag water-proof and mosquito-proof with a poncho and a head-net. It's no use. We'll fight them awake and sopping tonight.

I wonder what's going to happen to us these next three months. Everything's easy so far.... We're over here, you see, to shoo Mr. Bear from the bacon.

June 27—First, we swam the horses across the Beluga. It's no worse than landing them from a ship, except as risking a basket of eggs is worse than risking eggs singly. We hand-corralled them with cinches on shore at low tide, when we thought they couldn't jump back up the bank, not because the current lessens—it never does. But up the bank they dashed through the ropes, and a dozen times we fought them back through the alders. With all inside the rope at last, King and I swept them into the river with it, like minnows in a net, the others shouting and stoning. They hesitate. Plunge. The current wiggles them as they stand upright at first, churning the water with their fore hoofs; strews them out in irregular parabolas toward the far shore, some swimming madly, and as they weaken, drifting down; others calmly, at last reaching upstream or colliding with the weaker ones. Then the tightness in your heart relaxes, for they all snort in chorus, and it bewilders you to see them struggle up the slimy bank, one by one, scattered out for half a mile.

Till noon we were packing them with the solid fifty-pound sacks—flour, bacon, beans, two bags to each horse—and loading the boat with the mountain-climbing outfit, instrument boxes, and all unwieldy stuff. The Professor suddenly decided, consulting no one, to take the river trip with Miller alone. So Simon is with us. We didn't want him, and King tried to make me protest to the Professor, but I wouldn't. So I'm in charge of the main outfit, for ten days at least, through what's said to be the wettest, most desperate mushing in Alaska, responsible for three men I never knew a month ago: a little New York Jew, a young sourdough, and a Montana packer who was with Brooks of the Geological Survey when he crossed this stretch. He (King) says the Indian trail we follow runs about west into the foot-hills of the Tordrillo Mountains; then is lost, and we must hit due north to Skwentna River.

"Dunn," said the Professor, as we parted, "under average conditions it is to be expected that we shall meet at the Skwentna ford in rather more than eight days." I hope so. Anyhow, new trails open in the old wilderness of life....

Later, and God knows where. The real thing just hit us. This winter trail we follow led from the birchy Beluga straight out into tundra, through line after line of ratty spruces, where you sink ankle-deep into sick, yellow moss, and wobbly little ridges separate small ponds. Suddenly every horse was down, kicking and grunting helplessly in the mud. They lost their heads. They seemed to like to jump off into the ponds. We tugged, hauled, kicked at the brutes; unpacked the sacks, lugged them to shore, pulled on tie-ropes, tails; batted heads, poured water down nostrils till they hissed like serpents. One was out, another was down. Oh, our beautiful oaths. Hot, hungry, dizzy, insane with mosquitoes, we struggled waist-deep in yellow muck, unsnarling slimy cinches, packing, repacking the shivering, exhausted beasts. It was endless. Torture.

We kept to dry gullies toward the river-bed, we kept to tundra; but always the train tore through the iron-fingered scrub spruce, ripping packs, snagging hoofs, tumbling us at the end of lead lines. Mount Sushitna [Susitna] tormented us, floating, patched with snow over the sickish forest; and the long, low hill we're aiming for, laid out in green squares of tropic grass and alders, seemed forever to recede. I call it Alice's Hill, after "Through the Looking Glass." Remember her perverse garden.

Jack went off at half-cock. "Just the sort of a —— trail a —— old woman like that —— Brooks would follow," he yelled; and when I said this was a pretty hard deal, the first crack out of the box, he shouted, "What yer blamin' King for? It ain't his fault."

All had been down for the tenth time, and a horse can't stand more. Someone said, "Camp." We'd gone only four miles; it was six o'clock. Fred looked at me. "It's up to you, you're the Professor," he drawled. Responsibility bit.

So, we've camped. No grass for the horses; mud water, and yet Fred, who moves so calmly and surely when all seems down and lost, who isn't supposed to touch a fry pan, has volunteered to bake the bread. Wonderful man—or is it he thinks I can't?

I've put a cheese-cloth door in the tent—oh, just to whet the 'skeet appetites. Jack is snoring, exhausted. The horse blankets we try to sleep in—we've nothing else, the Professor swiped the sleeping bags—are soaked. Goodnight.

June 28—Two days' travel, and we've gone eight miles! At this rate, we won't see McKinley till winter.

Calvin, when he manufactured his own hand-made hell, must have been to Alaska. Oh yes, King says that last year the ground had not thawed out here as much as this. But, by Heaven, we'll make it.

Yesterday was only a hint; watering the brutes' nostrils was child's play to how we kicked their necks and eyes today; being dragged and snagged through the scrub was fun to how we've been hunting Alaska over just now for shipped packs, to how we'd meet a pond after a mile-long detour, and have to track back again with the same antics.

The old White, Big Buckskin, who is much too aged and heavy for this game, the Bay Mare carrying our dunnage, would all flounder together into each pond. Still Alice's Hill and Mount Sushitna, north at the head of the Inlet, mocked us. Still the sickish, tufted spruces dwarfed one another in plague-procession down into the stinking yellow sphagnum of these hot ponds. We fished the soaked food sacks out from the little white flowers floating on top. Sank to our knees at every step, seeming to lift a ton on each boot.

Hot, hungry, dizzy, we fell into camp by this grassy stream. I kept on alone over the mile-long tundra beyond it, to see the worst ahead for tomorrow. Responsibility was not wearing me. If we don't get through, it will be no fault of ours. Glossy snows cloaked Mount Spurr (11,000 feet) in the southwest. I floundered across a backbone of red moss, climbed its lower slopes twice, to more tundra and fearful mud holes. This damned winter trail! You can't write the thoughts you have alone on the tundra, dragging onward three men by a trail leading from nowhere to nowhere, where we shall never pass a soul nor see sign of man for months. Sand-hill cranes with scarlet wings and red heads floated away, with squawks like wood-wedged axes. Twice I sank to rest in the moss, and found I was crawling on. I tried to smoke, but it only sickened me. . . .

But now I have eaten—*eaten*—six enormous bannocks, six plates of Bayo beans, four cups of tea like lye, and I feel better than I have ever felt, in any state of intoxication, by anything. Alaska proves the law of compensation. I have just shaved, with the tin reflector, which bakes the bread, for a mirror.

King is spreading Simon's mosquito goo on his face, just to prove it's no good. Simon, who has catarrh, is snuffing things up his nose from a crooked glass tube. Jack is telling how once he cleaned up a temperance hotel....

Shortly after Dunn and his companions reached the Skwentna ford, the Professor and Miller came floating in to camp, and the combined party soon set out. They covered fifty more miles of wet ground before crossing the Alaska Range and turning to the northeast. By then, they had been on the trail two months and were down a man. Jack had gotten ill and decided to turn back with an allocation of ten days of rations and an axe.

The group set up base camp at 2,000 feet, where McKinley's nearly sheer ice walls stretched more than 18,000 feet above them. As they began the ascent, they cut foot and hand holds into ice that began to incline more and more precipitously. There weren't enough axes to go around—Jack having taken one—and Dunn was forced to attempt the climb of Mt. McKinley with the aid of a ten-foot willow tent pole.

At 10,800 feet, the group stood on a knife-edged summit and realized that they were at a dead-end. They were less than halfway up the mountain, had little remaining food, little remaining summer, and had to give up. After returning to base camp, they continued traveling east, and, at a pass in the Alaska Range, turned south. They had planned to float the rivers that flowed south to Cook Inlet, but upon reaching the place where they had stashed the Tyonek trader's borrowed boat, they learned that Jack had taken it.

Dunn thought that the expedition was a failure, but, in making a five-hundred-and forty-mile circumnavigation of the mountain, the men achieved a feat that would not be repeated for the next seventy-five years. Furthermore, they had discovered an until-then unknown pass on the eastern side of the mountain that led to the headwaters of the Chulitna River.

Before Dunn left for McKinley, editor Steffens had advised him that, no matter what happened, he should tell the truth when he wrote about the trip. Thus, *The Shameless Diary of an Explorer* and a series of articles Dunn wrote about the venture for *Outing Magazine* were different from the usual glorified accounts published in the day. Dunn included stories like the one about Simon putting a bullet in one of the horses while trying to shoot a mud hen, and Fred's comment about the incident: "Alasky is no place for little boys with girls' guns."[7] As Dunn wrote, "The passions of the trail bring out the best in men and the worst, and all in scarlet."[8]

Meanwhile, Dunn's assessment of the Professor—"of a leader's qualities, [he] has shown not one"[9]—guaranteed that when Cook made his second attempt on McKinley, Dunn wasn't invited along. On that venture, Cook fabricated photographs that purported to show him at the top of the mountain. That claim and another that he was the first to reach the North Pole were both proven false, and Cook eventually went to federal prison for mail fraud in connection with a sale of oil stocks.

Dunn returned to Alaska to climb the top of a volcanic island in the Aleutians as it erupted from the sea and to make the first ascent of Mount Wrangell. He traveled in Siberia and Turkey, served as a war correspondent and naval intelligence officer, and accompanied General John Pershing on his pursuit of Pancho Villa in Mexico.

Upon retirement, Dunn lived in Katonah, New York, and devoted himself to horticulture and to writing novels and poetry. He died on December 24, 1955, after a long illness and was buried at Newport. In an obituary in the *New York Times,* Lincoln Steffens said, "Dunn could write, and Dunn could bite, and he bit and wrote his way through with us for months."[10]

Dunn's autobiography, *World Alive* (1958), was published after his death and included a snapshot of him with his friends, Franklin and Eleanor Roosevelt, at their home. Dunn alone is dressed in a bathing costume.

Notes

Epigraph: Dunn, *Shameless Diary* (New York: The Outing Publishing Company, 1907), 17.

1 Edward Hoagland, introduction to Robert Dunn, *The Shameless Diary of an Explorer* (1907; repr., New York: The Modern Library, 2001), vii.

2 Robert Dunn, *World Alive* (London: Robert Hale Limited, 1958), 11.

3 Richardson, quoted in Dunn, *World Alive,* 22.

4 Dunn, *World Alive,* 29.

5 Ibid., 44, 45.

6 Dunn, *Shameless Diary,* 18.

7 Ibid., 49.

8 Ibid., 4.

9 Ibid., 36.

10 "Robert Dunn, 78, Explorer, Is Dead," *New York Times,* December 25, 1955.

14

AGNES HERBERT

Invitation to a Card Game

We went to Alaska to shoot, and—we shot.

At the front of *Two Dianas in Alaska,* Agnes Herbert faces the camera, unsmiling and earnest. She is dressed in a Native-made knee-length caribou parka and has a firm grip on the barrel of the rifle standing beside her. Herbert was a wealthy English widow with a passion for shooting and was determined to prove that she was as tough and independent as the men with whom she hunted.[1]

On the way to Alaska, Herbert and her cousin, Cecily, sailed from England to New York, where they paid the outrageous sum of fifty cents to take a bath. On their cross-country train trip, they met Miss Mamie Potts, a Mississippi Christian Scientist, who debated en route which of her suitors she should marry.

"Husbands ain't come by easy," Miss Potts said. "What you two gals need to do is to go out and scratch for 'em."[2]

When the women reached Butte, Montana, Cecily said that she wanted to stop for a visit with her brother, but the excuse proved to be a ruse. Actually, Cecily planned to meet Ralph Windus, a friend hunting bighorn sheep and wapiti with the man Herbert would identify simply as the "Leader" and, in the alternative, as "Shikári"—an Urdu term for "hunter."[3] These four English hunters—Herbert, Cecily, Ralph, and the Leader—had previously been on safari together in Somaliland, and Herbert had written about that venture in *Two Dianas in Somaliland* (1908). When Ralph and the Leader learned that Herbert and Cecily were going to Alaska, they invited themselves along.

At Victoria, the group engaged the schooner *Lily,* manned by a Scandinavian captain, Clemsen. The boat was filthy, but it was cleaned and then packed with bedding, cushions, books, knickknacks, and foodstuffs. Among the party's gear were reindeer-skin sleeping bags, wool-lined khaki coats, and rubber-soled hunting boots. Tents from Victoria's Chinatown were made to order, weighed a mere seven pounds, and would later shed rain beautifully. Since there was no camel transport in Alaska, the beds and chairs the party had enjoyed in Africa would be left behind, but they carried an arsenal of weapons—small bore rifles, a .375 bore, and a .256 Mannlicher. In their rifle cases, they took along .12-bores, a .35 Winchester, a .22 Winchester, a .410-bore collector's gun, and .450 cordite rifles.

When the hunters reached Kodiak Island, they hired Russian Aleut guides Ivan, Pete, Steve, and Ned. The price the men demanded—a dollar and a half a day—seemed justified, for in the field the men would be responsible for skinning the animals, cleaning their heads, and curing the skins. Loaded onto the *Lily* were *bidarkas* (sealskin kayaks) for river travel, flat-bottomed dories for shallow-water landings, and fur parkas hand-sewn by Natives using sinews and ivory needles.

On Kodiak, Herbert and her cousin simultaneously fired into a ten-foot *Ursus middendorffi,* largest species of brown bear in the world, which, as it fell, looked to Herbert like nothing so much as an annoyed chauffeur. On the Alaskan Peninsula, Herbert and the Leader tracked a wounded bear into the alders. The animal sprang up an arm's length away, and, when Herbert shot it, fell so close that the Leader had to jump to safety. After Herbert killed a charging female, she adopted its cub—but it soon expired from eating the half-raw beans and greasy cocoa it was given by the *Lily*'s crew.

After taking the heads of three-thousand-pound walruses, the hunters sailed to the mouth of the Kuskokwim River where they hoped to hire local guides to take them inland to hunt caribou, sheep, and moose. The group's plan was to travel up the Kuskokwim in their *bidarkas* and, at the river's headwaters, abandon the boats and proceed on foot, crossing the divide between that river and the Susitna. Captain Clemsen, meanwhile, was to return the Kodiak guides to their homes, then sail to Cook Inlet, where he would engage other guides who would paddle up the Susitna and bring the English hunters back down to the coast.

That elaborate plan met with a hitch, for, at the Kuskokwim, the Yupik chief was reluctant to allow his people to travel into a part of the country unknown to them.

"Him say, no good, you bet,"[4] Kodiak guide Steve translated.

Fortuitously, a Native turned up who had led another party of white hunters to the sheep grounds, and he agreed to go. This time, the price demanded—a dollar a day per man—seemed fair, for once the group left the Kuskokwim and headed overland for the Susitna, their guides would have to pack the supplies, equipment, and trophies on their shoulders.

The hunt started in April and continued through the summer in weather that ranged from bright, clear, crisp sunshine to howling winds, rain, and hail. As autumn approached, the mornings grew colder. When the party reached the headwaters of the Kuskokwim, they crossed the divide and traveled through caribou country, where Herbert shot a caribou with antlers spanning forty-nine inches.

At the time of the following excerpt, Herbert and the Leader are hunting *Ovis dalli*, bighorned sheep. They are accompanied by their Kodiak guide, Steve, who elected to stay with the hunting party rather than return to his home. By now, the hunters and their guides are largely relying on game for food.

AGNES HERBERT

Invitation to a Card Game[*]

We were really anxious to bag a ram to fill our larder, for we were trenching on the stores again. The men were exceedingly anxious to be allowed to try and shoot a ewe, as a native is permitted to do at all times and seasons, but we managed to stave the thing off by saying confidently that we hoped to return from the next stalk with a quantity of meat.

The following morning dawned bright and clear, and it did not need our glasses to tell us that the hillside opposite our camp was dotted with myriad moving sheep. It was a "hen" party, though, for counting up to one hundred and ten we could not spot a decent head among the number.

We set off along our side of the river, Steve following in our wake, and commenced the ascent of the cañon, whose slopes were some 1,500 feet high, and fairly sheer, in places really precipitous. At the summit, crossing an undulating bit of plateau country, a fine ram got up from nowhere, and standing a moment in terror-stricken amazement, actually bolted straight towards us. At sixty paces off, it pulled up in a great slide, with fore-feet planted well together, head slightly lowered, a formidable-looking creature.

Place aux dames, in our shoot, anyhow.

I fired and missed ignominiously. It seems a ridiculous thing to clean miss

*From *Two Dianas in Alaska* (1909), 243–51.

so large a mark as an *Ovis dalli* ram at sixty paces. But when winded, after a long, hard climb, the hands are apt to be very unsteady and an odd trembling of the limbs affects a certain number of us.

I felt very small as the Leader raised his rifle to mend matters. All this takes a long time to tell, but it happened in the fraction of a moment really. The ram, not moved by my fusillade, presented a most desirable chance, standing broadside now, quivering. He seemed almost magnetized with terror.

Bang!

The bullet passed over the back of the sheep, and for that animal the spell was broken and he bolted incontinently, slipping and sliding down the slopes.

"You might say it for me too, will you?" I said to the Leader, who was saying things to his rifle, as he regarded it closely, as though wondering if he might portion some part of the blame to the weapon.

Steve was heartbroken. Why not kill a ewe and be done with it? We could get any quantity, he said, without travelling so far. Just as though our object on the trip was to keep these natives going with unlimited provender!

At that moment, a bullet hit the ground about four paces from us; another fell ominously close to Steve, who ran round and round in a circle in a most ridiculous manner, as though by keeping moving he might avoid the hail of lead. Another and another bullet struck the rocks near us, and we were just about to fly on the wings of terror to some likely bit of cover when suddenly, on the peak above us, a tatterdemalion figure appeared on the sky line, and slowly sauntered down to us.

He showed no surprise at seeing us, expressed no regret for making targets of us, and he did not seem in the least inquisitive as to whence we came or why. He stood leaning nonchalantly on his rifle and let us admire him. He knew we were doing so, and indeed we could not help it. A great sombrero curved on the red-grey hair, which fell to his shoulders, a wavy beard grew to his waist, and in the interregnum between it and the top of his trousers was a band of red leather stuck full of cartridges. A scarf of red was knotted about his throat, and ever and again we caught a glimpse of a lump of Cassiar gold, big as a pigeon's egg, doing duty as a tie-pin. This romantic figure of the mountains, who had been doing his best to send us out of this world, said he guessed his bullets had fallen "kinder close." He was real mad at missing a fine ram, so blazed away anyhow.

"Rather a waste of cartridges," I said thoughtfully.

"Say so, ma'am," our friend answered, "but you waste them or words these times."

He invited us to lunch with him upon the mountains, striding on ahead the instant the invitation was given, as though he were a Pied Piper we must fain follow. So he was to Steve, for at the first mention of food, that worthy practically ran the trail at the heels of our host-to-be. Round the green slopes, climbing still at an easy gradient. And set in a little cleft of an overhanging rock, a titanic mass of granite, with three sides of the walls readymade, stood a crude, stern homestead, with frontage of the grey, grim rocks. It had all the appearance of Druidic remains. It was Alaskan beginnings really, or perhaps endings. I don't know. No window, an entrance for a door, a pile of wood ashes where a fire had been, a roof of alder branches, banked outside with earth. There was no furniture whatsoever, a heap of blankets lay in dishevelment in a dim corner.

The forequarter of a sheep hung on an outstanding point of rock, most convenient walls had this small domicile, with hat stands and pegs readymade.

Presently strips of mutton frizzled on the stones before a small wood fire. Help from on high to Steve, who scarce waited for the flesh to warm through ere he seized it with greedy fingers and devoured it *au naturel.* This was the simple life if ever it was lived.

"Guess you are speculating what I'm doing here?" said our host, in between moments of gnawing a mutton chop. We had no bread or biscuit.

"I confess to a slight feeling of curiosity," replied the Leader, "but of course—" Slight feeling of curiosity! I nudged him furtively. I did hope he would not pretend we were not consumed with inquisitiveness. The detective-like propensities which lie dormant, unless they are active, in every woman, were all alert in me now, and I judged, and considered, and decided the case every five minutes.

"'Twas a game of poker." The red-grey head nodded towards the Pacific Coast, as though locating the scene of the catastrophe. "*He* cheated, and—wal, I shot him dead!"

We went on eating, to all appearance quite unconcernedly, though I remember being thankful that Steve sat out of earshot.

"You'll not give me away," said the great rugged creature, with a kind of certain confidence. "I'm glad I told you. Guess it's kind of lonesome up here."

"How long must you remain?" I asked, a wave of pity for the broken man surging in me. "Surely you will not winter at this altitude?"

"No," he said dully, "when winter comes I'll turn trapper and take to the woods."

A group of four rams passed below, pulling up to graze; the Leader picked up his rifle, handling it as though he was glad to be recalled to the present, sighted carefully, and bang! Another try. The rams raced off, but one lagged behind, going with difficulty. A well-planted bullet finished the business, and the sheep jumped clean into the air, an expiring effort, then fell a-heap.

As the Leader ran forward down the hill to investigate, he put his foot into a pitfall that waited for the unwary, and fell heavily. He was in great pain, too great to bear sympathy just then. At the first shock of anything of the kind, the instinct of a man in pain is to creep away like an animal and hug his wounds in silence. The woman who attempts to offer sympathy, at the first onslaught of the anguish which is sufficient to wring a man's brow, stands a very good chance of hearing—*sotto voce*, of course—desires expressed that some beneficent being or other would take her away and wring the ministering angel's neck!

Very rude, but—my advice to ministering angels is don't commence to minister until the psychological moment. Then bring up the sympathy in carloads, and you cannot overdo it.

The big romantic murderer helped to carry the fallen Leader to the Druidic cottage, and, most unlike a murderer—I have really very little experience of the genus, this was the first murderer I have met in society—helped to ascertain the damage. He diagnosed the case as a sprained ankle, and put his country seat at the Leader's disposal.

Steve went back to camp with orders to bring up my tent and some stores to this roof of the world where we had to sojourn awhile whether we would or no, as the Leader could not put his foot to the ground.

It was a land flowing with milk and honey for our men. This spirit of the mountain had but to wave his wand, and lo! a sheep, ram, or ewe, it mattered not, fell before it.

I made some bread from hops and cooked the dough in the ground in a tin pan, with glowing wood ashes set around and over it. The poor murderer had not tasted bread since he fled up here, a month ago. He had mixed up flour with water and cooked it over the fire. My bread was to him what a lump of cake would have been to me.

Below the Druidic cottage, on a rock platform, guarded on all sides by forbidding precipices, a pair of golden eagles had an eyrie. The friendly murderer told me of it, thinking I might like to see it. He called the eagle residence "a nest." Somehow it seems to me that such a word, the simplicity of which strikes home to all of us, is out of place in connection with the egg-home of the King and Queen of the air. Eyrie is much higher sounding, therefore more suitable.

Nest is almost *lèse majesté.* A King would be out of place in a nest. He might possibly condescend to inhabit an eyrie.

Leaning over the edge of the cliff, with my obliging friend the murderer hanging on to my coat with a good firm grip, I could see the great heap of nest, four feet or more across, and with my glasses two young birds, fully plumaged, sitting dolorously inside. A second family, perhaps. I don't know. But it was late in the season for young birds to keep to their breeding place, unless indeed the youthful eagles go on using the eyrie until they are quite big and able to fend for themselves under any conditions.

I watched the parent birds for hours, as with mighty sweeps they cleft the air, circling with scarcely moving pinions over infinite space, magnificent creatures of the rugged cliffs. I never saw the young ones make any attempt to fly. They simply sat there, Micawber-like, and waited for something to turn up.

The second evening after the accident, as we sat by a small wood fire—it had to be small because the men grumbled so at hauling wood such a distance—overlooking a scene of grandeur which baffles description, our host suggested a game of cards. Poker! I fairly trembled. I frequently cheat at cards, either to end the game or from sheer lack of interest, and almost invariably revoke. If it is possible to revoke at poker I should do so, without a doubt. It really was not safe, whatever might not the consequences be!

I said very firmly but politely that unfortunately I do not play cards, and as for the Leader, it was a standing joke that he did not know one card from another.

"Read, then," commanded this extraordinary being, "read out of that book you carry in your pocket."

I drew out my Shakespeare, and obediently set to work on *Julius Caesar.* My audience said that Julius Caesar "fairly beat the band," whatever that might mean. It was appreciative though, for presently he would know if "Julius," as he called him, ever lived. Shakespeare, too, was he anybody? Did I suppose that Julius Caesar was as great a soldier as General Howe of Bunker's Hill—it was easy to read the hero-worship in the haggard eyes—and this Shakespeare, would he be as handy with his pen as Mrs. Beecher Stowe?

It was an odd quartet. Julius Caesar, Shakespeare, General Howe, and Mrs. Beecher Stowe. Never mind, different as they are, each name rings forever down the corridors of time.

As soon as the Leader could move—four days afterwards—we trekked away, for we had so much to do in a very given time, Cecily and Ralph to meet, the moose hunting, and the locating of our new men who were to come up from Cook's Inlet.

We left our friend of the Druidic cottage as much of our stores as we could possibly spare, and the last we saw of his solitary figure was the grey-red hair waving in the breeze and the glint of his fiery tie.

When the hunting party met the guides hired by Captain Clemsen at the Susitna, the heads and skins of fox, brown bear, black bear, walrus, caribou, sheep, otter, porcupine, timber wolf, and moose all had to be loaded into *bidarkas* for the start of the trip home.

Cecily had apparently taken Miss Potts's advice, for she and Ralph were engaged and going hunting in Mexico. The Leader co-authored *Two Dianas in Alaska*, he and Herbert each writing alternate chapters. Although Herbert never revealed his identity, the Leader may have been C. R. E. Radclyffe,[5] an Englishman who also hunted in Alaska and who wrote about the experience in *Big-Game Shooting in Alaska* (1904).

In 1913, Herbert was married to a commander of the Royal Navy, and she seems to have then stopped hunting. She did continue to write, authoring books for young readers as well as travel books, including one about her home, the Isle of Man. She was a member and officer of the Society of Women Journalists and, in 1931, was named an Officer of the British Empire.[6]

Notes

Epigraph: Agnes Herbert and a Shikári, *Two Dianas in Alaska* (London: J. Lane, 1909), 1.

1 Mary Zeiss Stange, foreword, *Two Dianas in Alaska* by Agnes Herbert (1909; repr. Mechanicsburg, PA: Stackpole Books, 2004), v–vi.

2 Herbert, *Two Dianas in Alaska* (1909), 5.

3 Simpson and Weiner, eds., *Oxford English Dictionary*, 15: 262.

4 Herbert, *Two Dianas in Alaska* (1909), 195.

5 Stange, foreword, *Two Dianas in Alaska* (2004), vii–viii.

6 Ibid., xiii.

15

HUDSON STUCK

Mistakes at Sixty Below

> Alaska is not one country but many,
> with different climates, different resources, different
> problems, different populations, different interests; and what
> is true of one part of it is often grotesquely untrue of other
> parts.... Not only do these various parts of Alaska
> differ radically from one another, ... they are
> in reality different countries.

Between 1904 and 1920, Hudson Stuck was the Episcopal archdeacon of Alaska. His territory, almost all of it wilderness, covered the basin of the Yukon River as it snaked through the middle of Alaska from east to west. In winter, Stuck traveled by dogsled and, in summer, on a thirty-two-foot boat named *Pelican.*

Stuck was born in England but, yearning for wide-open spaces, immigrated to Texas, where he worked as a cowboy and a schoolteacher before attending Episcopal seminary. Upon ordination, he returned to Texas, where he campaigned against lynching, founded a night school for mill workers, started a home for indigent women, and helped secure legislation curbing child labor.[1] He was named dean of the cathedral in Dallas but had no use for power or for material goods. Looking for the sort of vigorous outdoor life advocated by Theodore Roosevelt, he asked to be sent to Alaska.

Stuck's *Ten Thousand Miles with A Dog Sled,* according to the *New York Times,* was so conversational that it seemed as if the author "were sitting at a friendly fireside and telling tales about his rambles."[2] By the time the book was published, Stuck might have actually mushed 15,000 miles, but there were those, he said, who had traveled further. The Alaska mailman, for example, had to keep moving no matter the temperature or the condition of the trail.

Stuck said that a person in that job could easily mush twice as far in a season as he had.

It was offensive, Stuck wrote, for writers such as Jack London to portray Alaskan Natives as baronial slave owners and hostile savages. In truth, the Alaskan Indian was "timid" and "peaceable,"[3] and the Eskimo "gentle, industrious, [and] good-humoured."[4] Stuck said that the greatest threats to the Natives' well-being were not cold or loneliness but white liquor traffickers and "rapacious" traders who provided gambling dens and barrooms on their premises. "It is pitiful to be compelled to teach savage people not to despise the whites," he wrote.[5]

He had harsh words for missionaries who encouraged Natives to exchange their furs for cotton garments and to call themselves silly names, like Mr. Pretty Henry or Mrs. Monkey Bill. What did it matter if an Indian didn't like canned fruit or had no idea when Columbus discovered America? Why should a Native be turned into "an imitation white," Stuck asked? An honest, hardworking Native could "be very much of a man in that station of life in which it has pleased God to call him."[6]

In the winter of 1905, Stuck set out with his dogs and sled to visit the church's most inaccessible mission, at Point Hope on the Arctic Ocean. In the course of four months, he would make a 2,200-mile circuit, traveling mostly on Alaska's "natural highways"[7]—the frozen creeks and rivers. Stuck left Fairbanks on November 27 with his friend E. J. Knapp and a young Indian guide. On his sled, he carried five hundred pounds of supplies, including his tent, stove, bedding, and cooking gear. He traveled with enough food for both humans and dogs, separate meals having to be prepared for each at the evening's campsite.

At the portage over Twelve-Mile Summit, the three men had to cut steps uphill in the ice and relay their supplies to the top. On the descent, the party was trapped in a blinding snowstorm, and the dogs ran ahead downhill—the men's lives being saved only because stakes marked the trail.

Circle City, a settlement named by those who mistakenly believed the Arctic Circle ran through their camp, had been at one time the largest log-cabin town in the world, at its height housing almost 3,000 prospectors. By 1905, when Stuck arrived on this winter tour, it was nearly deserted, most residents having moved on. Once he had passed Circle, Stuck would be on the most dangerous part of the Yukon River—the "flats," a low-lying, forested, boggy region of wetlands where the river spread out into multiple channels. The thermometer at Circle registered about sixty degrees below zero, but the area was well traveled. Since Stuck anticipated that others would have broken trail, he didn't believe he'd encounter a problem.

A significant danger of winter travel in Alaska resulted from "overflow." Rivers are continually fed, and thus, even though frozen on the surface, still flow in winter. Pressure from running water can get trapped beneath the surface ice, build up, and break through, flooding the ice on top. Thus, a thin layer of ice might belie the fact that moving water lies just below.

At the time of this selection, Stuck is in his second Alaskan winter. He is still a tenderfoot and has much to learn.

HUDSON STUCK

Mistakes at Sixty Below[*]

A certain arctic traveler has said that "adventures" always imply either incompetence or ignorance of local conditions, and there is some truth in the saying. Our misadventure was the result of a series of mistakes, no one of which would have been other than discreditable to men of more experience. Our course lay for seventy-five miles through the Yukon Flats, which begin at Circle and extend for two hundred and fifty miles of the river's course below that point. The Flats constitute the most difficult and dangerous part of the whole length of the Yukon River, summer or winter, and the section between Circle City and Fort Yukon is the most difficult and dangerous part of the Flats. Save for a "portage" or land trail of eighteen or twenty miles out of Circle, the trail is on the river itself, which is split up into many channels without salient landmarks. The current is so swift that many stretches run open water far into the winter, and blow-holes are numerous. There is little travel on the Flats in winter, and a snow-storm accompanied by wind may obliterate what trail there is in an hour.

The vehicle used in the Flats is not a sled but a toboggan,[†] and our first mistake was in not conforming to local usage in this respect. There is always a very good reason for local usage about snow vehicles. But a toboggan which had been ordered from a native at Fort Yukon would be waiting for us, and it seemed not worthwhile to go to the expense of buying another merely for three days' journey.

*From *Ten Thousand Miles with a Dog Sled* (1914), 13–21.

†A toboggan has no runners or skis but sits directly on the snow.

The second mistake was in engaging a boy as guide instead of a man. He was an attractive youth of about fourteen who had done good service at the Circle City mission the previous winter, when our nurse-in-charge was contending single-handed against an epidemic of diphtheria. He was a pleasant boy, with some English, who wanted to go and professed knowledge of the route. The greatest mistake of all was starting out through that lonely waste with the thermometer at 52° below zero. The old-timers in Alaska have a saying that "travelling at 50° below is all right as long as it's all right."

If there be a good trail, if there be convenient stopping-places, if nothing go wrong, one may travel without special risk and with no extraordinary discomfort at 50° below zero and a good deal lower. I have since that time made a short day's run at 62° below, and once travelled for two or three hours on a stretch at 65° below. But there is always more or less chance in travelling at low temperatures, because a very small thing may necessitate a stop, and a stop may turn into a serious thing. At such temperatures, one must keep going. No amount of clothing that it is possible to wear on the trail will keep one warm while standing still. For dogs and men alike, constant brisk motion is necessary; for dogs as well as men—even though dogs will sleep outdoors in such cold without harm—for they cannot take as good care of themselves in the harness as they can when loose. A trace that needs mending, a broken buckle, a snow-shoe string that must be replaced, may chill one so that it is impossible to recover one's warmth again. The bare hand cannot be exposed for many seconds without beginning to freeze; it is dangerous to breathe air into the lungs for any length of time without a muffler over the mouth.

Our troubles began as soon as we started. The trail was a narrow, winding toboggan track of sixteen or seventeen inches, while our sled was twenty inches wide, so that one runner was always dragging in the loose snow, and that meant slow, heavy going.

The days were nearing the shortest of the year, when, in these latitudes, the sun does but show himself and withdraw again. But, especially in very cold weather, which is nearly always very clear weather, that brief appearance is preceded by a feast of rich, delicate colour. First a greenish glow on the southern horizon, brightening into lemon and then into clear primrose, invades the deep purple of the starry heavens. Then a beautiful circle of blush pink above a circle of pure amethyst gradually stretches all around the edge of the sky, slowly brightening while the stars fade out and the heavens change to blue. The dead white mirror of the snow takes every tint that the skies display with a faint but exquisite radiance. Then the sun's disk appears with a flood of yellow light but with no appreciable warmth, and for a little space his level rays shoot out and gild the tree tops and the distant hills. The snow springs to life. Dead white no longer, its dry, crystalline particles glitter in myriads of diamond facets with every colour of the prism.

Then the sun is gone, and the lovely circle of rose pink over amethyst again stretches round the horizon, slowly fading until once more the pale primrose glows in the south against the purple sky with its silver stars. Thus sunrise and sunset form a continuous spectacle, with a purity of delicate yet splendid colour that only perfectly dry atmosphere permits. The primrose glow, the heralding circle, the ball of orange light, the valedictory circle, the primrose glow again, and a day has come and gone. Air can hold no moisture at all at these low temperatures, and the skies are cloudless.

Moreover, in the wilds at 50° below zero there is the most complete silence. All animal life is hidden away. Not a rabbit flits across the trail; in the absolutely still air not a twig moves. A rare raven passes overhead, and his cry, changed from a hoarse croak to a sweet liquid note, reverberates like the musical glasses. There is no more delightful sound in the wilderness than this occasional lapse into music of the raven. We wound through the scrub spruce and willow and over the niggerhead [sedge and grass tufts] swamps, a faint tinkle of bells, a little cloud of steam; for in the great cold the moisture of the animals' breath hangs over their heads in the still air, and on looking back it stands awhile along the course at dogs' height until it is presently deposited on twigs and tussocks.

We wound along, a faint tinkle of bells, a little cloud of steam, and in the midst of the cloud a tousle of shaggy black-and-white hair and red-and-white pompons—going out of the dead silence behind into the dead silence before. The dusk came, and still we plodded and pushed our weary way, swinging that heavy sled incessantly, by the gee pole in front and the handle-bars behind, in the vain effort to keep it on the trail. Two miles an hour was all that we were making. We had come but thirteen or fourteen miles out of twenty-four, and it was dark; and it grew colder.

The dogs whined and stopped every few yards, worn out by wallowing in the snow and the labour of the collar. The long scarves that wrapped our mouths and noses had been shifted and shifted, as one part after another became solid with ice from the breath, until over their whole length they were stiff as boards. After two more miles, it was evident that we could not reach the mail cabin that night.

Then, I made my last and worst mistake. We should have stopped and camped then and there. We had tent and stove and everything requisite. But the native boy insisted that the cabin was "only little way," and anyone who knows the misery of making camp in extremely cold weather, in the dark, will understand our reluctance to do so.

I decided to make a cache of the greater part of our load—tent and stove and supplies generally—and to push on to the cabin with but the bedding and the grub box, returning for the stuff in the morning. And, since in the deepest depths of blundering there is a deeper still, by someone's carelessness, but certainly by my fault, the axe was left behind in the cache.

With our reduced burden we made better progress, and in a short time reached the end of the portage and came out on the frozen river, just as the moon, a day or two past the full, rose above the opposite bank. One sees many strange distortions of sun and moon in this land, but never was a stranger seen than this. Her disk, shining through the dense air of the river bottom, was in shape an almost perfect octagon, regular as though it had been laid off with dividers and a ruler.

We were soon in doubt about the trail. The mail-carrier had gone down only two or three times this winter and each time had taken a different route, as more and more of the river closed and gave him more and more direct passage. A number of Indians had been hunting, and their tracks added to the tangle of trails. Presently we entered a thick mist that even to inexperienced eyes spoke of open water or new ice yet moist. So heavy was the vapour that to the man at the handle-bars the man at the gee pole loomed ghostly, and the man ahead of the dogs could not be distinguished at all. We had gone so much farther than our native boy had declared we had to go that we began to fear that, in the confusion of trails, we had taken the wrong one and had passed the cabin. That is the tenderfoot's, or, as we say, the chechaco's fear; it is the one thing that it may almost be said never happens. But the boy fell down completely and was frankly at a loss. All we could get out of him was: "May-be-so we catch cabin bymeby, may-be-so no."

If we had passed the cabin, it was twenty odd miles to the next; and it grew colder and the dogs were utterly weary again, prone upon the trail at every small excuse for a stop, only to be stirred by the whip, heavily wielded. Surely never men thrust themselves foolhardily into worse predicament!

Then I made my last mistake. Dimly the bank loomed through the mist, and I said: "We can't go any farther. I think we've missed the trail and I'm going across to yon bank to see if there's a place to camp." I had not gone six steps from the trail when the ice gave way under my feet and I found myself in water to my hips.

Under Providence, I owe it to the mukluks I wore, tied tight round my knees, that I did not lose my life or, at least, my feet. The thermometer at Circle City stood at 60° below zero at dark that day, and down on the ice it is always about 5° colder than on the bank, because cold air is heavy air and sinks to the lowest level, and 65° below zero means 97° below freezing.

My moose-hide breeches froze solid the moment I scrambled out but not a drop of water got to my feet. If the water had reached my feet, they would have frozen almost as quickly as the moose hide in that fearful cold. Thoroughly alarmed now, and realising our perilous situation, we did the only thing there was to do—we turned the dogs loose and abandoned the sled and went back along the trail we had followed as fast as we could. We knew that we could safely retrace our steps and that the trail would lead us to the bank after a while. We knew not where the trail would lead us in the other direction. As a matter of fact, it led to the mail cabin, two miles farther on, and the mail-carrier was at that time occupying it at the end of his day's run.

The dogs stayed with the sled. Dogs will usually stay with their sled. They seem to recognise their first allegiance to the load they haul, probably because they know their food forms part of it.

Our cache reached, we made a fire, thawed out the iron-like armour of my leather breeches, and cutting a spare woolen scarf in two, wrapped the dry, warm pieces about my numbed thighs. Then we pushed on the eighteen miles or so to Circle, keeping a steady pace despite the drowsiness that oppressed us, and that oppressed me particularly owing to the chill of my ducking. About five in the morning, we reached the town, and the clergyman turned out of his warm bed and I turned in, none the worse in body for the experience, but much humbled in spirit.

We had been out about twenty hours in a temperature ranging from 52° to 60° below zero, had walked about forty-four miles, labouring incessantly as well as walking, what time we were with the sled, with nothing to eat—it was too cold to stop for eating—and one of us had been in water to the waist, yet none of us took any harm. It was a providential overruling of blundering foolhardiness for which we were deeply thankful.

Stuck was an experienced climber and long wished to climb the mountain that the Americans had named McKinley and that the Indians knew as Denali—the latter name being the one by which Stuck insisted it be known. To his mind, Denali was not a "peak" but a "region," "a great soaring of the earth's crust" that "dominates the view whenever it is seen at all."[8] One could not doubt, Stuck said, whether he had seen the mountain. He either had—and knew it—or had not.

On June 7, 1913, Stuck was a member of the first party to reach Denali's highest point, the 20,320-foot south peak. He and three others had started out from Fairbanks, planning to reach the top of the mountain by mid-May, but their way was blocked by ice that had been eroded by an earthquake. It took the men three weeks to tunnel through the three miles of ice.

The first person to stand on the top of the mountain was Walter Harper—son of an Athabaskan Indian mother and white trader father—a distinction Stuck thought properly belonged to a Native. He wrote *Ascent of Denali* (1913) about the climb, and lobbied without success for the restoration of the mountain's Indian name.

According to conflicting accounts by two people, both of whom claimed to have been present, Stuck fell seriously ill in 1920 of either a cold that turned into bronchitis and then to pneumonia[9] or suffered a cerebral hemorrhage.[10] In either event, he died a month short of his fifty-eighth birthday. At his funeral, Fort Yukon Indians swept a trail through the snow, then bore his coffin from the church to the Native graveyard where he had asked that he be buried. Two spruce wreaths and a cross of red geraniums were laid on his grave. Weeks later, the flowers were frozen solid but still lay red on the snow.[11]

Notes

Epigraph: Hudson Stuck, *Ten Thousand Miles with a Dog Sled: A Narrative of Winter Travel in Interior Alaska* (New York: Charles Scribner's Sons, 1914), ix–x.

1 "Alaska Scrapbook," *Anchorage Daily News*, November 10, 2002, H4.

2 "Exploration: Adventures in Strange Lands by Many Travelers," *New York Times*, May 31, 1914.

3 Stuck, *Ten Thousand Miles*, 266.

4 Ibid., 134.

5 "Bad Whites in Alaska," *New York Times*, October 20, 1913.

6 Stuck, *Ten Thousand Miles*, 24.

7 Ibid., 4.

8 Ibid., 225.

9 "'Sky Pilot' of the North," *New York Times*, October 24, 1920.

10 Clara Heintz Burke, *Doctor Hap* (New York: Coward-McCann, 1961), 239.

11 "Letter from Dr. Grafton Burke of Fort Yukon, Alaska, to John Wilson Wood, Executive Secretary of the Department of Missions, the Protestant Episcopal Church," dated October 27, 1920. Wickersham Historic Collection, Alaska Historical Library, Juneau, October 12, 2010, http://www.observatorybooks.com/hudson_stuck.htm.

A cleanup, no. 11, Dexter, ca. 1903–1907.
Alaska State Library, P12-230.
B. B. Dobbs Photograph Collection.

PART III

INEXHAUSTIBLE OPTIMISM

The Mad Rush for Gold

For sixty-seven days, he had wandered in the mountains back of Nome, lost and bewildered. His grub stake consisted of a pound of bacon and few dozen crackers. With these articles of food, and such berries and roots as he could find, he subsisted for over two months.

James A. Hall,
Starving on a Bed of Gold, or, the World's Longest Fast, 1909

During the Great Gold Rush of Alaska, men in thousands came from all parts of the world. Many were ignorant of the hardships before them—the intense cold, the lack of food—and a journey through regions of ice and snow was a problem that awaited them.

Charlie Chaplin,
The Gold Rush, 1925

As the story goes, when one of Baranov's men brought him a handful of Alaskan gold, the Russian governor told the man to keep the news to himself. "Let the Americans and the Englishmen know that we have gold in these mountains, then we are ruined; they will rush in on us by thousands and crowd us to the walls—to the death."[1]

A handful of prospectors, having heard rumors of gold in Alaska, had migrated to the territory in the 1860s and 1870s, but the first real "rush" would be in response to the 1880 discovery of gold along Gastineau Channel. That mini-rush would be followed by larger ones, after the find in 1886 on Fortymile River and another on Birch Creek in 1893. The Birch Creek diggings were notable, with a million dollars in gold being taken out of the ground in the mines there in the summer of 1896.

In spite of the amount of gold recovered at Birch Creek that year, the diggings and the nearby mining camp at Circle City were nearly deserted by the time winter came. That August, gold was found along Bonanza Creek in the Canadian Yukon by a white prospector named George Carmack and his Indian brother-in-law. The Indian, whose name was Skookum Jim, said they found the gold "shining like cheese in a sandwich."[2] According to Canadian writer Pierre Berton, news of the Klondike strike spread up and down the Yukon River valley "like a great stage whisper," moving "as swiftly as the breeze in the birches, and more mysteriously."[3] As the price of a sled dog at Circle City rocketed from $25 to $1,500,[4] men and women on the Alaskan creeks dropped what they were doing and headed for the Klondike.

The stories in this section took place on Alaskan soil, but information about Canada and Canadian events is woven through them. Joined by two thousand miles of the Yukon River, main transportation route to the goldfields of both the United States and Canada, the region became all mixed up in the nineteenth-century mind by that little tsunami called "the gold rush." The Canadian Yukon and Alaska were consequently sometimes viewed and written about as a single place—the far northwest.

Much of Robert Service's poetry and Jack London's fiction was set in Canada rather than in Alaska, but, as historian Roderick Nash points out, "the distinction hardly mattered in the public mind."[5] Prospectors "neither knew nor cared," says David Wharton in his history of the Alaska gold rush, "whether they were in Canadian or American territory."[6] There were no maps, no towns, and, in many cases, no recognizable government authority, and geographic boundaries were of little moment to those trying to reach the gold. They would go wherever it was.

In the 1890s, the United States was facing economic depression. Those in desperate straits had good reason to dream of striking it rich. They were urged on by the *San Francisco Chronicle,* which claimed "Every river in Alaska is … filled with gold,"[7] and the bold headline in a Seattle newspaper that screamed, "GOLD! GOLD! GOLD!"[8] *Strand Magazine* reported, "All you have to do is to get there, and then it is your own fault if you don't return a millionaire."[9]

By the summer of 1898, between 100,000 and 200,000 people—some of them never having been farther north than Duluth—had started for Dawson and the Klondike River. A significant number invested a lifetime of savings in an effort to cure the disease known as "Klondicitis."[10] A California school child might not know the length of his own state's coastline but could report the length of the Yukon River.[11] Discussions on street corners, in saloons, at churches, and in Sunday schools were sure to be about the latest strikes. People sported buttons that read, "Yes, I'm going this spring,"[12] not knowing that, by the time they reached the Klondike, all the good claims would have been staked.[13]

No matter, for the tide was moving on. In 1898, gold was found on Alaska's Seward Peninsula, and many who had been disappointed in Dawson left for Norton Sound. In temperatures as low as twenty degrees below zero, they set out on foot, some pulling sleds, others bicycling down the Yukon.[14] In 1899, with gold trading at between seventeen and eighteen dollars an ounce, two million dollars was taken from the beaches at Nome, and another million was recovered from nearby creeks.[15]

Early Alaskan surveyor Addison Powell wrote, "In 1900, it was Nome, Nome; no place like Nome.... If you succeeded in convincing others that you were going north and not to Nome, you also succeeded in impressing them with the belief that you were an imbecile."[16] Then gold was found on the Koyukuk River, and in the Tanana River valley, and the restless wave kept moving, establishing—and then deserting—settlements at Ruby, Ophir, Dillman City, and Flat. There was a camp called Hope and another called Coldfoot, the latter named for those who arrived and got cold feet.

People went north in pairs: one to hold the sack, the other to shovel in the gold.[17] What they were looking for was placer gold (the Spanish word "placer" means "pleasure"), gold that had been eroded from the rock and washed into the beds of streams and rivers. Placer gold was recovered with a pan or sluice box. The gravel and dirt were washed away, and the precious metal was trapped in the bottom of the pan or in the riffles of the sluice. Placer gold was quickly depleted, and what remained was gold still encased in quartz—lode ore. The recovery of lode gold required manpower and expensive machinery—like that used at the Treadwell at Douglas Island—to blast away or crush the quartz. Under any scenario, finding—much less reclaiming—gold in the frozen ground of Alaska was grueling work for which many were unprepared.

They were unusual people nonetheless, described by one early prospector as the kind who "finish anything they start, or die in the attempt."[18] And one in ten of them was a woman, traveling with a spouse or a relative, a stranger, or alone.[19] A thirty-two-year-old who had left behind her husband and two sons in Chicago was crossing Chilkoot Pass when she twisted her ankle and broke down in tears. She was traveling with her brother George, who told her, "For God's sake, Polly, buck up and be a man! Have some style and move on!"[20] That woman, Martha Louise Purdy Black, did move on and later became the second female member of the Canadian House of Commons.

Following the prospectors came innkeepers, barkeepers, blacksmiths, gamblers, dance hall girls, restaurateurs, and prostitutes—not all of them honest. In 1900, thirty thousand men and women were "dumped" on the beach at Nome with no provision made for keeping the peace. According to Catholic priest Edward Devine, disreputable characters made "their presence felt in various and disagreeable ways."[21]

Of the hundred or two hundred thousand who joined the stampede, not many found gold—as few as three hundred clearing as much as $15,000.00.[22] Some concluded—not without good reason—that all the foofaraw had been a hoax. The Seattle Chamber of Commerce had hired a Harvard-educated journalist to blanket cities around the country with "fact sheets" and "news articles" that were in actuality thinly disguised advertisements for local merchants. As a consequence of the "rush," Seattle's 1890 population of 40,000 had ballooned to 240,000 by 1910, and the main beneficiaries were local tax coffers and businessmen's wallets.

Not everyone who left Alaska empty-handed looked back nostalgically on the experience, but even some of those who experienced extreme hardships were glad they had gone. Walter Curtin was trapped for eight months on a steamer frozen in ice. He saw one neighbor go mad in the long, dark winter, and watched another die of scurvy. Curtin arrived in Alaska with thirty-five cents in his pocket and went home with less. Thirty years after the fact, he said, "I made exactly nothing, but if I could turn time back, I would do it over again for less than that."[23]

Notes

Epigraphs: James A. Hall, *Starving on a Bed of Gold; or, The World's Longest Fast* (Santa Cruz: Press of the Sentinel, 1909), 79; *The Gold Rush*, written and directed by Charles Chaplin (United States: United Artists, 1925; restoration by Photoplay Productions, The Roy Export Company Establishment, 2003).

1 Baranov quoted by Henry Wood Elliott in preface to Ernest Ingersoll, *In Richest Alaska and the Gold Fields of the Klondike* (Chicago: The Dominion Company, 1897), iii.

2 "Discovery in the Klondike," Educators' Resource Guide to the Klondike Gold Rush of 1898, February 15, 2011, http://www.nps.gov/archive/klse/Resource_Guide.htm.

3 Pierre Berton, *The Klondike Fever: The Life and Death of the Last Great Gold Rush* (New York: Alfred A. Knopf, 1972), 51.

4 William R. Hunt, *North of 53 Degrees: The Wild Days of the Alaska-Yukon Mining Frontier* (New York: Macmillan, 1974), 25.

5 Nash, "Tourism, Parks and the Wilderness Idea in the History of Alaska," in *Alaska in Perspective,* ed. Sue E. Liljeblad (Anchorage: Alaska Historical Commission / Alaska Historical Society, 1981), 9.

6 David Wharton, *The Alaska Gold Rush* (Bloomington: Indiana University Press, 1972), 105.

7 Carolyn Jean Holeski and Marlene Conger Holeski, eds., in *In Search of Gold: The Alaska Journals of Horace S. Conger, 1898–1899* (Anchorage: The Alaska Geographic Society, 1983), xii.

8 Beriah Brown, "GOLD! GOLD! GOLD!," in an article published in the *Seattle Post-Intelligencer* on July 17, 1897, that started the stampede, according to "The United States in 1897," Educators' Guide to the Klondike Gold Rush of 1898, National Park Service, February 15, 2011, http://www.nps.gov/archive/klse/Resource_Guide.htm.

9 William G. Fitzgerald, "The New El-Dorado on the Klondike," *The Strand Magazine* 14, no. 82 (October 1897): 419.

10 William B. Haskell, *Two Years in the Klondike and Alaskan Gold Fields, 1896–1898* (1898; repr., Fairbanks: University of Alaska Press, 1998), 521.

11 Ibid., 522.

12 Ibid., 521.

13 William Hunt, *North of 53 Degrees*, 81.

14 Ibid., 90–91, 107.

15 Ibid., 99.

16 Addison Powell, *Trailing and Camping in Alaska* (New York: Wessels & Bissell, 1910), 174.

17 Ibid.

18 Unidentified man quoted by Berton, *Klondike Fever*, 432.

19 Claire Rudolf Murphy and Jane G. Haigh, *Gold Rush Women* (Anchorage: Alaska Northwest Books, 1997), 11.

20 Ibid., 71.

21 Edward J. Devine, *Across Widest America, Newfoundland to Alaska, with the Impressions of a Two Years' Sojourn on the Bering Coast* (Montreal: The Canadian Messenger, 1905), 148.

22 "The Gold Fields," Educators' Guide to the Klondike Gold Rush of 1898, National Park Service, February 15, 2011, http://www.nps.gov/archive/klse/Resource_Guide.htm.

23 Walter Curtin quoted by Berton, *Klondike Fever,* 429.

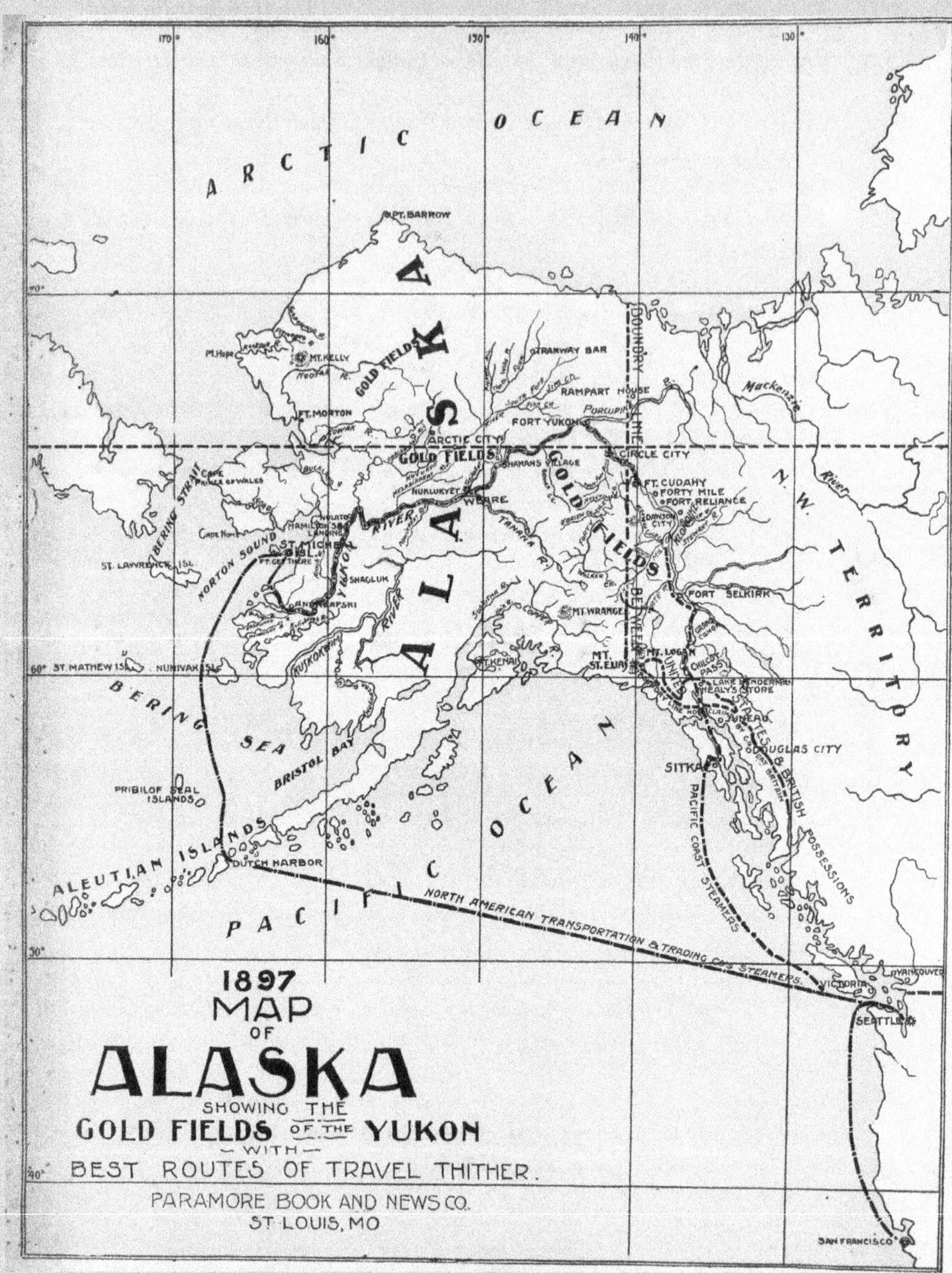

Map of Alaska showing the goldfields of the Yukon, 1897.
Rare Maps Collection, UAF-M0425m, Alaska and Polar Regions Collections, Elmer E. Rasmuson Library, University of Alaska Fairbanks.

Boundary line on Chilkoot Pass, Alaska, 1898.
Alaska State Library, P41-009.
P. E. Larss Photograph Collection.

Miles Canyon, n.d. Alaska State Library, P39-1222.
Case and Draper Photograph Collection.

Floating down the Yukon, ca. 1897–1910.
Alaska State Library, P232-248. Klondike Gold Rush Photograph Collection.

Steamer *Monarch* at Eagle, Alaska, n.d. Anchorage Museum, AMRC-b64-100. John Urban Collection.

The *Ohio* in an ice pack, ca. 1900–1910.
Alaska State Library, P155-78.
William E. Hunt Photograph Collection.

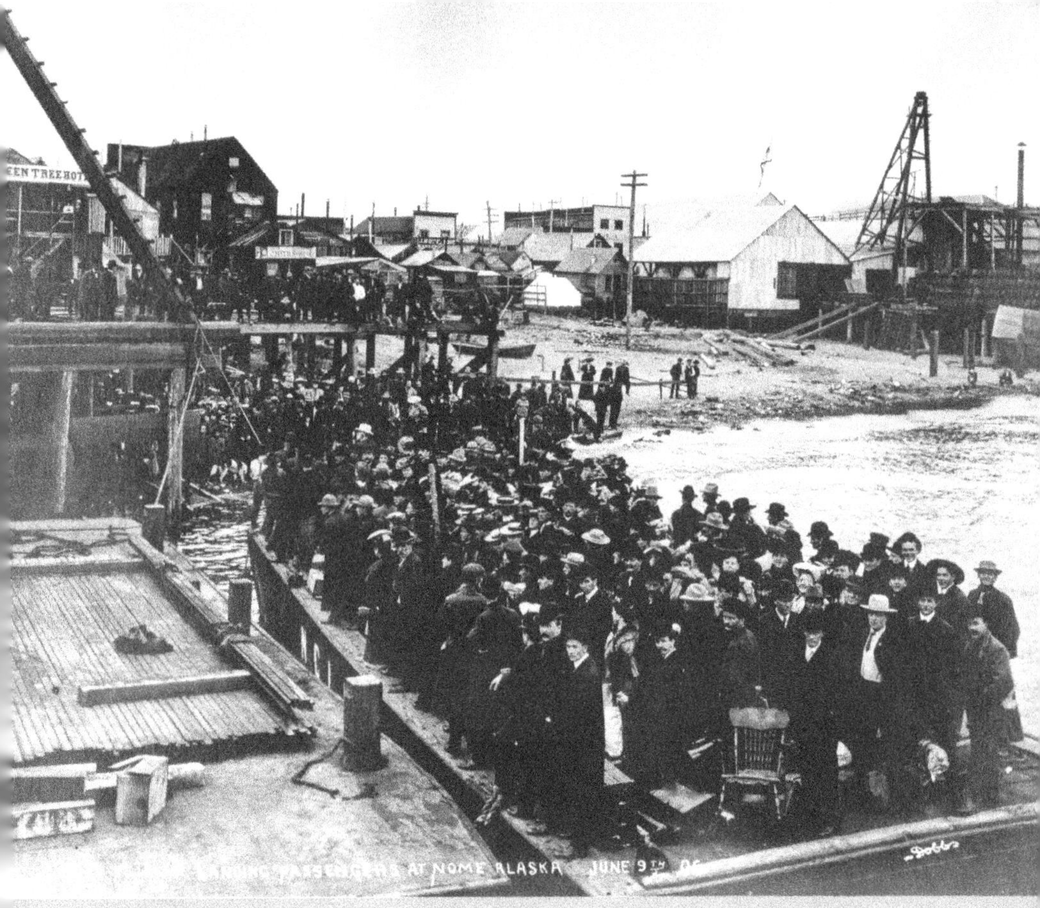

Landing passengers at Nome, Alaska, June 9, 1906.
Alaska State Library, P12-099.
B. B. Dobbs Photograph Collection.

Nome, Alaska, July 1900. Alaska State Library, P155-1-27.
William E. Hunt Photograph Collection. Photograph by B. B. Dobbs.

“Miner’s cabin in the hills back of Juneau,” n.d. Alaska State Library, P175-18.
US Army Signal Corps Photograph Collection.

Nome in the "Good Old Summertime," Diamond Fruit Company, ca. 1903–1907. Alaska State Library, P12-063. B. B. Dobbs Photograph Collection.

Miners at McCarthy's Camp, Copper River, ca. 1908.
Alaska State Library, P124-16.
Eric A. Hegg Photograph Collection.

Nome, dog team pulling boat, ca. 1906.
Alaska State Library, P12-090.
B. B. Dobbs Photograph Collection.

16

ERNEST INGERSOLL

Outfit for an Argonaut

> Nowhere else on earth will the student of human nature find more to interest him than in the mining camps of the frontier.... The sudden gathering of all classes, races and ages, widely separated in birth and breeding, character and customs and tongue, confronted by the greatest hardships, surrounded by the extremes of human joy and human sorrow, brings about a situation that forms a basis for many startling chapters in the book of life.

In his introduction to *In Richest Alaska and the Gold Fields of the Klondike,* Smithsonian scientist Henry Elliott presented a stark picture of what awaited the Alaskan prospector. Mosses, lichens, shrubs, ferns, and grasses covered the ground, thus every foot of territory had to be uncovered before one could find what lay below. Success, Elliott said, would be "purely accidental."[1] No ranches or farms were available to supply provisions, and the climate confined a person to one place between November and June. At the same time, the potential for gain was great. Elliott estimated that less than one-thousandth of Alaska's mineral wealth had been tapped. Besides, an Alaskan prospector would breathe only healthy air and be untroubled by sickness of any kind—a claim that scurvy victims would have disputed.

The author of *In Richest Alaska,* Ernest Ingersoll was, like Elliott, a Smithsonian scientist. He had also had served as a US Treasury agent in Alaska and had studied fur seals in the Pribilof Islands. When the *Excelsior* arrived in San Francisco on July 14, 1897, with its freight of gold dust and nuggets and its news of the Klondike, Ingersoll was on hand to witness the resulting delirium, which he claimed spread from ocean to ocean within ten minutes of the ship's docking. The *Portland* reached Seattle three days later, with sixty more miners and another seven hundred thousand dollars in gold onboard, and the nation's mania spiraled out of control.

In the weeks and months that followed, the "rich and poor, weak and strong, venturesome and timid"[2] were all on their way to Alaska and the Klondike—many of them with absolutely no mining experience. Crowds in West Coast ports nearly rioted as incoming passengers were unable to disembark due to those shoving to get onboard. Ingersoll began *In Richest Alaska* just a few months after the news of the Klondike reached the outside world and the rush was showing no signs of abating. It was anticipated that migration to the north would be even greater when the Yukon River opened in the spring of 1898.

Ingersoll interviewed some of the passengers who had arrived in San Francisco on the *Excelsior*—one of them a former YMCA secretary Ingersoll called Professor Lippey, but whose name is correctly spelled Lippy. According to Ingersoll, Lippy returned from the Klondike with $85,000 in gold; Pierre Berton says that Lippy's take was closer to a million.[3] Lippy was accompanied by his wife, a small woman with skin tanned as brown as her eyes. She had been the first white woman to cross the pass at the head of Lynn Canal that marked the boundary between Alaska and Canada, and reported that, in spite of a steady diet of canned foods, she and the Professor were returning in perfect health. While they were in the goldfields, Mr. Lippy had seen to the mining and she had taken care of the housework.

Ingersoll also interviewed Mrs. Gage, a "wide-awake American" who said that there was "an immense amount" of gold in the Yukon and who believed that the stories of probable future starvation in the north were unfounded. Gage said that life on the frontier was "fascinating," and that a man or woman who succeeded at it "rarely gets to like anything else."[4] She, like others returning from the north, was so besieged by those seeking information about the goldfields that she had to hide in the drawing room of a railcar as she traveled home.

For those contemplating the trip, Ingersoll described the most frequently used routes to the goldfields. The all-water route from Seattle, the "rich man's route," crossed the Pacific, went through the Aleutians to St. Michael on the Bering Sea, then up the Yukon River to the goldfields of Alaska and Canada. The whole trip was on the water, via steamship across the ocean and then by riverboat up the Yukon, and was thus easier. It was also longer, more expensive, and only available in the summer.

The alternate itinerary, known as the "poor man's route," crossed the trails at the head of the Lynn Canal. This route was closer to the goldfields, cheaper, and shorter. It could be accessed nine months of the year, but was much more arduous. After a sail up the Inside Passage to the head of Lynn Canal, a footpath crossed the Coastal Range, either via White Pass above Skagway or Chilkoot Pass above Dyea. Those crossing either pass were required by the Canadian government to carry with them a year's worth of supplies, which weighed as much as a ton.

Prospectors with sufficient wherewithal could hire Indian packers, some of whom were so strong that it was said one of them had toted a piano on his back. Those who could not afford such luxury relayed their supplies up the trail and over the mountain, fifty pounds or so at time, on sleds or on their backs. Goods in the process of being relayed were cached at places all along the trail, where they apparently were left undisturbed until their owners returned. It could take a miner as long as three months to ferry his supplies to the Canadian lakes on the other side of the passes. The trails were themselves no picnic, with the last hundred and fifty feet of the climb up the Chilkoot so steep that one man likened it to "scaling the walls of a house."[5]

After crossing the mountains, depending on which pass they had taken, travelers descended to either Lake Bennett or Lake Lindeman. There, on Canadian soil, they were set for the next stage of the journey—building a boat to negotiate the lakes and rivers that led to the Yukon and to Dawson and Alaska. They would do this, that is, if any of the trees for miles around remained standing, if they could figure out how to whipsaw logs, and if they succeeded in assembling a craft that would float upon launch.

These neophytes were Ingersoll's audience. He attempted to provide all of the information a gold seeker might need, but avoided giving a recommendation on one important topic: where to stake a claim. "To be well prepared is half the battle won,"[6] he confidently wrote.

Here is some of Ingersoll's best advice for those contemplating the journey.

ERNEST INGERSOLL

Outfit for an Argonaut[*]

To be sober, strong, and healthy is the first requisite for anyone who wants to battle successfully for a year or two in the frozen lands of the far North. A physique hardy enough to withstand the most rigorous climate is an abso-

*From *In Richest Alaska and the Gold Fields of the Klondike* (1897), 79–94.

lute necessity. With a temperature varying from almost one hundred degrees above zero in midsummer to fifty, sixty, and even seventy below that point in winter, with weeks of foggy, damp, thawing weather, and with winds that rage at times with the violence of hurricanes, the man with a weak constitution is bound to suffer untold hardship. No one with weak lungs or subject to rheumatism ought to think of wintering along the Yukon.

In short, making the venture means, according to one who has tried it, "packing provisions over pathless mountains, towing a heavy boat against a five to an eight-mile [an hour] current, over battered boulders, digging in the bottomless frost, sleeping where night overtakes, fighting gnats and mosquitoes by the millions, shooting seething cañons and rapids and enduring for seven long months a relentless cold which never rises above zero and frequently falls to eighty degrees below."

If a man is able to meet these conditions, he is almost sure of making a good living and takes chances with the rest in making a fortune. It is not alone to the physical side of the question that one should look. Temperament counts for a great deal in a miner's life. Men should be of cheerful, hopeful dispositions and willing workers. Those of sullen, morose natures, although they may be good workers, are very apt, as soon as the novelty of the country wears off, to become dissatisfied, pessimistic, and melancholy.

Good judgment is also a prime requisite. Once in the atmosphere of the gold country, one hears constantly of newly-found placers which are reported to be vastly richer than anything yet discovered. With each such report, scores of miners leave diggings which are vastly superior to those which they propose to seek six, twenty, or one hundred miles away. If one is constantly on the jump from claim to claim, there is evidently no time left for the only work that counts, separating the gold from its containing earths. One of the returning miners on the *Excelsior* said that the hardest work he had to do in the Klondike region was to keep pegging away at his claim, which, by the way, was a very good one, and give a deaf ear to the stories of fabulous wealth being found just beyond the nearest range of mountains. These stories are often put in circulation by people who are anxious to see certain claims forsaken by their owners that they themselves may step in and become the owners.

As to the outfit, Joseph Ladue, who has spent years in this country and who is given credit for having founded Dawson City, says in regard to this:

"It is a great mistake to take anything except what is necessary. The trip is a long, arduous one, and a man should not add one pound of baggage to his outfit that can be dispensed with. I have known men who loaded themselves up with rifles, revolvers, and shotguns. This is entirely unnecessary. Revolvers will get you into trouble, and there is no use of taking them with you, as large game of any character is rarely found on the trip. I have prospected through this region for some years and have only seen one moose. You will not see any large game whatever on your trip from Juneau to Dawson City, therefore do not take any firearms along."

In addition to the great inconvenience of carrying a great deal of luggage, it is a matter of continual expense. It is said that the Indians are disposed to gauge a man's ability to pay by the amount of baggage he takes with him, and scale their prices accordingly. At 15, 20, or 25 cents a pound for packing over the Chilkoot Pass, it makes considerable difference whether a man has with him a hundred weight or half a ton of freight. Then there are steamer charges, wharfage fees, and often portage expenses to be defrayed, to say nothing of customs duties. One hundred and fifty pounds of baggage is all that is allowed for a passenger on the Yukon River boats and those sailing from Seattle and San Francisco for Alaskan ports.

The general practice as to clothing for miners who remain over winter is to adopt the dress of the natives. Water boots are made of seal or walrus skins; dry weather, or winter boots from various skins, fur trimmed. Trousers are made of Siberian fawn and marmot skins, while the upper garment, combined with a hood, called tarka [parka], is made of marmot trimmed with long fur, which helps to protect the face of the person wearing it. Flannels can be worn under these, and not be any heavier than clothing worn in a country with zero weather. For bedding, woolen blankets are used, combined with fur robes. If the former are used, it is well to be provided with two pairs.

As to provisions, it is impossible to lay down any definite scheme. The first consideration is to have enough to last for the journey from the coast to the interior. Figuring on thirty days as the shortest time possible in which this trip can be made, the supply ought to be about as follows: Twenty pounds of flour, twelve pounds of bacon, twelve pounds of beans, four pounds of butter, five pounds of vegetables, five pounds of dried fruits, four cans of condensed milk, five pounds of sugar, one pound of tea, three pounds of coffee, one and one-half pounds of salt, five pounds of cornmeal, a small portion of pepper and mustard, and baking-powder.

To one accustomed to camp life, there are many things in the way of utensils and apparatus generally that can be dispensed with, which, to the man new to such modes of living, are, or seem to be, absolutely necessary. A pretty complete outfit includes matches, cooking utensils and dishes, frying pan, water kettle, duck [cloth] tent, rubber blanket, bean pot, drinking-cup, two plates, tea-pot, knife and fork, large cooking pan, small cooking pan. A fine addition to the culinary department will be a good assortment of fish-hooks, gill nets, and fishing tackle. These ought to be graded through the medium and small sizes. Alaskan fish are for the most part gamey.

Ample provision must be made for the boat, raft, and sled building, which is a feature of every journey overland. To this end these items will be found not only useful but absolutely necessary: One jack-plane, one whip-saw, one cross-cut saw, one rip-saw, one axe, one hatchet, one hunting-knife, one two-foot rule, six pounds of assorted nails, three pounds of oakum, five pounds of pitch, 150 feet of rope.

Inasmuch as gnats and mosquitoes abound all over the Alaskan interior, some means of protection from their assaults must be provided. Mosquito netting is recommended, and it is well to buy that with the smallest mesh obtainable. Snow spectacles and a simple medicine chest ought to find a place in every outfit. One man ought never to try the trip alone, and where four or five pool their interests, one tent, one stove, and one set of tools will suffice for the party.

After the supplies for the trip to the mines have been decided upon, the more extensive task of laying in provisions for the stay can be taken up. A good, safe rule is to estimate on remaining on the Yukon a full year. If one decides later to prolong the time, it will be easier to send back or go back to Juneau for further supplies than to be burdened with them during the first months of life in camp, and more especially when making the first trip over the mountains.

A miner who, after spending long years in the Colorado camp, went to Alaska to tempt fortune on the Klondike, gives the following list his endorsement as containing everything necessary for one man for one year: Flour, 400 lbs.; cornmeal, 20 lbs.; rolled oats, 36 lbs.; rice, 25 lbs.; beans, 100 lbs.; sugar, 75 lbs.; dried fruits (apples, peaches, apricots), 75 lbs.; yeast cakes (6 in pkg.), 6 pkgs.; candles, 40; dry salt pork, 25 lbs.; evaporated potatoes, 25 lbs.; evaporated onions, 5 lbs.; butter; bacon, 150 lbs.; dried beef, 30 lbs.; extract of beef (4 oz.), 1/2 doz.; baking-powder, 10 lbs.; soda, 3 lbs.; salt, 20 lbs.; pepper, 1 lb.; mustard, 1/2 lb.; ginger; coffee, 25 lbs.; tea, 10 lbs.; condensed milk, 2 doz.; soap (laundry), 5 lbs.; soap (toilet), 5 cakes; matches, can of 60 pkgs.; tobacco; compressed soup, 3 doz.; compressed soup vegetables, 10 lbs.; Jamaica ginger (4 oz.), 2 bottles; stove, 1; gold pan, 1; granite buckets, 2; knives and forks, 1 each; spoons, 3 tea and 3 table; Quaker bread-pan, 1; cups, 2; plates (tin), 3; whetstone, 1; coffee-pot, 1; picks and handles, 1; sleds; hatchet, 1; saws (whip), 1; saws (hand), 1; shovel, 1; nails, 20 lbs.; files (assorted), 1/2 doz.; axe and handle, 1; draw knife, 1; plane, 1; brace and bit, 1; chisels (assorted), 3; butcher knife, 1; compass, 1; revolver, 1; evap. vinegar, 1 qt.; rope (1/2 inch), 100 ft.; medicine case; pitch; oakum; fry pan, 1.

As a general rule, miners find it to best advantage to buy the larger part of their outfits in Juneau rather than in the United States or on the Yukon. Buying in the United States, one has to pay the freight to Juneau or Skaguay [Skagway], and perhaps wharfage at those points. The prices prevailing in Juneau for the necessary commodities are not prohibitory at all. But the same cannot be said of the tariff in vogue among the storekeepers of Dawson City.

Of course, a few months will make a great difference in these matters. Already the steamboat companies doing business on the Yukon are making plans to send thousands of tons of food, supplies, and clothing to the gold fields when the ice breaks up next summer. Their efforts will be largely supplemented by private enterprises of one kind and another, so that it is confidently expected that the exorbitant rates which now obtain on the Klondike will be materially reduced next summer.

A good clothing outfit for a year's stay is this: Two pairs heaviest wool socks, one pair Canadian laragans or shoe packs, one pair German socks, two pairs heaviest woolen blankets, one oil blanket or canvas, one mackinaw suit, two heavy flannel shirts, two pairs heavy overalls, two suits heavy woolen underwear, one pair rubber boots (crack-proof preferable), one pair snow-shoes, heavy cap, fleece-lined mittens.

In conclusion, here are a few pointers dictated by experience for the benefit of the Klondiker. For the most part, their observance will involve but little trouble, and, on the other hand, will add vastly to one's comfort while in the frozen lands:

Don't waste a single ounce of anything, even if you don't like it. Put it away and it will come handy when you will like it.

Shoot a dog, if you have to, behind the base of the skull; a horse between the ears, ranging downward. Press the trigger of your rifle. Don't pull it. Don't catch hold of the barrel when thirty degrees below zero is registered. Watch out against getting snow in your barrel. If you do, don't shoot it out or the gun may and probably will burst.

If by any chance you are traveling across a plain (no trail) and a fog comes up, or a blinding snowstorm, either of which will prevent you from taking your bearings, camp and don't move, no matter what anyone may urge, until the weather becomes clear again.

Keep all your drawstrings on clothing in good repair. Don't forget to use your goggles when the sun is bright on snow. A fellow is often tempted to leave them off. Don't you do it.

Establish camp rules, especially regarding the food. Allot rations, less while idle than when at work, and also varying with the seasons, a man requiring less food, or at any rate less of certain kinds in warm than in cold weather.

Keep your furs in good repair. One little slit may cause you untold agony during a march in a heavy storm. You cannot tell when such a storm will overtake you.

No man can continuously drag more than his own weight. Remember this is a fact.

Be sure during the winter to watch your footgear carefully. Change wet stockings before they freeze, or you may lose a toe or a foot.

When your nose is bitterly cold, stuff both nostrils with fur, cotton, wool, or anything else soft enough. The pain will cease.

Don't try to carry more than forty pounds of stuff over a stiff climb, at least the first day.

Keep your sleeping bag clean. If it becomes inhabited with vermin, freeze the inhabitants out.

White snow over a crevasse, if hard, is safe; yellow or dirty color, never.

Don't eat snow or ice. Go thirsty until you can melt it.

Choose your bunk as far from tent door as possible.

The man who knows little now will come back knowing more than he who knew it all before starting.

In his final chapter, Ingersoll provided an update from some passengers who had just arrived from Dawson. Due to the burgeoning population, comestibles could not be purchased for "love or money,"[7] and the coming winter was predicted to bring both food shortages and problems from lack of sanitation. Those sailing for Alaska, Ingersoll warned, should be prepared to face "the ghastly triumvirate"—starvation, typhoid fever, and exposure to the deadly cold.[8]

Notes

Epigraph: Ernest Ingersoll, *In Richest Alaska and the Gold Fields of the Klondike* (Chicago: Dominion Company, 1897), 95. The work was also printed as *Gold Fields of the Klondike and the Wonders of Alaska* (Philadelphia: Edgewood Publishing Company, 1897).

1 Henry Elliott, introduction to Ingersoll, *In Richest Alaska*, iv.
2 Ingersoll, *In Richest Alaska*, 19.
3 Berton, *Klondike Fever*, 97.
4 Ingersoll, *In Richest Alaska*, 25.
5 Berton, *Klondike Fever*, 250–51.
6 Ingersoll, *In Richest Alaska*, 79.
7 Ibid., 490.
8 Ibid.

17

ROBERT C. KIRK

Heartbreak on the White Pass

"There be Skagway," said the mate, "and over there on the flat is Dyea. You will soon be ashore, and you can take your choice—Chilcoot or White Pass—and I guess from all accounts they're both bad enough."

Nothing disturbed "the peace and quiet of the great Metropolis"[1] of San Francisco on July 14, 1897, wrote Englishman Robert Kirk, until the *Excelsior* steamed into harbor, bearing news of the Klondike. According to Kirk, it was those lurid headlines and the fantastic press accounts of sudden wealth that caused mayhem.

As he explained in *Twelve Months in Klondike,* gold was displayed in San Francisco shop windows and reporters on both the East and West Coasts vied for stories of the staggering riches being brought into town. Exaggerated news reports—many of them based on rumors and half-truths—built hopes, inflamed passions, and focused the world's attention on a previously unknown portion of the globe.

A photo at the front of Kirk's book demonstrates the sort of publicity that contributed to the rush. A bearded gent stands behind a stack of bulging sacks as wide as his arms and as high as his chest above a caption that reads, "Half a Million in Gold Dust Ready for Shipment."[2] The response was dramatic. Overnight, steamship companies were organized and flooded with customers demanding to know what clothing to wear, what food to take, and what were the chances of staking a good claim. The only people with sound information about the region—returning miners—were hounded by interviewers.

All sorts prepared to go north. An Irish washerwoman planned to have her children hunt nuggets at night and attend school by day—forget the fact that no schools were available. A dancing teacher intended to give lessons to miners and Indians, and to prospect in his spare time. Thousands who made the trek north could ill afford to take the loss—many were manual laborers squandering hard-earned savings on outfits and passages for Alaska.

The Alaska Commercial Company, owner of the *Excelsior*, immediately overhauled the steamer and announced a return sailing. The company promised to get its passengers to St. Michael in time to travel up the Yukon before freeze-up, and all berths were sold within hours. The ship left San Francisco with a "seething, surging mass of humanity eager to get a glimpse of the departing gold-seekers"[3] crowding the docks and streets. When the boat reached St. Michael, the promised riverboats were nowhere in sight, and as few as 10 percent of the *Excelsior's* passengers would reach Dawson before winter set in.

Back in San Francisco, boats sailed north at the rate of three or four a week. It was too late to take the route up the Yukon, but the passes at the head of the Lynn Canal were still open, and that's where Robert Kirk decided to go. He booked passage on the *Willamette*, a ship that Kirk knew as the *Willammette*, a converted coal carrier pressed into service by the Pacific Coast Steamship Company. There was coal dust in every corner of the ship, but there had been no time to clean it. When the vessel left San Francisco, it was loaded with two hundred passengers, sixty horses and mules, and tons of cargo. By the time the *Willamette* sailed from Puget Sound, she had been loaded with even more and was carrying eight hundred passengers, their freight, and three hundred animals—with no standing room available.

The *Willamette's* captain, whom Kirk identifies only as Holmes, had been sailing for three score years and ten and had never lost a ship. This voyage was to be his first through the Inside Passage, as well as his last, for he was set to retire upon completion of the trip. For a captain unfamiliar with the route, navigation of the Inside Passage was no easy matter, since a ship had to wend in and out among the islands of southeastern Alaska, cross rocky shoals, and travel rough, open waters. With such a large number of passengers onboard—some of them from "the rougher element"[4]—the ship was insufficiently staffed, so Holmes appointed a committee to maintain order and a fire patrol to keep smokers away from the flammables.

Onboard were Washington ranchers, Montana miners, Puget Sound steamboaters, clerks, tradesmen, laborers, and a few women. The decks were crowded with patent medicine hawkers, storytellers, newspapers readers, and card players. As the *Willamette* floated by Indian settlements, log cabins with moss roofs, and totem poles, Native women paddled along in hollowed-out log canoes, their faces painted with burnt cedar soot mixed with grease as protection from the sun.

Some of Kirk's fellow passengers had been to Alaska before, so he interviewed them on the question of which of the two trails at the head of Alaska's Lynn Canal was preferable: the one over Chilkoot Pass—which Kirk, like many others, called the Chilcoot—or the one over White Pass? What he learned was that each trail had its own proponents.

Those in favor of the forty-mile White Pass thought it more "modern," having been blazed more recently. The trail was said to be a series of easy grades and flat surfaces over which horses and mules could handily transport goods. By contrast, the thirty-two-mile Chilkoot was said to be so steep it was nearly impossible.

But then Kirk heard from those who preferred the Chilkoot. According to them, the White Pass trail was a series of bottomless bogs where horses sank out of sight. Prospectors who tried to cross it were the very "pictures of despair and misery."[5] The shorter Chilkoot was the trail to take, and those who had chosen it had no trouble reaching Lake Lindeman.

Given these conflicting views, Kirk decided to investigate further before committing to either route. He got off the boat at Skagway, where the passengers' freight was taken ashore on a barge called a lighter. Goods were offloaded haphazardly and piled indiscriminately on the beach. Frantic men and women rushed about, trying to reclaim their possessions and find a place to camp.

In the following passage, Kirk describes Skagway and what he found out on the trail.

ROBERT C. KIRK

Heartbreak on the White Pass[*]

The Pack Train saloon, one of the largest tents in the town, was the common meeting point for the Klondikers, who gathered there at nighttime to discuss proposed improvements on the mountain trail. Drinks and cigars were a shilling (twenty-five cents) each, this being the customary price in the rival saloons. Men who had already become disgusted with the trail had placed their tents along the road and opened a shop or store with their wares. A doctor had appeared on the scene, and there were blacksmiths, boat-makers,

*From *Twelve Months in Klondike* (1899), 27–40.

and carpenters. The road through the town was crowded at all times with hundreds of men and a few adventurous women, hurrying madly along with all sorts of vehicles and pack animals.

With the arrival of each succeeding steamer, bearing hundreds of passengers, the confusion became greater, and this was only finally surmounted by the laying out of several additional streets along which the travelers might pass. Lawlessness was held somewhat in check by the various miners' committees that had been appointed, and the fear of meeting with summary punishment at the hands of these men probably operated as a restraining check on the evil intentions of thieves and others.

It became necessary for me at that time to journey across the mountain trail to see for myself the conditions and hardships that would have to be encountered if we chose that route, and also to try and sift the truth from the mass of misinformation we had listened to on the ocean steamer. Accordingly, I left the vessel at daybreak on the morning after our arrival, and started in the direction of the mountains, carrying with me a camera, a blanket, and three days' provisions.

The course lay at first across a flat, swampy piece of ground, heavily studded with timber, for a distance of four miles; then it left the valley and disappeared into a ravine between two mountains. For some unknown reason, the man who had originally blazed the trail chose to follow up and down a succession of high mountain ridges in order to approach the White Pass summit, rather than pursue the easier and more natural passage along the banks of the river.

After ascending and descending these high ridges for a continuous distance of ten miles, during which there were many unnecessary descents, the trail re-crossed the same stream that we had followed near Skagway, and at an elevation of but a few hundred feet above the sea. The route along these mountainsides and over the different summits was tortuous in the extreme, and the descents were often so great that the course of the trail lay in a series of zigzags. Mud holes and swamps of moist, black loam were encountered in all the ravines, and the trail among the mountainsides lay among rocks and between boulders of great size.

Sometimes we reached altitudes of probably twelve or fifteen hundred feet, and from these places we had fine views of the granite summits around us, mountain torrents beneath us, and the blue spectral glaciers beyond us towards the sea. Sometimes the trail led to the edge of a precipice, sometimes over great areas of glacier-ground rock, and over swamps and through forests where travel was extremely difficult.

When we had passed the bridge crossing the turbulent stream, we ascended a zigzag trail over the highest and last mountain before reaching the summit. This was undoubtedly the worst incline of all, and the descent to the stream again, after we had gone along the summit for some distance, was even more steep and so difficult that a misstep might have meant disaster. Then it became necessary to ford the stream again before ascending the final summit. By this time, we had got well out of the large timber, and there were no poles of sufficient size to bridge the stream. A chain of rocks extended diagonally through the water to the opposite bank, and the few men who had preceded us had crossed on these. But this little stream was fed by melting glaciers higher up in the mountains, and in the afternoon it had twice the volume it had in the early morning before the effect of the sun's rays was felt on the glaciers. The rocks upon which we were to cross were submerged in this seething, roaring mass, but their position could be reasonably well guessed by the surface indications.

Since it was important that we should cross, we took off our clothing and made it into a roll, in the center of which were our cameras, and, with the bundle fastened to our shoulders and a long slender pole in our hands for support, we cautiously forded the stream. The roar of the water was so loud that we could not hear the words of encouragement from those on shore, and the speed of the ice cold water was such that when it struck us it shot upwards, completely drenching our clothes, but without injuring our cameras.

We dressed on the opposite bank and proceeded over a bald, bare mountain, upon which no trees nor shrubs could grow, until we reached the summit of White Pass. Looking ahead, we could see nothing but a great expanse of rockbound country, but after we had traversed this, we came upon a chain of three lakes, across which the Klondikers who afterwards came with tons and tons of supplies ferried their goods in small boats, thereby saving several miles of rocky trail. Beyond these lakes, the trail led over hills and swamps, through forests and past stagnant pools of water, a section that afterwards proved the hardest part of the journey to the worn out men and horses. The trail ended at the head of Lake Bennett, an estimated distance of forty-five miles from Skagway.

While we were travelling back to the coast, we arrived at the ford late one afternoon and found half a dozen Klondikers on the opposite bank who had waited there half a day hoping someone would come from the direction of Lake Bennett and bring the poles across the stream from where we had left them. After the usual preparations, we crossed on the submerged rocks as we had done before, and the others were able to proceed. We reached the steamer, which was still busy discharging her cargo, after an absence of four days.

Skagway had grown so during these four days that we could scarcely recognize it. I searched for an hour for a certain blacksmith's tent where I had left some mule shoes, and finally found that the "street" in which it stood, instead of being the main street as it was when I had been there before, was out in the "suburbs," the town having grown more rapidly in another section. The streets were filled with a greater number of people, who were hurrying frantically among the stumps and roots that still occupied the roadways, carrying provisions out towards the mountains.

The scenes on the Skagway, or White Pass Trail, can never be described so that the reader will get an adequate idea of the suffering and hardships endured by the men and horses while crossing. Hundreds of men gave up in despair and returned to their homes in the United States after having tried the trails for a few days and become utterly discouraged. The ones who finally succeeded in getting their winter supply of provisions to Lake Bennett did so only after weeks of incessant toil and exposure to the weather and a considerable outlay in money. Many died from pneumonia and spinal meningitis, brought on presumably by sleeping on the damp ground; others were drowned in fording the streams and crossing the lakes, and some were so exhausted by continued overwork that they were forced to return to their homes to recuperate their lost health.

Hundreds of horses were killed because in falling over rocks they broke their legs, making it necessary for the travelers to shoot them, and when men began to realize more and more the fact that they were totally unable to transport their goods across the mountains without the aid of these animals, the price of a horse rose to sixty pounds (or three hundred dollars). The horses would arrive in Skagway in excellent condition, but a week's work carrying packs, weighing perhaps two hundred and fifty pounds, over the trails always left unmistakable signs of hardship. Then they had, too, little feed and rest. Hay and grain were both expensive and difficult to pack to the different points along the trail, and many a horse worked under these exceptionally trying conditions, beneath the warm sun and almost continual rainstorms, with little or no food.

As they approached the rockier summits, vegetation grew considerably less, and what grass they could find usually made the animals sick and unfit for work. And when the marsh lands were reached that lie between Lake Bennett and the three little lakes close to White Pass summit, many of them tottered under their heavy loads and sank into the black mire unable to rise. By actual count, there were over two thousand dead horses on this last stretch of ground in September 1898, and it was possible at that time for a man to walk half a mile over the swamp without stepping from the carcasses.

The condition of the trail grew rapidly worse after August 15, and it became almost impossible for a horse to journey to the summit, a point that very few outfits had reached, because, rather than pack directly through it to Lake Bennett, they all chose to carry their goods about three miles at a time, and then return for other loads. This method of crowding all the traffic at one time on the first ten miles of the trail resulted in numerous blockages and consequent loss of time, and the swamps and bogs were so torn up by the trail that horses frequently sank deep in the mire and had to be got out by means of ropes and poles. The work of digging them out of the bogs was so great that on many occasions men drew their revolvers and shot the animals rather than spend half a day extricating them.

The trail was so narrow in many places that horses were unable to pass, and it frequently happened that the horses journeying coastwards would have to stand for an hour at a time while the mountain-bound caravan was passing; and this loss of time, together with the wretched condition of the bogs, made it imperative that the gold seekers should halt in their work and repair the trail before it should become wholly impassable. Meetings were called, committees appointed to handle the gangs of men, and several days were spent "corduroying" bogs by laying logs across the surface, blasting out slippery rocks, and making log bridges. Many of the adventurers objected to working on the trail, and, in order to keep those from packing with their animals while the others repaired the trail, it was closed by the Klondikers and no one was allowed to pass for two days.

But the Skagway Trail was a total failure as far as the summer of 1897 was concerned, and scarcely 10 percent of the men who started from Skagway ever reached Lake Bennett. Whenever the men gave up to return home they would offer to sell their provisions, which, of course, would have a value depending on the distance they had been moved up the trail. It often happened, however, that these disheartened men were unable to sell even a pound of provisions, because their fellow travelers already had more than they could get to the lakes, so the little *cache* of stores was abandoned beside the trail, and during the following winter enterprising merchants in Skagway sledded the goods to town and sold them.

On August 18, the *Willammette* sent her last lighter of goods to Skagway and then steamed across to Dyea to land a hundred of us, who had seen enough of the Skagway route, and had determined to undertake the crossing of the Chilcoot Pass without the formality of first seeing it. We thought that, in any event, it could be little worse than the White Pass route....

By the following summer, Kirk was one of the twenty or twenty-five thousand living in tents and cabins in Dawson and its suburbs—Klondike City, Portland Addition, and West Dawson. Among their number, Kirk said, one could have recruited a crew to sail a ship or to run a railroad. All of them—doctors, lawyers, bank clerks, and undertakers—had spent months sacrificing to reach the goldfields and were wandering about at a loss, wondering why they had come.

Like many others, Kirk shared bear stories. A prospector who returned to his tent at the end of the day and found an intruder eating his bacon and flour might be able to get off a single shot, but the infuriated animal would be upon him before he could fire another. One old-timer took a stick to the mother bear and three cubs he found in his cabin and soon beat a hasty retreat, first to the roof of his cabin, then up a tree. When it was finally safe to come down, he found that everything edible in his cabin had been devoured.

In the winter, Kirk's cabin was difficult to heat since it was built of green logs. He thawed his water bucket each morning before breakfast, and his only light at night came from a bear-grease candle. To ease the monotony of a long winter, Kirk trained the field mice who lived under his bunk to eat out his hand and let them run about the cabin with impunity.

Notes

Epigraph: Robert Kirk, *Twelve Months in Klondike* (London: William Heinemann, 1899), 23–24.

1 Kirk, *Twelve Months in Klondike*, 1.

2 Ibid., frontispiece.

3 Ibid., 8.

4 Ibid., 13.

5 Ibid., 19.

18

MARY E. HITCHCOCK

Ho for the Land of Gold!

Mr. A . . . had quarreled with his partner and made the usual division—cut the tent in half, the boat in twain, and even divided the stove.

When Mary Hitchcock announced that she and Edith Van Buren were going to the Klondike, their friends thought that they were candidates for the insane asylum. How could people like Hitchcock, the widow of a naval commander, and Van Buren, a grandniece of President Martin Van Buren, trade the luxuries and comforts of home for deprivation and hardship in the north? The answer was simple: the two women had no intention of sacrificing anything.

Into their packing crates went gowns, linens, silver, china, easy chairs, a hundred-pound gramophone, musical instruments, a library, an ice cream freezer, cases of paté, truffles, canned asparagus, lobster, oysters, and a seventy-by-forty-foot tent. They would take along their Great Danes, canaries, parrot, and two dozen pigeons. It seemed that the only thing they planned to leave behind was their maid—a girl too young and pretty for the Klondike.

Of the thousands who went to the Klondike that year, Pierre Berton says that Hitchcock and Van Buren may have been the only ones who were "merely . . . sightseers."[1] If they happened to make money, so much the better; if they experienced a loss, they could afford it.

"All in life is a lottery,"[2] Hitchcock wrote, as she recounted her grubstaking of some "trustworthy" miners.

The women took the all-water route to Alaska and, when they reached St. Michael, found the Yukon so low that the boats headed for Dawson had all run aground. While waiting for the river to rise, the two women lunched with the officers of an American man-of-war and Hitchcock took the Great Danes, Ivan and Queen, for a run onshore where they were chased by cows.

Prices in Dawson were rumored to be outrageous, one man having raffled a frozen turkey for three hundred dollars, and a tent site running a thousand dollars a month.

When the first boatload of prospectors came downriver from Dawson, the passengers disembarked with bags so heavy it didn't take an X-ray to reveal the gold inside. Some wore animal skins stuffed with gold draped around their necks like sausages, and Hitchcock overheard a woman say, "They're just carrying their gold that-a-way for effect."[3] Two men were doubled over by the weight of a box suspended from a stick resting on their shoulders. They were followed by a parade of those afflicted with frostbite, scurvy, and snow blindness.

When their riverboat, the *Leah*, was ready to sail, Hitchcock and Van Buren had only an hour to get their baggage and the flustered animals—the pigeons fighting and the parrot scolding—transferred. They were assigned bunks on a newly constructed barge that would be towed behind the riverboat, and that basic accommodation would have to do, for the women had made up their minds to "close [their] eyes to anything which must be endured because it could not be cured."[4]

Joe Ladue, a former storekeeper who was by then famous as the founder of Dawson, was onboard. Hitchcock wanted his advice on how she could make her fortune, and arranged an introduction. Ladue told her that people in Dawson were dying like flies, and he predicted an epidemic. Alarmed at the news, Van Buren sent Queen back home. Hitchcock, on the other hand, believed the danger was exaggerated and refused to part with Ivan. When the *Leah* left St. Michael, the elated passengers paraded on the deck, waved their hats and handkerchiefs, and sang. As the *Leah* steamed upriver, Hitchcock often sat on deck, practicing the zither and mandolin and writing in her diary. One of her neighbors in Dawson would later say that her writing kept her as "busy as a cat with two tails."[5]

The *Leah's* operator, the Alaska Commercial Company, had promised its passengers they'd be the first to the goldfields that season. As the following passage shows, that promise led to a friendly rivalry between the men and women on the various boats travelling the Yukon as it snaked its way across the middle of Alaska.

MARY E. HITCHCOCK

Ho for the Land of Gold![*]

Tuesday, July 12th

Pandemonium let loose! Last night, after a sunset so glorious that it surpassed all others, we retired as usual at eleven. At 2 a.m., we tied up to the bank at Koserefsky. We had been anticipating with great pleasure a visit to the church and the wonderful gardens, but, unfortunately, the hour of arrival was not propitious and we again sought repose in sleep.

Alas! that was impossible, for, having no officer on the barge at night, the Indians were allowed to board her and roam at will, not only on the narrow ledge outside our windows but to congregate in groups before our doors or tramp through the hall, chattering like magpies. Then came the whistle from an approaching steamer, and we were soon aware that the long-expected *Alice,* from Dawson, was being secured to the barge.

In a few moments, many of her two hundred passengers had landed on our decks, and were loudly calling for those whom they hoped to find on board. The same advice was reiterated on all sides—"Turn back. Don't go to Dawson. People are dying there like rats in a trap."

Only one man was affected sufficiently to follow this counsel, and his companions said that he was dreadfully homesick and only too glad of an excuse. It was nearly 4 a.m. when the *Alice* left and broad daylight, but we settled down to sleep, when the howling of the pack of dogs belonging to the purser reached our ears; then came the opening of the pantry, preparations for breakfast, and another day had begun.

Late this evening, the *Leah* sounded a whistle which told us we were to stop, so hasty preparations were made for a walk on shore, but no plank was put out, only a man got off to inquire if the husband of Mrs. ——, one of our passengers, was there. The story quickly went the rounds that, while she was on her way to meet him in Dawson, he, learning of her intention, had "skipped," and was "hurrying out." She traced him to this little settlement, where he had evaded her by three hours.

As we wended our way to our cabins, we found them with great difficulty, the night being unusually dark. Lamps have been hung in the mess hall, but the stewards say that the oil was forgotten, as well as soap and many other articles usually supplied; we are thankful, however, at being safely carried

[*]From *Two Women in the Klondike* (1899), 67–90.

this far on our trip, but there are plenty of "kickers" who complain at getting so little for three hundred dollars.

Thursday, July 14th

We started for a tramp with Ivan, but the native dogs, which dared not face him, set upon him in a pack when his back was turned, causing him to be ignominiously sent on board. A large rowboat from the Koyukuk, containing two men and a woman wearing a sunbonnet, interested us greatly, and still more, when the latter told us that just around the bend, in a boat with a tent, was Mr. N., partner of one of the men whom we have "grub-staked" and whose stories of life on the Koyukuk were so thrilling that we were strongly tempted towards that river rather than to make the trip to Dawson. His nuggets were so large and so valuable, his plans so wonderful, that had it not been for fear of the Indians, who we were told were very savage, we should have joined our man and his family.

After dinner, we were comfortably ensconced in our easy chairs in the bow of the barge, admiring the scenery, which was still wonderfully beautiful, the air balmy and soft as that of springtime at Lenox, when someone wished aloud for an ice. Edith said, "Your wish can easily be granted, if you can get our freezer from down below." Up jumped J. and two other men, and in a few moments, the freezer was on deck, taken to the steward, who supplied the sugar, cream (tinned, of course), and extract, and half an hour later we indulged in the first ice-cream, according to all accounts, that had ever been served on the Yukon.

Many boats have passed us to-day containing from two to eight miners returning home. Everyone shouts the same question, "How far ahead is the other steamer?" (meaning the one belonging to the Columbia Navigation Company, which started two days before us.) Latest information is that we are separated only by four hours. Consequently, we are wild to overtake her and most impatient at any detention.

Just before retiring, J. came to me and said, "I'll give you ten dollars for your freezer."

"It cost fifteen before paying fifteen cents a pound freight," I replied. After some reflection, he offered Edith twenty dollars for her half, but she told him that he could not have it at any price.

Friday, July 15th

Towards evening, the *Margaret* was seen coming toward us and excitement was rife as she tied up alongside. They also warned us to turn back, as had those in the small boats passed during the day; but such advice only creates laughter, as the constant repetition seems ridiculous to those who have more than half finished so long a journey. The *Margaret* was crowded to that degree that men were sleeping on tables, under tables, and even on the cords of wood on deck, and they informed us that, as there are still thousands waiting to "go out," there was little chance for newcomers to secure transportation down the Yukon.

Saturday, July 16th

All day, we had steamed without stopping. At last, in the distance, we beheld great stacks of wood piled high on the shore, so all made preparations for a short tramp, until the captain shouted, "How much for the wood?" "Fifteen dollars a cord," was the reply. "Keep it"—and on we went. Just beyond, another lot was plainly visible, but for that seventeen dollars a cord was asked; at the third place, twenty, which caused the passengers to discuss the likelihood of being called on to fell trees in order that the Alaska Commercial Company should not be obliged to pay such exorbitant prices.

We remained on deck until eleven, hoping to catch a glimpse of Rampart City, but found that we were not to make that settlement until 2 a.m. We might just as well have remained up, for when we did get there, sleep was impossible. One of the passengers had brought out some whiskey and was treating the crowd in the hall before our door. Such a babel of voices! And we were told the following day that, the supply of whiskey in Rampart having given out, her citizens were offering our passengers nine dollars a bottle. We breathed a sigh of relief as the whistle blew, the men rushed for shore, and we slowly steamed away. Then came the howling and yelping of the dogs, which lasted until drowned by the clattering of dishes and preparations for breakfast.

Sunday, July 17th

Poor Ivan [who had been chained up by the steward and called "a d——d nuisance"] was let loose from the terrible heat of the engine-room and the howling of the other dogs, which is so racking to the nerves that we now fear his good habits may be spoiled and his training prove non-effective by association with these "Siwash" mongrels. To think that sixty dollars was the price paid for such quarters and companionship just from St. Michaels to Dawson, and we supply the dog's food! How we longed for Sunday peace and quiet after such a night, but it was not to be.

Scarcely were we again on our way when our ears were pierced by the rasping noise of a badly played violin, which had to be endured until the bell rang for luncheon. Later in the day, the sky grew dark, then leaden colored. A storm was brewing. Nervous women, terrified at the thought of a thunderstorm amidst the mountains, flocked into the dining room like a herd of sheep—only to be together. The scene soon became one of most imposing grandeur, in which I reveled, seated alone in the bow of the boat, well protected by cap and mackintosh, as the rain came down in torrents.

Shortly after, the Doctor came to ask if I would not like to talk with the famous Hank S., saying, "You don't want me to bring him out here in the rain, so let us all sit inside." Following the Doctor, I soon came face to face with the new passenger, one of the noted miners of this part of the world, who, having passed eight years in Alaska, had left Dawson only eight days previously. Consequently, his conversation was of intense interest, but he gave us the same advice we have received from all others: "Better turn back, even at this late date, for typhoid fever and malaria are raging. Even those on the hill are not free from what may soon become an epidemic, and there are not steamers enough to transport those waiting to leave."

Mr. S. showed us the big nugget he had first panned out, a ring made from gold taken from one of his claims, and told of the man who had first grubstaked him, to whom he was able to send twelve thousand dollars in ninety days. But grub-staking is rarely so profitable, for many tales do we hear of these men who, after striking it rich, forget those who have assisted them in time of need, sell their claims, carrying the result where it cannot be reached by the rightful owner, who, according to miners' laws and agreements, is entitled to one-half.

Monday, July 18th

During the entire trip, men have been complaining from time to time that their cargo was being ruined. Notwithstanding this, matters were left without investigation until one of the captain's favorites went down to procure some articles from her trunk. She returned most unhappy over its condition and must have gone at once to him, for scarcely had we finished dinner, when he accompanied her to the hatchway, had it opened, sent some of his men down and had all trunks brought on deck. Up they came, covered with mould, then wet mattresses, and small tents mildewed; the passengers on all sides looked on, groaning. "What a shame!"

"D——d outrage!"

"Our goods packed where they can be ruined and the Company's goods nicely stored in high, dry space on the steamer!"

However, we are lucky to have our boxes up, even though our stores are still in the dampness, and we are told that our beautiful new tent is not fit to be seen.

Tuesday, July 19th

Not a star has been visible in the heavens since we left St. Michaels, and tonight, as we sat in our little corner of the barge, peacefully discussing that and other astronomical subjects, we were startled by an unusual invasion of mosquitoes, which attacked so ferociously that even our shields afforded little protection, and we were driven to our cabins, there to wage war until 5 a.m., when the attack suddenly ceased. We fell into a delicious sleep, which lasted about fifteen minutes, then chairs were dragged from under the tables, and the stewards, who were sweeping the dining-room, engaged in loud conversation. Groans were heard on all sides, and when the bell rang calling passengers to breakfast, they would gladly have had quiet and sleep in preference to all the delicacies of the season.

Wednesday, July 20th

We are all indignant this morning. The *Sovereign* passed us at six o'clock and here we are three hours later, tied up again to the bank, and have been for the last hour and nobody knows the reason why, although questions have been freely asked. We are chafing under the detention.

Thursday, July 21st

We passed [Fort Yukon] without running in, but congratulated ourselves, as we saw the *Sovereign* not far ahead, that plans were being made to overtake her. To our great disgust, however, we were soon tied up to another wood-pile where we remained until midnight, groaning and suffering under attacks of myriads and myriads of ravenous mosquitoes and vicious gnats.

We sought refuge in the dining-hall where many of the passengers were playing whist, cribbage, and muggins.

Friday, July 22nd

Awakened this morning by the *Victoria's* being tied up outside of our cabin window, shutting off light and air, and we were obliged to make it still darker by drawing the curtains, as there were men on her decks, conversing in loud tones. To the usual slamming of chairs and dishes, loud whistling was added, until the noise became deafening. From eleven till two, we were tied up to the banks. At noon, to the anger and disgust of all the passengers, the *John C. Barr*, of the North American Transportation Company, passed us, those on board waving handkerchiefs and hats, hurrahing, hurling shouts of derision, calling that they would wait for us in Dawson, etc.

At 4.30 p.m., we reached Circle City, and were delighted to see the *John Barr* tied to the banks, but alas! She pushed off even as we arrived and her passengers shouted, "We will deliver our own messages in Dawson, thank you, and will not trouble you, who have tarried so long by the way, to give them." The plank was soon out, and here some half-dozen passengers left us to tempt fortune in a strange land.

We had two new and entertaining arrivals who contradicted many of the stories we had heard of Dawson. In fact, all stories in this part of the world seem to be told but to be contradicted. According to the newcomers, Dawson is exceedingly healthy, prices are very low—bacon only twenty cents a pound, whereas we are paying fifteen cents a pound freight, while this, added to the original price and duty to be paid, would prove it wiser to start empty-handed and purchase provisions at the journey's end.

Our pigeons have attracted great attention, and we have received many fine offers for them but prefer "squabs on toast." The man who wants the ice-cream freezer has gradually increased his bid, which now stands at eighty dollars, as he has heard he can get ten dollars a glass for ice-cream!

As Joe Ladue had predicted, diseases were indeed spreading among the populace at Dawson. In an effort to escape contagion, Hitchcock and Van Buren crossed the Klondike River to a Dawson suburb and erected their tent there. They set up the four-hundred-pound, twenty-eight-hundred-square-foot tent on a hill where it could be seen from afar. The "Big Tent," as it was known, threatened to fly away in high winds and to collapse under heavy rains. It was so difficult to heat that the women slept in a smaller tent inside. Butter was stored two feet down in the permafrost, so there was no need for refrigeration. Their fine clothes had been ruined by mold in the *Leah's* wet hold, but Hitchcock realized that skirts were impracticable for wood gathering and that silken hose were useless in mukluks.

Each woman acquired a number of claims in her own right—Hitchcock herself may have had more than a hundred.[6] She didn't focus at length on gold hunting but did provide a lot of detail about the meals she and Edith fed their guests. With a disappointed Cockney prospector acting as their servant and cook, they served the US consul general anchovies on toast, roasted moose, scalloped tomatoes, and asparagus salad, and they treated their neighbors, the "boys" in nearby tents, to tinned lobsters, oysters, and homemade ice cream.

Summer drew to a close, and Van Buren predicted that she would suffer a "direful death"[7] if forced to winter in Dawson. The women sold their library at a loss and their remaining canned goods at a profit. In the last week of September, with snow falling and the Yukon threatening to freeze over, the women made their escape on a cramped, dirty riverboat headed for Lake Bennett.

Before her climb over White Pass, Hitchcock donned two suits of wool flannels, a jersey, and a cloth jacket, and she engaged a newspaper boy to carry her sealskin wrap. Of the experience, she said this: "Another word of warning! Never overburden yourself with heavy clothing for an eight-mile tramp."[8]

At home in New York, Hitchcock lectured at the Waldorf Astoria about her northern venture and received so much correspondence that she had to employ two secretaries. In an interview with the *New York Times*, she encouraged women to take the trip. A female "could go quite alone and ... would receive the most courteous treatment and the best advice that could be given about taking claims."[9]

Notes

Epigraph: Mary E. Hitchcock, *Two Women in the Klondike: The Story of a Journey to the Gold-Fields of Alaska* (New York: G. P. Putnam's Sons, 1899), 127.

1 Berton, *Klondike Fever,* 316.

2 Hitchcock, *Two Women in the Klondike,* 45.

3 Ibid.

4 Ibid., 50.

5 Ibid., 312.

6 Terrence Cole, introduction to Hitchcock, *Two Women in the Klondike* (1899; repr., Fairbanks: University of Alaska Press, 2005), xviii–xxi.

7 Hitchcock, *Two Women in the Klondike* (1899), 387.

8 Ibid., 442.

9 "Klondike Reminiscences," *New York Times,* February 5, 1899.

19

J. D. WINCHESTER

The Mosquitoes' Bugle on the Koyukuk

What won't men do for gold? Here they were exposed to weather sixty and seventy degrees below zero, living in tents, and relaying their packs. I knew of a party who got lost and had to eat their dogs and the rawhide lacings on their moccasins.

In Captain J. D. Winchester's house, it was his wife who first caught gold fever. She read about a woman who collected sixty dollars of gold in her dishpan from her husband's first washing in the Klondike. Then, Winchester caught the fever too, as he later wrote in *Captain J. D. Winchester's Experience on a Voyage from Lynn, Massachusetts, to San Francisco, Cal., and to the Alaskan Gold Fields*. When he learned that a group in his hometown were planning a trip to Alaska, he decided to investigate.

The organizer of the Lynn Mining Company was W. H. Hooper, a man who sounded like a socialist, with lots of talk about those "held down by the heel of the oppressor" and the "redemption" that lay in Alaska. In Alaska, Hooper claimed, "a poor man could drive his stakes with no millionaire bosses to say that he should not."[1] Winchester and twenty others decided to sign up.

They each put up $250, $50 of it payable up front, and purchased the *Abbie M. Deering*, a sailing ship badly in need of repairs. While being treated for bedbugs with an explosive chemical, the boat caught fire, and the resulting damage led to further delay and more expense. Nonetheless, once the repairs were made, it was an eager group that set sail from Lynn on November 10, 1897. Winchester, a merchant marine and the only seafaring man of the party, was at the helm. None of the men knew how to operate the sails, so Winchester had his work cut out teaching them. For some reason, the navigator,

Mr. Rounds, kept the charts locked in his cabin and refused to let Winchester see them, so he never knew where he was sailing.

The ship was soon renamed the *Diver*, "for the vigorous way in which she dove into a sea, giving many of us a good wetting, in spite of every precaution."[2] Hooper insisted on first sailing north to visit his family and friends in Nova Scotia, and only then did the ship turn south, traveling down the coasts of North and South America, around and through the Strait of Magellan, and up the eastern coasts of the continents toward California.

As things developed, Hooper turned out to be not a socialist but a crook. He refused to account for the money the men had entrusted to him and cheated them on the purchases he had made. He bought too little material for sleeping bags, and when the men sewed them, some bags were too short to reach their owner's shoulders. The drinking water barrels were contaminated with oil, and the water was thus unusable. Hooper had purchased so little food that, near the end of the voyage, the cook could offer the men only fritters made with salt water dressed with sour molasses. As the men were eating hard biscuits into which kerosene had leaked, they learned Hooper and Rounds were snacking on dried fruit hidden in their cabins.

When the *Diver* sailed through the Golden Gate, that narrow neck of water separating San Francisco from Marin County, it had been five months since she left Massachusetts. It was clear the company would have to be dissolved, and, with the help of lawyers, the *Diver* and its equipment were sold and the proceeds divided. As for Hooper, he was never seen again.

Many of the prospectors crowding the streets of San Francisco were headed for Kotzebue Sound, the location of the most recent finds. Anything that could float, from a dory to a whaling ship, was being fitted for the journey. Many craft were unseaworthy—one boat loaded with forty passengers sank before it left San Francisco Bay. Winchester located a ship that looked sound, and he and three other men from the *Diver* booked passage for Seattle, paying an extra dollar and a half for a private room.

In Seattle, the streets were clogged with hurdy-gurdies, vendors, and patent medicine men. Pickpockets roamed at will, and armed bandits forced people to surrender their cash. Winchester watched one man walk into a store, stick a gun in the proprietor's face, and say, "If you cheat, I will make trouble for you."[3] He read in the *Post-Intelligencer* that a man could earn ten to fifteen dollars a day and get all the gold he wanted in Alaska, and his "fever" went up another twenty-five degrees.

A fellow named Chase offered a combination fare that included passage to Alaska by steamer and then up the Yukon by riverboat. He was charging only a little more than others were asking for the first leg of the trip alone, so the party of four booked passage with him. When Chase could not get his boat ready in time to sail, he agreed to transfer the men's paid-up fares to the *Haydn Brown.* Thus, when that ship left the dock in Seattle on the 25th of May, onboard were Winchester, his three companions, and three hundred others—"tinkers and tailors, barbers and sailors, farmers and cowboys and rangers, all ready now to move on."[4]

As the *Haydn Brown* sailed toward the Aleutian Islands and into the Bering Sea, her passengers dined on half-cooked beans with raw pork and a sticky paste of oatmeal and water called "muss." When the ship reached St. Michael in June, Winchester had been underway for eight months—and he wasn't to the goldfields yet. Only then was it discovered that Chase hadn't transferred the men's paid-up fares to the *Haydn Brown* as he had promised he would do but, instead, had skipped with the money. The *Haydn Brown's* captain ordered the four *Diver* men off his ship. One went off on his own, while Winchester and the other two, Ryan and Lepage, were put ashore with a little money, their freight, and Ryan's violin.

Then Winchester realized that the reports of work and good wages were untrue. Many disappointed prospectors were stranded at St. Michael, living in tents and depending on the charity of others who themselves had nothing to spare. By agreeing to work their way up the Yukon and to pay $300.00 each if they found gold, Winchester, Ryan, and Lepage secured passage on the riverboat *Rock Island.* Once the boat was underway, they were awoken at night to load wood from the shore, since the riverboat ran on steam and required a steady supply, and by day were forced to tote hundred-and-fifty-pound sacks of coal. Besides that, some mysterious illness had so debilitated Winchester that he was confined to his bunk.

At the Koyukuk, the three men heard of a big strike upriver. Anxious to end their engagement on the *Rock Island* and to settle in before winter, they decided to get off rather than continue up the Yukon. To ascend the Koyukuk, they needed a boat, and the only ones available for sale were out of their reach, but they spotted an old Indian fishing boat and gave a man on the bank $10.00 for it.

In the passage that follows, Winchester describes the next leg of his trip on that boat, the little *Mary Ann.* Though he only alludes to it, Winchester's mysterious illness persists and is, in fact, growing worse.

J. D. WINCHESTER

The Mosquitoes' Bugle on the Koyukuk[*]

Sunday morning came and we were all ready. I did not care about starting out on Sunday, but the mosquitoes were biting just the same as they did any other day and I asked the boys what they thought. They were all ready to go, so we loaded up our boat and with Lepage ahead with the tow rope—for the current was swift and banks steep—we warped her along toward the mouth of the Koyukuk. Some men hailed us, claiming we would never get up the river with that load on our boat but we did not answer, for we felt sure we could and were not discouraged.

After we got around the bend, we could row. Ahead of us was a high, rocky bluff that gave us a little trouble to get around. After that we could row, and we got to the mouth of the river sometime in the night, where we were told that our boat was too deep and that we never could get up the river with that load. We heeded not their warning but, pushing along, we were told to keep to the right bank and we would go along all right. We did so as soon as practicable but the trouble was we got no sleep.

After we had been three nights without sleep, we landed on the bank where there was a breeze blowing and had a sort of restless sleep. We had been so long without it that we were troubled with nervousness, and I could not close my eyes so long as I heard the mosquitoes' bugle. We did not stop long but were up and away again and soon began to feel the need of sleep. We tied our boat to an old stump that was off in mid-stream while we were getting our dinner—if you could call it such. We had not taken time to cook and our meals consisted of hard bread and condensed milk—a very weak diet for the work we had before us.

I had made a mosquito net and had it over my hat; when I went to light my pipe it caught fire and, by the time I got it away from my face, it was completely destroyed. The Alaska Union launch passed by and hailed us, asking where we wanted to go. We answered "up the Koyukuk," and they replied we were on the wrong river—we would have to go back.

This worried us a little, for we had no charts and it was hard to feel just confident unless we saw some landmark. Yet I did not intend to turn back, and why that man should lie I could not tell.

[*]From *Captain J. D. Winchester's Experience* (1900), 166–72.

There was another little steam launch on the river and we found out that it belonged to the Kelly party from New York. She was trying to take two heavy boats up the river, loaded with stores, by relaying. We had made a sail, and with a fair wind we were stemming the current all right.

We saw a large boat lying on the side of the bank so we landed, and found three men of the Kelly party cutting wood. They were one of the relays and were waiting their turn to be towed further up. They told us we were on the Koyukuk and that this Alaska Union Company was a set of vagabonds. They did not wonder at their trying to send us down the river again. It was one of their tricks.

I saw that two of this party were disgusted with Alaska and were willing to go back. We bade them good-bye and sailed away with more confidence in ourselves, for we knew that men would lie to make mischief and we would be on our guard hereafter.

We made a landing on the point of an island where there was a good breeze blowing, thinking to cheat the mosquitoes and get some rest. But after we landed and cooked something to eat, the wind died out and they swarmed down on us.

Ryan and I walked the beach until I thought I should drop. We then woke Lepage up, got in our boat, and rowed up stream again. If we had known enough to have made a smoke, we might have got rid of some of the mosquitoes, but it never entered our minds, and we had to stand and take it. I saw that there was a coolness between Ryan and Lepage and their sulky, glum visages made it very unpleasant for me, as it was a case that needed harmony.

We had seven hundred miles of river to get over and what there was ahead of us to overcome we did not know. We were told that when we got to Treat's Island we were half way up, but we had no way to determine how many miles we made in a day and the river was nothing but crooks and turns. We did not set our tent nights but slept out on the banks in our sleeping-bags, not knowing but that some wild animal would come along and eat our heads off. We cared little, so long as we could sleep.

Some nights we would wake up and find it had been raining and we were soaked. Our pillows sounded like a bee's nest when the bees are fighting mad and trying to get out. These mosquitoes were a torment to us. Our hands were swollen to twice their natural size and our faces were a pitiful sight. Although we wore netting over us, they could get through and punish us for trying to keep them out. The river was low and we had quite an easy time of it, for the current was not swift and there were sand-bars all bare that broke the force of the stream, making dead water for us. All this helped and we figured we were making about fifteen miles per day, but I think now that ten miles was about all that we could do.

The shores all along were muddy and when we landed we would sink nearly to our knees. The first fierce struggle we had was with a sand bar. There was a shoal channel between it and the shore but not deep enough for us to get through. On the other side of the bar was our only hope and we had a struggle to get there, for the bar was uneven, full of gully holes and then shoaled up again. We dared not get overboard for fear of getting into one of these holes and the current was racing over this point. We conquered at last and sent Ryan on the bar with the rope while we towed her along, but she took a sheer that Ryan could not manage and, after being dragged off into the water, he let go the rope and Lepage and I went down the river like a race horse, leaving Ryan standing on the bar. We got to our oars and reached the bank after a hard row, where Ryan joined us.

After getting off the bar, we thought we would try the other side of the river, but found we could do nothing there. Our only hope was this sand bar, so we came back to the place we had left and after a hard time of it we got by. We found that the river was rising by the junks of froth that came floating down. The wind was against us about all of the time and we could not use our sail. After this we had to use new tactics, for the river had changed. The crooks were more elbow style and we would cross the river to where the current was easy and there was good sand bottom; for as the current came rushing around a point it would cross over to the other bank, where it would gully out and the trees would slide in, making a mass of fallen trees that was impossible to pass, while on the other side there was easy water, with a good chance to tow our boat along until we came to the point that we would have to rope around until we could get a chance to cross over.

There were some difficulties also on the opposite side of the river. Some trees and limbs stood upright as they had grown, while some leaned over our boat as if threatening to fall and swamp us. At other places, the bank hollowed out ready to dump another lot of trees. This is the way we got around that point. Lepage was the most sure-footed and he took the rope, passing it outside of all the trees. When he got all the rope, we would shove off and pull until we got to the end and then pass it again. This was dangerous work for Lepage, for he had to go out on trees that were lying in the river and by the crooks of the bank. We little knew when the bank would give way, but in this manner we managed to work the river.

One day we tried a slough* for a rest and risked the chance of getting out at the other end. We made a good cut-off, but found a bar across the other end and the water pouring in. We worked some time to get through but found it impossible, so we had to turn back. We had then been on the river three weeks and the boys were doing pretty well for men who never had worked a boat before and had taken their first lesson on the Koyukuk. But one trouble was that, after they had learned so much, they thought they knew it all and sometimes conflicted with my orders which made bad work for me. Still this is natural to all beginners and I had to overlook it.

Lepage was very quick to learn, and used good judgment on working the river. He was very active in his movements and that is a good feature in boating; but he was growing ambitious and had to be called down. He was sulky, which he claimed was Ryan's fault, and so the harmony that ought to have existed was wiped out, and jealousy and gloom ruled in its place. Lepage had a jealous nature that showed itself every little while, when he could not keep himself from his dark thoughts—but it was Ryan's fault. He said he could get along with me alright if it was not for Ryan.

The mosquitoes were thinning out, the gnats taking their places, and these little pests were ten times worse than the mosquitoes, though they would let you rest nights. They would stop their work at seven, but about five in the morning would start in again at full blast. The mosquito net was of no use, for they would sift through it, and after they got in would fight to get out. They swarmed about us all day, filling our ears, eyes, mouth and nostrils. They would bury themselves in our hair and burrow into the flesh, bringing the blood.

We had not met a human being for three weeks, and we felt there was nobody on the river but us. One night after we had pitched our tent, I was cooking supper, and Ryan and Lepage were securing the boat for the night, when suddenly I heard the command of "Hands up!" and looking up, I saw three men standing with revolvers pointed at us. Before I could say anything, they burst into a laugh and came forward. I had not seen them before, but I shall never forget the feeling of welcome as I grasped their hands for a friendly

*Winchester explains, "The slough is a side channel made by the overflow of water. When there is an ice jam the water opens a new way for miles, running parallel with the river before finding its way out to the stream again. In time the water washes out this new channel, which always affords a very convenient shelter for men in a boat or canoe, when the wind is high on the river, and it is always easy to find one of these sloughs for they are plenty along the banks of the river" (161–62).

shake. They had mistaken us for another party but were glad to meet us.

They belonged to the launch *Serene*, formerly of the Kelly party, that broke up down the river, and four of them took what provisions they wanted and came along. The rest went back to Nulato with the remainder of the stores to sell them out. We were out of tobacco and begged a smoke of them, and they went to the boat and brought us a pound, for which we were very grateful.

They were going up to Arctic City and we spent a pleasant evening talking together and, when they left us, we were alone once more to fight our way along. Lepage grew sulky and would not talk, because they addressed their conversation mostly to Ryan. He did not like the *Serenes* and hated Ryan the more. I was delighted with my new acquaintances and felt revived after their visit, for I was about half sick before.

We shouldered the tow line once more and started up the river, looking for Treat's Island, and though we did not know what the island was like, supposed that we would find the mouth of the passage easily. We followed the trail of some boats ahead, seeing their tent stakes where they had tented nights. Sometimes a piece of sawed wood from some steamer was a sign that we were on the right river; then there would be a place where wood had been cut. This is the way I navigated without chart or compass and was confident I was right.

When they finally reached Beaver City, the three men decided to stop. Winchester was so sick he could no longer walk, so the task of cabin building fell to Ryan and Lepage. The resulting windowless hovel was dark and impossible to heat, and Winchester was immobilized in a cold bunk while Ryan and Lepage turned to prospecting—gathering wood, building fires to thaw a few inches of ground, digging the thawed earth, and setting it aside for sluicing in the spring. The steps would have to be repeated until bedrock—and theoretically gold—was reached. A thousand prospectors were in the Koyukuk region that winter, and, like many of them, Winchester, Lepage, and Ryan—despite possessing six claims—found no gold.

A doctor examined Winchester, decided that rheumatism was what ailed him, and prescribed citric acid. But the captain thought acid was bad for rheumatism and refused to take it. He continued to decline and became so weak that he could only crawl. He had a fever and couldn't eat because his mouth was swollen and his teeth were loose. When he was near death, another doctor diagnosed scurvy and prescribed raw potatoes. The nearest fresh vegetables were a hundred miles away, but Winchester sold candles to raise money and sent away for some. His three pounds of onions and seventeen pounds of potatoes arrived frozen, but they were tasty nonetheless and saved his life.

Winchester had only partially recovered when he and Ryan decided to leave Beaver City and head for home. The sled Winchester was riding on kept turning over, and Ryan abandoned him, leaving the captain to make his way back to the cabin. Some of his Beaver City neighbors had warned Winchester that Lepage had designs on his life, but when the ice went out, it was Lepage who sailed the little *Mary Ann*, with Winchester in it, down the Koyukuk and the Yukon rivers to St. Michael.

From there, the US government shipped Winchester and other broken-down miners back south. Some of them had lost limbs, others their companions. Nevertheless, many were making plans to return to the goldfields as soon as they recovered.

When he reached his home in Lynn, the captain had been gone a year and ten months. He'd found no gold, but his wife must have been relieved that he was alive. When he wrote about his experiences in the north, he included thirty-seven sketches he'd made along the way. One was of him, Ryan, and Lepage navigating the little *Mary Ann* past the sweepers on the Koyukuk.

Notes

Epigraph: J. D. Winchester, *Captain J. D. Winchester's Experience on a Voyage from Lynn, Massachusetts, to San Francisco, Cal., and to the Alaskan Gold Fields* (Salem, MA: Newcomb & Gauss, 1900), 207.

1 Winchester, *Captain J. D. Winchester's Experience*, 10.

2 Ibid., preface.

3 Ibid., 135.

4 Ibid., 137.

20

JOSIAH EDWARD SPURR

A Bureaucrat Comes to Call

> The history of the prospectors in any new country, especially in Alaska, would be record of intensely interesting pioneering. . . . They penetrate the deserts, they climb the mountains, they ascend the streams, they dare with the crudest preparation the severest danger of nature. Some of them die, others return to civilization and become sailor or car-conductors or janitors, but they are the stuff that keeps the nation alive.

Josiah Spurr headed an 1896 US Geological Survey team sent to investigate the "diggings" in Alaska—the placer mines at Fortymile, Birch Creek, and other places. Gold had not yet been found in the Klondike, so most miners heading north were going to Alaska. Apart from some prospectors, few of Spurr's fellow passengers on the Inside Passage knew much about Alaska or were aware that gold had been found there. One lady onboard asked Spurr what he would do for food. "Will you depend on the farmhouses along the way?"[1] she asked. Another passenger told Spurr he'd have to spear whales for dinner.

At the front of *Through the Yukon Gold Diggings*, a full-length photograph of Spurr and his two companions, who are identified only by their last names—Schrader and Goodrich—carries the caption, "We of the Flannel Shirt and Unblacked Boot." The three men stand with geological tools in hand, sport full beards, and wear their field clothes—black shirts, black pants held up by suspenders, and high-topped black leather boots. Draped over their heads are white cloths that hang down across their shoulders, and clapped over those cloths are black felt hats. As Spurr said, frontier dress was "varied, picturesque, and unconventional."[2]

In Juneau, Spurr purchased food supplies: three pounds per man per day—beans, bacon, dried fruit, flour, sugar, cheese, an essential pot of strawberry jam, and tea, which was preferable to coffee because it weighed less and lasted longer. He also bought kettles, frying pans, a tent, blankets, and netting and gauntlet gloves to ward off mosquitoes. For boat building on the other side of Chilkoot Pass, he obtained lumber, a whipsaw, chisels, hammers, nails, screws, oakum, and pitch.

When the party reached Dyea, Spurr's Indian packers refused to carry the boat-building lumber unless it was sawed in half. That would have made the boards useless, so Spurr left them behind. At Lake Lindeman, he found an eighteen-foot dory for sale and the men floated away sooner than they would have had they been delayed by boat building. The purchased dory turned out to be so sound and reliable that the party named it *Skookum,* a Chinook Indian word meaning "strength and courage."

The first diggings Spurr visited were along the Fortymile, a river that crossed the Alaska-Canada border. The mining camp, known as Forty Mile, was on the Canadian side, while the "diggings" were on American soil. When Spurr arrived, the region was in decline, most prospectors having departed for more recent finds along Birch Creek.

While at the camp, Spurr attended a "squaw" dance. Native women entered the saloon and parked their babies against the wall. As an old fiddler sawed away, the miners and the Indian women shuffled wordlessly about the room. At evening's end, the women packed up their babies and headed home. Prices at Forty Mile were high, with a hundred-by-hundred-and-fifty-foot lot in town costing between $7,000 and $8,000. Available supplies were also expensive, since everything was shipped in from Seattle and San Francisco, which were four and five thousand miles away, respectively.

The mining operations were spread out and typically far removed from the camps. Spurr covered as much as twenty miles a day, and his feet grew chafed from his leather boots, so he bought a pair of Indian moccasins and found that he could trot along the trail fifteen miles before noon. From the Fortymile, Spurr headed for Circle City, where he was to meet Leroy Napoleon "Jack" McQuesten, an early trader on the Yukon who gave unlimited credit on the expectation that he would be repaid when a prospector "struck it."[3]

In the excerpt that follows, Spurr is on his way to visit Hog'em Gulch, a place named for the prospector who tried to "hog" claims by staking them for his wife, his wife's brother, a niece of his wife's friend, and so on—even for people whose names he made up.

JOSIAH EDWARD SPURR

A Bureaucrat Comes to Call[*]

From Forty Mile, we floated down the Yukon again, and in a day's journey, camped at the mouth of Mission Creek, not then down on the map. It had received its name from miners who had come there prospecting. Several of them were encamped in tents, and they came over and silently watched our cooking, evidently sizing us up.

"When did you leave the Outside?" asked a blue-eyed, blonde, shaggy man.

The Outside means anywhere but Alaska—a man who has been long in the country falls into the idea of considering himself in a kind of a prison and refers to the rest of the world as lying beyond the door of this.

"In June," we replied.

"How did the Harvard-Yale football game come out last fall?" he inquired eagerly—it was now August and nearly time for the next!

"Harvard was whipped, of course," we answered.

"Look here," he said, firing up, "you needn't say 'of course.' Harvard is my college!"

I was engaged in reinforcing my overalls with a piece of bacon sack. I could not help being amused at this fair-haired savage being a college man.

"That makes no difference," I replied. "Harvard's our college, too—all of us."

"What are you giving me?" he ejaculated, and at first I thought he looked a little angry, as if he thought we were trifling with him; and then a little supercilious, as he surveyed the forlorn condition of my clothing, which the removal of the overalls I wore had exposed.

"Hard facts," I said. "Classes of '92 and '93. Lend me your sheath-knife."

"Why-ee!" he exclaimed. "Ninety-three's my class. Shake! Rah, rah, rah! Who are we? You know! Who are we? We are Harvard ninety-three—what can we do?—WHAT CAN WE DO?—We can lick Harvard ninety-two—cocka-doodle-doodle-doo—Harvard, Harvard—ninety-two—hooray!"

The next day we tramped over to American Creek together where some new gold diggings were just being developed. The Harvard miner had had no tea for several months, as he told us (and one who has been living in Alaska knows what a serious thing that is), so we brought a pound package along to make a drink for lunch. At American Creek, we got a large tomato can outside of a miner's cabin, and the Harvard man offered to do the brewing.

[*]From *Through the Yukon Gold Diggings* (1900), 156–74.

"How much shall I put in?" he asked.

"Suit yourself," was the answer.

He took a tremendous handful. "Is this too much?" he asked, apologetically. "You see, I haven't had tea for three months, and I feel like having a good strong cup." We assured him that the strength of the drink was to be limited only by his own desires. He was tempted to another handful, and so little by little, till half the package was in the can. When he was satisfied, we told him to keep the remaining half pound for the next time. He was disappointed.

"If I had known you intended giving it to me," he replied, "I wouldn't have used so much."

There were some paying claims already on this creek—it was a little stream which one could leap at almost any point—and on the day we arrived we saw the clean-up in one of them. It was very dazzling to see the coarse gold that was scraped from the riffles of the sluice-boxes into the baking-powder cans which were used to store it. There was gold of all sizes, from fine dust up to pieces as big as pumpkin seed, but this was the result of a week's work of several men, and much time had been spent in getting the claim ready before work could begin. Still, the results were very good, the clean-up amounting, I was told, to "thirty dollars to the shovel"—that is, thirty dollars a day to each man shoveling gravel into the sluices.

On the edge of the stream, the rock, a rusty slate, lay loosely. One of the miners was thrusting his pick among the pieces curiously and, on turning one over, showed the crevice beneath filled with flat pieces of yellow gold of all sizes. They were very thin and probably worth only about five dollars in all but, lying as they did, the sight was enough to give one the gold fever, if he did not yet have it. The Harvard man and his companion were immediately seized with a violent attack and set off down the stream to stake out claims, meanwhile talking over plans of wintering here, so as to be early on the ground the next spring.

The next night we reached that part of the river where Circle City was put down on the map we carried, but, not finding it, camped on a gravelly beach beneath a timbered bluff. When we went up the bluff to get wood for our fire, the mosquitoes fairly drove us back and continued bothering us all night, biting through our blankets and giving us very little peace, though we slept with our hats, veils, and gloves on. We afterwards found that Circle City had at first been actually started at about this point but was soon afterwards moved further down to where we found it the next day.

We had been looking forward to our arrival in this place for several reasons, one of which was that we had had no fresh meat for over a month and hoped to find moose or caribou for sale. As our boat came around the bend and approached the settlement of log huts dignified by the name of Circle City, we noticed quite a large number of people crowding down to the shore to meet us and, as soon as we got within hailing distance, one of the foremost yelled out:

"Got any moose meat?"

When we answered "No," the crowd immediately dispersed and we did not need to inquire about the supply of fresh meat in camp.

We landed in front of the Alaska Commercial Company's store, kept by Jack McQuesten. On jumping ashore, I went up immediately in search of information and, as I stepped in, I heard my name called in a loud voice. I answered promptly "Here" with no idea of what was wanted, for there was a large crowd in the store, but, from the centre of the room, something was passed from hand to hand towards me, which proved to be a package of letters from home—the first news I had received for over two months. On inquiry, I found that the mail up the river had just arrived and the storekeeper, who was also postmaster *ex officio,* had begun calling out the addresses on the letters to the expectant crowd of miners and had got to my name as I entered the door—a coincidence, I suppose, but surely a pleasant and striking one.

We obtained lodgings in a log house, large for Circle City, since it contained two rooms. It was already occupied by two customhouse officers, the only representatives of Uncle Sam whom we encountered in the whole region. One room had been used as a storeroom and carpenter-shop, and here, on the shavings, we spread out our blankets and made ourselves at home.

The building had first been built as a church by missionaries, but as they were absent for some time after its completion, one room was fitted up with a bar by a newly arrived enterprising liquor-dealer, till the officers, armed in their turn with the full sanction of the church, turned the building into a customhouse and hoisted the American flag on a pole fashioned out of a slim spruce by the customs officer himself. The officers, when we came there, were sleeping days and working nights on the trail of some whisky smugglers who were in the habit of bringing liquor down the river from Canadian territory in defiance of the American laws.

There were only a few hundred men in Circle City at this time, most of the miners being away at the diggings, for this was one of the busiest times of the year. These diggings were sixty miles from the camp and were only to be reached by a foot trail which led through wood and swamp. Several newcomers in the country were camped around the post, waiting for cooler weather before starting out on the trail, for the mosquitoes, they said, were frightful. It was said that nobody had been on the trail for two weeks on this account and blood-curdling stories were told of the torments of some that had dared to try, and how strong men had sat down on the trail to sob, quite unable to withstand the pest. However, we had seen mosquitoes before, and the next morning struck out for the trail.

It was called a wagon road, the brush and trees having been cut out sufficiently wide for a wagon to pass. Taken as a footpath, however, it was just fair. The mosquitoes were actually in clouds; they were of enormous size, and had vigorous appetites. It was hot, too, so that their bites smarted worse than usual. The twelve miles, which the trail as far as the crossing of Birch Creek had been said to be, lengthened out into an actual fifteen, over low, rolling country, till we descended a sharp bluff to the stream. Here a hail brought a boatman across to ferry us to the other side, where there stood two low log houses facing one another and connected overhead by their projecting log roofs.

This was the Twelve Mile Cache, a road-house for miners, and here we spent the night. Each of the buildings contained but a single room, one house being used as a sleeping apartment, the other as kitchen and dining-room. The host had no chairs to offer us, but only long benches, and there were boxes and stumps for those who could not find room on the benches, which were shorter than the tables.

We ate out of tin dishes and had only the regulation bacon, beans and applesauce, yet it was with a curious feeling that we sat down to the meal and got up from it, as if we were enjoying a little bit of luxury—for so it seemed to us then. There were eleven of us who slept in the building which had been set apart for sleeping; we all provided our own blankets and slept on the floor, which was no other than the earth, and was so full of humps and hollows and projecting sharp sticks where saplings had been cut off, that one or the other of the company was in misery nearly all night, and roused the others with his cursing and growling. The eight who were not of our party were miners returning from the diggings with their season's earnings of gold in the packs strapped to the backs. They all carried big revolvers and were on the lookout for possible highwaymen.

In the fine, bright morning light, we noticed a sign nailed up on the dining cabin, which we had not seen in the dusk of the preceding evening. It was a notice to thieves, and a specimen of miners' law in this rough country.

NOTICE
TO WHOM IT MAY CONCERN
At a general meeting of miners held in Circle City
it was the unanimous Verdict that all thieving and
stealing shall be punished by
WHIPPING AT THE POST AND
BANISHMENT FROM THE COUNTRY,
the severity of the whipping and the guilt of
the accused to be determined by the Jury.
SO ALL THIEVES BEWARE.

From Twelve Mile Cache to the diggings, we travelled over what was called the Hog'em trail, since it led to the gulch of that name. It ran for the whole distance through a swamp and was said to be a very good trail in winter—in summer it was vile. We had been informed of a way which branched off from the Hog'em route and ran over drier ground to a road-house called the "Central House," but we were unable to pick up this; and we discovered afterwards that it had been blazed from the Central House, but that the blazing had been discontinued two or three miles before reaching the junction of the Hog'em trail, the axe-man having got tired or having gone home for his dinner and forgotten to come back. So people like ourselves, starting for the diggings, invariably followed the Hog'em trail, whether they would or not, and those coming out of the diggings and returning by way of the Central House followed the blazes through the woods till they stopped, and then wandered ahead blindly, often getting lost.

The next day's journey was again twelve miles, over about the same kind of trail. Crossing a sluggish stream which was being converted into a swamp by encroaching vegetation, we were obliged to wade nearly waist deep, and then our feet rested on such oozy and sinking mud that we did not know but the next moment we might disappear from sight entirely. Further on, the trail ran fair into a small lake whose shores we had to skirt. There was no trail around, but much burnt and felled timber lay everywhere, and climbing over this, balancing our packs in the meantime, was "such fun." Sometimes we would jump down from a high log, and, slipping a little, our packs would turn us around in the air and we would fall on our backs, sprawling like turtles, and often unable to get out of our awkward position without help from our comrades.

At the end of the second day we arrived at Hog'em Junction, where the Hog'em trail unites with that leading off to the other gulches where gold is found. Here was the largest road-house we had seen. There were fifteen or twenty men hanging about, mostly miners returning or going to the diggings, and a professional hunter—a sort of wild man, who told thrilling stories of fighting bears.

We ate breakfast and supper at Hog'em Junction, paying a dollar apiece for the meals, and, when we learned that the bacon which was served to us had cost sixty-five cents a pound, the charge did not seem too much. No good bacon was to be had, that which we ate being decidedly strong, and even this kind had to be hunted after at this time of the year.

The Hog'em Junction innkeeper paid twenty dollars for a case of evaporated fruit, such as cost a dollar in San Francisco. Condensed milk was one dollar a can and sugar eighty-five cents a pound. The previous winter, beans brought one dollar a pound and butter two and a half dollars a roll. In summer, all prices were those of Circle City, plus forty cents freighting, plus ten cents handling. So a sack of potatoes, which I was told would cost twenty-five cents in the state of Washington, cost here eighty-five dollars. Even in Circle City the prices, though comparatively low, were not exactly what people would expect at a bargain counter in one of our cities. Winchester rifles were sold for fifty dollars apiece and calico brought fifty cents a yard. Luckily, there were few women folks in the country at that time!

Alaskan prospectors customarily offered any passing stranger a meal and place to sleep, even if the only bed they had to share was a single, but the hospitality at Hog'em Gulch, if it could be called that, was surly and grudging. By contrast, five prospectors at Forty Mile issued Spurr invitations for dinner—and some of the prospective hosts were "loath to be put off with the plea of previous engagement."[4] Any prospector who found himself out on the trail and in need was welcomed to take supplies from a miner's cabin, the only requirement being that he leave a note acknowledging the items he had taken. No questions were asked, and repayment was never expected.

Most of the miners Spurr met in Alaska were politically astute and well-read—works of science and philosophy being their special favorites. "A gulch that had a full set of Shakespeare considered itself in for rather a cozy winter; and there were regular Shakespeare clubs, where each miner took a certain character to read," Spurr wrote.[5]

At the end of their summer tour, Spurr, Goodrich, and Schrader returned to San Francisco, where their long beards, shaggy hair, and worn-out mining clothes inspired catcalls on the streets. After having been in Alaska, the three geologists found the conventional dress of the city folks disagreeable. "The white collars and cuffs of the men, in particular, irritated me,"[6] Spurr said.

Two years after that initial trip to Alaska, Spurr returned as head of a second US Geological Survey. On that expedition, which Spurr also wrote a book about, he covered over 1,300 miles and, among other things, traced the Susitna River to the Yentna and the Yentna to the Skwetna. While this second survey was significant, it was Spurr's work on the expedition of 1896, said one official, that helped "establish the presence of a gold belt 300 miles in length in Alaska."[7]

Notes

Epigraph: Josiah Edward Spurr, *Through the Yukon Gold Diggings: A Narrative of Personal Travel* (Boston: Eastern Publishing Company, 1900), 227.

1 Spurr, *Through the Yukon Gold Diggings*, 15.

2 Ibid., 23.

3 Berton, *Klondike Fever*, 23.

4 Spurr, *Through the Yukon Gold Diggings*, 132.

5 Ibid.

6 Ibid., 274.

7 Morgan B. Sherwood, *Exploration in Alaska, 1865–1900* (New Haven: Yale University Press, 1965), 144.

21

JOSEPH GRINNELL

Pluck on the Kowak

In this year of our Lord 1898, men are flying northward like geese in the springtime. That not more than one of us has ever set eyes on a real, live nugget passes for nothing; we shall naturally recognize "the yellow" when we see it.

Twenty-one-year-old Joseph Grinnell was the youngest of the twenty-member Long Beach and Alaska Mining and Trading Company, also known as the LBAM & T Co. Bound for Kotzebue Sound, they traveled on their seventy-two-foot schooner, *Penelope*, and were led by preacher/undertaker C. C. Reynolds, a man described by Grinnell as "a rollicking fellow … given to much mirth."[1] Reynolds's best friend was a medical doctor named Coffin who went along in the event of medical "contingencies."

Before leaving home, Grinnell had promised his mother that he would keep a journal and, in the event of disaster, would put it in a corked bottle and set it adrift. When he returned to California, Mrs. Grinnell published the journal as *Gold Hunting in Alaska*, noting in a preface that she had not edited the journal but had reproduced it just as her son kept it, "written in pencil on any sort of paper at hand … 'for the folks at home.'"[2]

When their sailing ship was stuck in the becalmed Bering Sea, the congenial members of the LBAM & T sang, wrote verse, and watched their captain demonstrate clog dancing. As the *Penelope* sailed past ships loaded with tough-looking miners, the LBAM & T gave their company yell: "*Penelope, Penelope,* zip, boom, ah! Going up to Kotzebue! Rah! Rah! Rah!"[3]

Grinnell was a trained naturalist and on his second trip to Alaska. He was keener on birds, insects, and flowers than on gold, and rescued the birds his shipmates had shot for sport. In Alaska, he sighted birds he had never seen, like the rare Emperor Goose, and sat up until three a.m., cleaning and preserving sea bird skins for his collection.

"I am doing my best to educate them in bird lore," he wrote of his companions, "but whenever I get off the long Latin names, they give me the 'ha-ha.'"[4]

The LBAM & T had left California in mid-May but were delayed by late spring ice in the Bering Sea. Thus, it was nearly two months before they reached Kotzebue Sound. Upon reaching Cape Blossom, the men had to assemble the riverboat they'd brought along. That smaller boat, the *Helen*, would ferry the party and their supplies up the Kowak (now Kobuk) River, where they planned to prospect. With boat builders working around the clock, Grinnell was responsible for preparation of two of the four daily meals, one at 6 p.m. and another at midnight. He traded ten gingersnaps to an Indian for three fifteen-pound salmon and fed the men meat from the ducks he shot for their skins.

Grinnell's father was a physician and had worked for Indian agencies in the American West, and Grinnell himself was born on a Comanche reservation. He had, he wrote, "learned to love … [the Indians] before I could speak"[5] and, in Alaska, became friends with the neighboring Eskimos, learning some of their language and teaching them English. He said that gold hunters were doing "more harm [to the Natives] in a few days than the missionaries can make up for in years."[6] He hoped that Sheldon Jackson would be able to put a stop to the liquor sales that whites were so freely making to the Natives.

The company would all go upriver on the *Helen*, except for the captain and two crewmen who would remain with the *Penelope* at Cape Blossom in an effort to keep it from being crushed in ice as the winter closed in. At the time of the following selection, the party has arrived at what would be the site of their winter camp. It is dawning upon the men that finding gold may not be as easy as they had envisioned.

JOSEPH GRINNELL

*Pluck on the Kowak**

Penelope Camp, Kowak River, Aug. 28—Here we are, one hundred and seventy miles from the mouth of the Kowak River and hard at work on our winter cabin. The *Helen* is almost a failure, else we should have been much farther up the river. The river is swift and has many rapids which we could not stem.

*From *Gold Hunting in Alaska* (1901), 18–22.

The boat is slow. Her wheel is too small. She will be remodeled this winter. It took five days to come this far, and, as there are two more loads to bring up, we thought it best to halt. We have been here a week and the walls of the cabin are nearly done, so that we are on the eve of owning a winter residence on the Kowak. We are expecting the *Helen* back soon with her second load.

The Kowak River, though scarcely indicated on good-sized maps, is as large as the Missouri. At our camp, it is nearly a mile across and very deep on this side, with sand bars in the middle. Other folks are having a harder time than we. Only three out of the dozen or more river steamers are a success. One is fast on a sand bar, and it looks as if she would stay there.

Some of our crowd think we had a hard time, but, when we compare our lot with that of others, we see it differently. Hundreds are toiling up in the rain, towing their loaded skiffs mile after mile along muddy banks. We have not had an accident worth mentioning unless it be the loss of a water pail. We took the wrong channel once coming up and steamed twenty-four hours up a branch river. It was the Squirrel River and, although but a tributary to the Kowak, is as large as the Sacramento and San Joaquin combined. It was so very crooked that at one point where we stopped to wood up, I climbed a hill and could see its route for several miles. Our course went around the compass once and half way again.

When we got back to the Kowak, we made good time until we reached the first rapids where our trouble began. The *Helen* would swing around and lose all she had made every few minutes when the current struck her broadside. Finally, a squad of us took to the river bank with a long tow-rope and, foot by foot, she was towed past the critical points. There were six of these rapids. When the wind blew, there was fresh trouble; it would catch on the side of the "house" and blow the boat around in spite of us. She almost got away from us once and we were in danger of being dragged off the bank, in spite of the fact that we dug our heels into the ground and braced with might and main. It was a tug of war. And such is gold hunting in the Far North!

Many others had a still harder time. We passed thirty of these parties in one day towing their provisions, while many lost their boats. There must inevitably be great suffering here this winter. Men have not realized what a long winter it will be and are poorly provisioned.

Our crowd is becoming a trifle disappointed as to the gold proposition and of course the general discontent is infectious. Hundreds are going back down the river every day, spreading defeat and failure in their path, and yet they have done no actual prospecting. This is a large country and a year is none too long to hunt, but with many parties the result is that, after panning out a little sand, the job is thrown up.

Birds are all right here, if there isn't any gold. I have been into the woods only twice so far, but secured another rare specimen of Hennicott's Willow Warbler. There is a bear in the woods back of camp. I have "laid" for him three times, but he is very shy.

Sept. 1—The *Helen* came with her last load yesterday, and our whole crowd is together again excepting the three men with the *Penelope.*

After a big pow-wow, it has been decided to divide for the winter. Ten men are to take the *Helen* with supplies and push up the river as far as possible. They think they can do some mining during the winter. We, who are destined to live together here for eight months, are Dr. Coffin, C. C. Reynolds, Harry Reynolds, Clyde Baldwin, Cox, Brown, Rivers, Wyse, and myself. Time will prove if this is a congenial combination. We shall resemble California canned goods in our narrow limits and the winter will show our "keeping qualities."

Camp Penelope, Kowak River, Sept. 13—Our cabin is done. It measures 25 x 30 feet. We moved in on the 7th. The river rose very high and threatened to inundate our tents. The place where they were is now under water. Our cabin roof was not a success. It was too flat. On the night we moved in, it rained heavily, and about 2 a.m., we were roused by the water pouring in on our beds and our precious supplies. The roof could not be repaired without rebuilding it, so we spread it all over with flies and tent cloth, which froze stiff for the winter, and now we are dry.

When the cabin was started, it was intended for our whole party, but there is no room to spare even now with only nine occupants. The foundation was leveled on the side of the knoll, so that the top of the hill is nearly as high as the roof and the earth is banked the rest of the way over the wall. That leaves no point for the north wind to strike the house.

We made a lean-to on the west and the door from the cabin opens into it. We have two windows, which we brought with us, fitted on the south. The interior of the cabin is a single room, seven feet high. It has a gable a foot or two higher, which gives "ample breathing space," as I told the boys, but which I have my eye on as a storeroom for my collection. The roof above this structure is fearfully and wonderfully made. If it had a trifle more pitch to it, to make it shed water, it would be better. A heavy ridge-pole and stringers run lengthwise, and over these are closely laid poles, the butts at the eaves along the sides, and the slender tops bent over and cinched on the opposite side of the roof.

Above the poles is packed a thick layer of moss. Above the moss is a layer of heavy sod with the dirt side up. Above all is a layer of spruce boughs like shingles. These boughs grow thick and flat, with needles pointing the same way, so they make good roofing.

The logs of the walls are chinked tightly with the moss. The floor is the natural sand. We did not cut the timber from near the house on account of the protection it gives us from the north winds. Trees large and long enough for building purposes are not very numerous, and we had to carry them a good ways. A few are as large as twenty inches at the butt, but mostly they are from ten to fifteen inches. It is all that eight of us can do to struggle along with one of these logs, they are so heavy, and we put them on rollers sometimes. Four of the men can easily carry one of the twenty-four-foot logs, but a green spruce log of any size is always heavier than it looks.

I have initiated "Brownie" into the secret mysteries of the cook stove and am one of the regular laborers now, working hard ten hours a day. Yet it is fun, for we are working for ourselves, with but the clean woods all about us, and there is a fascination in chopping up the spruces, their delightful fragrance permeating everywhere.

Sept. 19—Six of us have just returned from a trip up the Hunt River—Harry Reynolds, Wyse, Cox, Rivers, Clyde and myself. I was culinary officer as usual. We had the eighteen-foot sealing boat and it was loaded pretty heavily. The whole of us had to work for it, one in the stern of the boat to steer, one wading at the tow-line as near the boat as possible, to lift it over snags, and the other four tugging at the tow-line.

We wore hip boots and, outside of them, oilskin trousers tied around the ankles. Even with this outfit, we were constantly getting into the water all over. Rivers got a soaking the first day. He shot a duck and jumped out of the boat in pursuit. The bottom is so plain through the water that it is deceptive, and he went in up to his waist, but he grabbed the side of the boat to keep from going under. He got his duck—and a ducking thrown in.

I shot two geese the first day out, which gave us a couple of meals. They were young and so fat, I could not save their skins, but I made a drawing of one of them so that I could be positive of their identity. Looking them up when I got home where my books are, I found them to be the Hutchins goose. The doctor and I shot two white-fronted geese on the banks of the Kowak. We see a good many, but they also see us and we have to do a good deal of sneaking through the bushes to get any.

On the fourth day out, Clyde and I thought we would explore a little cañon.

Harry Reynolds had washed out several pans of sand from different bars on the way up but had not found a trace of gold. Clyde and I hoped to have better luck and started out in high spirits with spade and pick and gold-pan to do our first prospecting.

We found a brook in the cañon where we panned some without success. Finally, we found a place where the stream ran over bed-rock. The rock had cracks and fissures running crosswise with the stream, so we reasoned that, if there was gold above, particles would have been caught in these cracks. We dammed the brook and turned the stream to one side, exposing the fissures in the rock. We then gathered several pans of sand from the niches, examining it with wistful eyes, but no trace of gold did we find. So we gave it up on that stream.

We found nothing save Fool's Gold. We kept on up the cañon and, as it was yet early, decided to climb the mountain peak. As we went up the spruces grew smaller and finally disappeared. The sides were barren save for a thin covering of moss and lichens and patches of stunted huckleberry bushes. These bushes, not more than three or four inches high, bore hordes of luscious ripe huckleberries, and, nearly every hundred feet in our climb, we would drop on our knees on the soft moss and fill ourselves, so often could we find room for more. Just as we were toiling up the last slope, a flock of twenty white ptarmigan flew up in front of us and circled down to another ridge. They, too, had been feeding on the huckleberries.

As we rested ourselves, sheltered in a niche of the summit crag, safe from the chilling wind, a little red-backed mouse ran from a crevice and scampered through the moss straight to a huckleberry patch, his own winter garden. Clouds began to gather on the highest peaks, and we started down, leaving them behind.

The moss was slippery and we found that we could slide down the steep pitches easier than we could walk or jump. I remembered seeing the little Sioux slide down the hills of Dakota in government skillets, and immediately sat down on my shovel, steering with the handle just as I had seen the Indian boys do, and made terrific progress. I was soon able to pick myself up, feigning to examine a ledge of quartz, while I rubbed my posterior, and looked back for Clyde.

He tried sitting in the gold-pan and started all right but soon found that he couldn't steer. He went at a frightful rate, tearing down the steep slide backwards, until he, too, found himself examining the geological strata while giving some attention to his anatomy. And then we had to hunt for the gold-pan which, from the musical sounds which grew fainter and fainter and finally died away altogether, must have got switched off into the bottomless abyss. Such is gold-hunting in far-away Alaska.

To pass time, Grinnell taught his companions German, studied physiology, and memorized parts of *A Glossary of Scientific Terms*. The resourceful men of the LBAM & T formed a literary society and presented lectures on "The Art of Printing" and "Reminiscences of an Undertaker." They debated whether slums could be eradicated and conducted Sunday services for neighboring miners and Eskimos, performing hymns on autoharp, clarinet, banjo, and violin. There were few outside visitors, but one of them was "The Flying Dutchman," a German mailman who came up the Kowak on ice skates and offered to take letters downriver to St. Michael for a dollar apiece.

Some members of the company went farther up the Kowak to prospect, but found nothing. As time passed, Grinnell noted the changing mood of the party. In early summer, all of the men had been determined to stay in Alaska for three years if it took that long to find gold. By fall, they had decided that two years would be long enough to try. In January, the men agreed to prospect during the coming summer and then return to California before Kotzebue Sound froze up. By February, they were wondering how soon they could start for home.

"Time, and plenty of it, seems to be an antidote for enthusiasm,"[7] Grinnell wrote. "Pluck is what is needed in these Arctic regions, besides plenty of flapjacks."[8]

When he ran out of preserving supplies, he said he gladly would have traded his LBAM & T stock for some plaster of Paris, cotton batting, and arsenic so he could continue to preserve specimens.

In June of 1899, the men bid *adieu* to their camp on the Kowak and departed for Kotzebue Sound. The *Helen* was loaded with so many jolly men that no one would have known that the members of LBAM & T were disappointed gold seekers. As for Grinnell, he had made two converts, Dr. Coffin, who had become a bird stalker, and "Uncle Jimmy," who was gathering birds' nests for Grinnell's collection.

In July, the company left Kotzebue Sound on the *Penelope*. Nome was then the center of attraction, so the group stopped at Anvil City to give prospecting one last try. There, they found their biggest nugget—one worth $4.13. As they sailed south, their new company yell was this: "*Penelope! Penelope!* Zip! Boom! Bah! Going home from Kotzebue! Rah! Rah! Rah!"[9]

Grinnell obtained master's and doctorate degrees from Stanford and became a zoology professor at the University of California, Berkley. He was the first director of Berkley's Museum of Vertebrate Zoology, a position he held until his death in 1939. He originated the Grinnell system, a method of keeping and maintaining strict field notes that is still used by professional naturalists today. Grinnell amassed an important collection of carefully documented specimens, field notes, and photographs of California's mammals, reptiles, and amphibians, and his philosophy of wildlife conservation and protection was so influential that it helped shape the policies of the National Park Service.[10]

Notes

Epigraph: Joseph Grinnell, *Gold Hunting in Alaska* (Elgin, IL: David C. Cook Publishing Company, 1901), 3.

1 Grinnell, *Gold Hunting in Alaska,* 3.

2 Ibid.

3 Ibid., 5.

4 Ibid., 8.

5 Ibid., 15–16.

6 Ibid., 16.

7 Ibid., 60.

8 Ibid., 17.

9 Ibid., 94.

10 "Joseph Grinnell (1877–1939)," Museum of Vertebrate Zoology at Berkeley, August 25, 2010, http://mvz.berkeley.edu/Grinnell.html.

22

MAY KELLOGG SULLIVAN

No Time for Sonatas

I had first-class health and made up in endurance what I lacked in avoirdupois, along with a firm determination to take up the first honest work that presented itself, regardless of choice, and in the meantime to secure a few gold claims.

May Kellogg Sullivan's husband gave her carte blanche to do as she pleased, but he had no money to give her with which she could do so. Fortunately, she had wealthy friends whose generosity enabled her to make seven trips to Alaska in ten years. *A Woman Who Went to Alaska* is about her first two trips, during the course of which she covered some twelve thousand miles. The book was published in 1902 and, by the following year, was in a sixth edition.

On her initial trip of 1899, Sullivan went to the Klondike to join her father and brother. Between Seattle and Skagway, she was assigned to a room with an "adventuress" who wore a sealskin coat, sported diamond earrings, and carried a silver-tipped umbrella. When the stranger offered Sullivan a glass of brandy, she had reached the limit, and Sullivan requested a different room. Although only a tiny space next to the engines was available, Sullivan preferred that to tight quarters with an unsavory character.

At Skagway, she crossed White Pass on the newly completed railway, switching to an open flatcar for the thrilling descent to Lake Bennett. Along the way lay "the bleaching bones of earlier argonauts and their beasts of burden."[1] When Sullivan reached Dawson, her father and brother were astonished to see her. They had been evicted from their hand-built cabin, allegedly as the result of a "land grab" by the government. As the three of them removed the family's belongings to a cramped barge in the river, Sullivan's father vowed that he would never again own a home in the Klondike. Sullivan complained that the eviction was arbitrary and further suggested that Canadian officials appeared to favor certain people when it came to recordation of claims. However, she praised the Mounties for their vigilance and quick redress of crimes. Thieving in Dawson was unknown. Murderers were summarily hung and prisoners were forced to carry their coffins through the streets. Also crowding those crooked, dirty streets were dog teams pulling carts loaded with supplies, and donkeys carrying everything from rubber boots to pickaxes.

In the year she arrived, Sullivan heard that fifty tons of gold worth some $25,000,000 had been taken out of the ground, but she thought that the figure was probably underreported, due to the Canadian government's 10 percent royalty on recovered minerals. By contrast, no royalty was collected in Alaska, and there were rumors of prospectors who snuck across the border with gold they had found in Canada.

At the end of that summer, Sullivan and her brother set out for their home in San Francisco. The first leg of their trip was a seventeen-hundred-mile journey down the Yukon through a region of Alaska she described as "almost unknown to man."[2] Passengers on her riverboat were reckless characters "given over to the pursuit of gold regardless of the manner of its getting"—gamblers, dance hall girls, musicians, drunks, and toughs.[3]

At the mouth of the Yukon, Sullivan transferred to the oceangoing *Bertha*, an incoming steamer headed for Nome. Like the riverboat, the *Bertha* was crowded with rowdy, drunken passengers. Staterooms were piled with flour sacks and supplies, so passengers slept on the floors or on piles of luggage. At Nome, the waters were so shallow that passengers and freight had to be transferred to open barges called lighters and ferried ashore. It took five days to unload all the incoming animals, cargo, and passengers, and, once that process was complete, gold bullion, disabled prospectors on stretchers, and the body of a suicide were brought onboard for the journey south.

In the summer of 1900, Sullivan returned to Nome, intending to stake claims. She sailed on the *St. Paul* with four hundred and eighty-five others, including thirty-five women and one child. The passengers included preachers, missionaries, doctors, lawyers, miners, and merchants. Members of an orchestra waited tables by day and gave concerts at night.

The *St. Paul* was one of the first boats to reach Nome that year. With the ship rolling on the waves, passengers descended a frail rope ladder onto lighters bobbing about on the sea. For the two-mile journey to shore, Sullivan had dressed in a shortened skirt, leggings, warm coat, and a cap and veil. As the lighter pulled away from the *St. Paul* and headed for the beach, the veteran of a previous Nome summer sang out, "We are bidding good-bye to all comforts now!"[4]

On that second trip, Sullivan traveled with an English woman, whom she called Madam, and the woman's son and daughter. As the lighter floundered through the waves, Sullivan could see heaps of baggage and a sea of white tents lining the beach. Nome's population had been swollen by Klondike miners who had heard about the strike on Norton Sound and headed downriver from Dawson.

To the new arrivals, the place "seemed good in their eyes—very good."[5] In this passage, Sullivan reports what it was like in those first days at Nome.

MAY KELLOGG SULLIVAN

*No Time for Sonatas**

The man who had predicted that we would find no comforts in Nome proved himself a true prophet. There were none. Crowded, dirty, disorderly, full of saloons and gambling houses, with a few fourth-class restaurants and one or two mediocre hotels, we found the new mining camp a typical one in every respect. Prices were sky high. One even paid for a drink of water. Having our newly-found Alaska appetites with us, we at once, upon landing, made our way to an eating house, the best to be found.

Here a cup of poor tea, a plate of thin soup, and questionable meat stew with bread were served us upon nicked china, soiled table linen and with blackened steel knives and forks for the enormous sum of one dollar a head; which so dumbfounded us that we paid it without a murmur, backed out the door and blankly gazed into each other's faces.

"Such prices will ruin us!" gasped the madam.

"That table linen! Ugh!" shuddered the young man.

"Fifteen cents in California for such a meal!" growled the English girl in her matter-of-fact way, and with wide distended eyes; while I found such amusement in watching the three faces before me that I barely found breath to remind them of the two tons of nice things in their own packing cases at the landing.

"If only they are soon landed," groaned madam, and we set off at our best gait to find the cases.

But we did not succeed. The freight was being unloaded from the ship,

*From *A Woman Who Went to Alaska* (1902), 94–104.

we were told, as rapidly as it was possible to handle it, but one lighter and a small tugboat in a very rough sea, unloading a ship two miles off the beach, must have time; and we waited. Only two or three lighters were to be had at Nome. Other large steamers were being unloaded, and hundreds of people were hourly being landed upon the beach. There was no shelter for them anywhere, every building was full, and confusion was badly confounded. To make matters worse, it began to rain. If we could only find our freight and get our tents, bed, supplies, etc., we would be all right, but it would be impossible that day we found, after making repeated excursions through the freight house and numberless inquiries at the office.

Something must be done, but what? I now remembered some Dawson acquaintances in town made the fall before while coming down the Yukon River with my brother. To one family of these I made my way. They were in the grocery and bakery business on a prominent corner on First Street and their signboard caught my eye.

Blessings on the heads of kind Mr. and Mrs. M. of Nome City! They were delighted to see me. They lived back of the store in one room, which contained their bed, stove, cupboard, baby-organ, table, chairs and trunks; but they also owned a one-room shack next door, which was vacant for a few days, being already rented to a dentist, who would make some repairs before taking possession. I could bring my friends and baggage into this without charge, if I wished, until we secured our freight, Mrs. M. said kindly, and I pressed her hand in real gratitude with many thanks.

"I am almost ashamed to show you the room," said the kind little woman, as she unlocked the door of the shack and stepped inside, "but it is better than no shelter in this rain, and you can have a fire in the stove," pointing to a small and rusty coal heater in one corner. "I wish I had some blankets or fur robes to lend you, but everything I have is in use. You are welcome to bring in as many friends as you like, if they will share the poor place with you; and you are quite safe here, too, for you see the barracks are just opposite," pointing across the muddy little alley down which a few boards had been laid for a sidewalk, "and the soldiers are here to keep order, though they do sometimes find it rather a hard job."

Then I thanked the little woman again most heartily, and, as I took from her hands the door-key and stepped outside into the rain to bring my waiting friends and baggage from the freight house, I offered a little prayer of thanks to our good Father, and hurried away.

At the steamer's landing, all was hurly-burly and noise. It was now late in the afternoon, still raining at intervals and muddy underfoot, though the weather was not cold. Finding my English friends, I told them of Mrs. M.'s kindness and offer of her room, which they were well pleased to accept with me, and we gathered up our luggage and started for the place.

Passing through the freight house on our way to the street, madam said, pointing to the figures of two women huddled in a corner: "See! Judge R. from the *St. Paul* has not found a room yet, and Mrs. R. and her friend, the nurse, are sitting there, waiting for the judge to return! His wife is nearly sick, and they have no idea where they can get a room. Judge R. has been looking hours for one without success," she said in a sympathetic tone.

"Let us speak to them," said I, going over to where the ladies sat.

Hearing their story and seeing for myself that both women were cold, hungry and disheartened, I decided on the spot to share Mrs. M.'s hospitality with them, made the proposal, which they very thankfully accepted, and we trailed off up the street laden with luggage.

Then madam's son was found, informed of the situation, [and] asked to bring Judge R. and a few loaves of bread from the shop, along with the remaining luggage, to our new camping place in the little board shack near the barracks.

Seeing us arrive and that the three elderly ladies looked worn and travel-stained, Mrs. M. urged us to come into her room and take tea and crackers which she had already placed upon the table. This invitation the older ladies gladly accepted, while the English girl and myself looked after our new lodgings.

Here now was a state of things indeed! The entire stock of luggage for seven grown persons was soon deposited in the middle of the floor. The room of which the shack consisted was about eight by ten feet square, set directly upon the ground, from which the water oozed at every step of the foot. Two small windows, a front and back door, with the small stove—that was all. These were our accommodations for the night, and perhaps several nights and days.

Then we two set to work with a will. We swept the floor, we gathered sticks for a fire, we threw boards down outside the door upon which to walk instead of in the mud, a pail of water was brought from a hydrant after paying twenty-five cents for it, and a box was converted into a table. Luggage was sorted, lunch baskets were ransacked, while tin cups, coffee pot, knives, forks and spoons were found, with a fresh white cloth upon which to spread the food.

When Judge R. finally appeared, it was supper time. He carried a tin fry-pan under one arm, a bag containing one dozen eggs, and a few slices of ham on a paper plate, for which articles he had paid the goodly sum of one dollar and seventy-five cents.

Waving the fry-pan above his old gray head, the jolly judge shouted: "See, the conquering hero comes! Oh, but I'm hungry. Say, how in the world did you get this place? I hunted four mortal hours and failed to find a shack, room or tent for the night. Four thousand people landed here today, and still they come. Jerusalem crickets! What a crowd! Everybody is in from Dan to Bearsheba! We will have fifteen thousand people here soon if they don't stop coming, and no shelter for 'em!"

Then changing his tone and glancing toward his wife, "And how is my dear little wifey by this time?" tenderly patting Mrs. R.'s white hand, which belonged to a woman tipping the beam at two hundred.

"Aren't you glad we came? I am."

Then rattling on without giving his wife a chance to speak, for her eyes had filled with tears: "I think I've got a 'case' already. Claim number four on D Creek jumped last winter while owner was away—jumper won't leave—talked with owner today—think I'll get the job," said the hopeful old judge, sitting on an empty cracker box and eating bread and cheese from his fingers.

"Eat your supper, dear," to his wife, who was taking nothing, "and you shall have a bed tonight—the best in Nome City. See! There it is now," pointing to a big roll of dark brown canvas done up with a few varnished sticks.

To all this, Mrs. R. shook her head, but she did not speak neither did she attempt to eat, for there was a big lump in her throat which prevented.

The rest of our party enjoyed the supper. Some sat on boxes, others stood up, but we ate ham and eggs, bread, butter and cheese, tea and crackers, pickles, jelly and jams, as being the greatest "comforts" we could find in the camp and we made them speedily disappear.

At last, the supper things were cleared away and remaining food repacked in the baskets. The patent cot was unrolled, set up and made ready for Mrs. R., who was the only one favored with a bed. The others finally faced the proposition and prepared, as best they could, their chosen floor space for their beds.

All slept in their clothing, for we had no bedding and the night was cold. The two men were banished to the outer air, where together they smoked and talked of affairs of the day, while we women unbuttoned our shoes, took out a few hairpins, cold-creamed our sunburned faces, and then, between jokes, stories and giggling, we settled ourselves, with much difficulty and hard snuggling, among our bags, raincoats, steamer rugs and wraps on the rough board floor for the night.

Coming in later, the judge spread his borrowed fur robe upon the floor beside his wife's cot [and] covered himself with one-half of the same, chuckling as he did so.

"I'm glad my bones are well cushioned with fat and that I'm old and tough and like this sort of thing. I say, wife, isn't it jolly?" And the portly and sunny old judge dropped off to sleep to keep me awake most of the night by his snoring.

If I slept little that night, I did not waste my time. My brain was busy forming plans of action. It was not wise to have only one plan, for that one might fail. Better to have several and some one of these would probably succeed.

I had little money. I would not go home. I would work. I was a good cook, though I had never done such work except for our own home folks. I knew that cooking was the kind of service most in demand in this country from women, for my travels in Alaska the year before had taught me that. I could teach music, and I could paint passably in water colors and oils. In fact, I had been a teacher of all three, but in Alaska these luxuries were not in demand. I could not expect to do anything in these directions, for men and women had come to Nome for gold, expected to get lots of it, and that quickly. They had no time for Beethoven's sonatas or water color drawings.

It was now an urgent question of food, shelter and work with all, and the man or woman who could the quickest devise ways and means, the one who saw the needs of the time and place and was able to supply those needs, was the one who could make the most money. Of course, being a woman, I was unable to do beach mining as could a man, and as many men expected to do. Those who brought large outfits and plenty of money with them were immediately obliged to hire help, but it was generally a man's help, like carpenter work, hauling and handling supplies or machinery, making gold washers and sluice boxes, or digging out the gold in the creeks. None of these could I do. On the steamer, all these things had been well talked over among ourselves, for others besides myself were wondering which way they should turn when they found themselves in Nome.

However, the first move to be made was to find our freight and baggage, and a spot upon which to pitch our tents, and the sooner that was done the better, as the best and cleanest camping places were fast being appropriated by the newcomers hourly landing.

Sullivan found the judge's snoring so grating that she bustled about the next morning and located a camping spot for herself and the English family at what was said to be the cleanest, driest, healthiest spot in Nome—the mouth of the Snake River. She got work as a cook, initially at a camp on Anvil Creek, and later in town at a restaurant run by Swedish women with whom she became friends.

Sullivan and the Swedes worked hard that summer and, by October, they were exhausted. They decided to winter at a mission on nearby Golovin Bay. The temperatures there plunged to forty below and Sullivan sewed clothes for Eskimo orphans, while other mission residents played the guitar, mandolin, violin, and harmonica. In the spring, Sullivan took work as a tutor for the children of a local white hotel owner and his Eskimo wife. A couple of armed thugs named Sim and Bub broke into her room and threatened her, and Sullivan decided she'd had enough and left for home. When she sailed, she took with her three mining deeds and a fox coat.

After the success of *A Woman Who Went to Alaska,* Sullivan wrote a work of fiction, *The Trail of a Sourdough* (1910). In the preface, she said that the stories she included in the volume might have been "more vividly, yes startlingly, told," but that she had instead exercised restraint, not wishing "to unduly disturb" her readers.[6]

Notes

Epigraph: May Kellogg Sullivan, *A Woman Who Went to Alaska* (Boston: James H. Earle and Company, 1902), preface.

1 Sullivan, *Woman Who Went to Alaska*, 10.

2 Ibid., 43.

3 Ibid.

4 Ibid., 92.

5 Ibid.

6 May Kellogg Sullivan, *The Trail of a Sourdough* (Boston: The Gorham Press, 1910), 5.

23

M. CLARK

Playing for Stakes

I caught a germ in Portland, Ore., where I was spending the winter. It completely unsettled my mind, even to the extent of causing me to come to Seattle to outfit for the trip to Nome. With my mental equilibrium destroyed, the dealers found it easy to sell me all the things they told me were absolutely necessary to life and health in the far North.

During the process of acquiring matériel for her trip to Alaska, M. Clark was taken in by a Seattle "sharper" who sold her a fifty-pound still. The man claimed that the device was necessary to remove poison from the beach water at Nome. Imagine, she said, toting around a still as big as a fifty-pound lard can on your back over the tundra. Once in Alaska, she abandoned it along with the coal oil burner that roared like "Vesuvius in full eruption"[1] the first time it was lit. Those fifty-pound stills, she wrote, could be found discarded at every camping place between Norton Sound and Nome. Clark concluded that all one needed in Alaska were a sleeping bag, a fry pan, grub, and cold, hard cash.

In her *Roadhouse Tales; or, Nome in 1900*, the author never revealed that her first name was Matilda, that she was married, or that she was accompanied on her Alaskan venture by two of her three children. Why the evasiveness? After her claim at Nome was stolen by a claim jumper, she was convinced that it wouldn't have happened had she been a man. So she decided to take on a different identity, dressing and acting as a man and carrying a gun.

Clark's husband was a disabled Civil War veteran and was confined to a Seattle hospital. As sole support of her children, she had struck out into Washington's Skagit River wilderness and opened a roadhouse for miners. Settling at a place she named Marblemount, she ran her hostelry and acted as postmistress and teacher for her children and for those of the local Indians.[2]

Like many others, she caught what she called the "germ" and decided to go to Nome. Her passage was on the *Centennial*, a boat built in England in 1859, rebuilt in the United States in 1878, used for the transportation of soldiers and horses to the Philippines, and then pressed into service by a commercial carrier to handle crowds headed for Nome. With perhaps 200 stowaways onboard, the boat left the dock at four in the morning. The passengers were headed for what Clark called the "Eldorado of golden promise where auriferous sands ... would make us all rich, if not millionaires."[3]

In this selection, Clark nears Norton Sound, a place where gold seekers thought their troubles would end. She was on her way to discover, as had L. H. French, another early traveler, that Nome's "richness was ephemeral."[4]

M. CLARK

*Playing for Stakes**

The talk on the boat was now all about "strikes" and "mines, "layers" and "stratas," formations and rocks. We were off Cape Desire. The sight of land had roused their mining instincts. They were all argonauts—no thought of failure seemed to enter their minds. "Whom the Gods destroy, they first make mad." We were nearing Nome and a storm had come up. The sea was lashed to a fury, the spray was thrown high above the [wheel]house. The passengers were sent to their state-rooms with a return feeling of stomach uneasiness. Nome in sight, and only a few hardy souls could venture on deck. It is wonderful what the powers of gold will do.

A fleet larger than the British used in their war with South Africa rides at anchor in these northern waters. A line of white tents longer than the waterfront of Seattle lay glittering in the midnight sun. A dark spot in the horizon showed where the old town was situated. Our long journey had ended. The game will now be played for stakes.

"To him that hath shall be given, and to him that hath not, shall be taken away, even that that he hath." The transportation companies are winning the game.

A few boats put off to the shore, but the lighters did not go until morning. The white glitter had in it no warmth for me. Like the Pitric life, it was full of sadness. What a weight of misery and wretchedness was hid in that line of white that skirted Behring sea. Hundreds were lying there, their blankets

*From *Roadhouse Tales, Or, Nome in 1900* (1902), 32–40.

spread on the wet sand, contracting disease that would shadow their whole life, even if they were fortunate enough to live through the terrible exposure.

Up and down the beach as far as eye could reach, close to the water's edge, and reaching back to the tundra, were stacked piles of all kinds of merchandise. Huge mounds of potatoes stacked in bulk because the sacks had rotted, as they were so long in transit; lumber piled at every place a lighter had docked; combination lock safes, trunks, valises were piled up under a guard. Great quantities of flour and bacon were corded up back from the surf. A few musical instruments showed here and there. Gold-washing machines were everywhere scattered along the beach waiting for a pay streak development. Dog teams were making fairly good wages. Horse teams were getting $10 and $12 an hour. If a storm came up, these goods so near to the water's edge would all be lost.

Everything was hurry and bustle. Frequently, the beach and streets would be blockaded and freighting stopped until the blockade was lifted. Carpenters were getting $1.50 an hour building cabins and setting up tents. Meals were from fifty cents to $2.50. Everybody was hurrying and rushing around, but what they were trying to do did not appear. As soon as a lighter came on shore, some of the passengers would seize their gold pans and try the beach. With a look of disgust, they would take their gold pan and rush up to another place. Hundreds, on business principles, were staking lots for the rise in real estate that everyone seemed to expect.

I began by visiting the postmaster. He had posters up, "Help Wanted." The mail was piled up waiting to be assorted. The street leading to the post office was frequently blockaded. You had to stand in line and wait sometimes for hours before you could reach the window. They gave out the mail in alphabetical order, and the ones at A, B, etc., were first served, and moved on to make room for the unfortunate ones whose initial came near the last. It took too much red tape to get this job. We then tried the business places.

"Sorry, but there are a dozen men for every job."

Then we tried for a cashier's place in a restaurant down the line. Our aspirations were getting lower and lower. They had reached zero when I applied for a job washing dishes. We were offered $10 a week. "What a fall was there, my countrymen." We had been certain of getting at least $10 a day. We thought of starting a restaurant, but the bottom was loosening and ready to fall out of the boom. A few more days and prices slumped. Wages were down, meals were down, and we were feeling just a little blue. Want and suffering was seen on every side. Thieves, cut-throats, thugs, on every hand. You had to camp right on your provisions or they would be stolen, almost from under your eyes. I turned in and rolled into my blankets. I was wedged in near the wall of the tent, where I alternately thawed and froze until morning.

Sometime along in the night, Mr. Leonard came into the tent, saying: "I saw a tough sight as I came in. A man with the smallpox is lying out here on a board, his teeth chattering with a congestive chill. His face is all broke out and blue with the cold. His blankets are under his head, but everybody is afraid to go near him. Like the Levites of old, they all pass by on the other side. His satchel is sitting by his side. He seems too sick to notice anything."

A few hours later, I heard a voice outside, saying, "That poor devil with the smallpox, out there on the board, is dead."

The sea was daily giving up the bodies of those who ventured in little boats, without knowing or not caring for the danger they encountered. The miners working the beach would tumble the corpses into a hole that had been worked out, with their shovels they filled in the sand, and the funeral was ended. Not one out of twenty of these men had either name or address to identify them by. Shooting affrays were almost of daily occurrence. The people who had rented their houses to parties staying "in," when they had gone "outside," came back to find the renters now claimed to be owners, by the "right of possession," and gun plays decided the ownership. Every steamer coming in brought a full contingent of steward's help, stowaways. These men were bound to subsist. They had no other way but to steal or starve.

Tents were going up so fast you could scarcely tell your own local habitation and abiding place from some other that looked exactly like it. Felix, the Seattle tent maker's name, was the one most familiar sign that met your eyes on every side. There are some laughable happenings, but they lie so close to tragedy that one can scarcely laugh. Forty thousand was now the estimated population of Nome. The white city of tents reached from Snake River to Nome River. The tundra was frozen, no rain, no water you could drink, that did not cost twenty-five cents for a pail full. No work, no gold, no nothing, but disappointment.

I started for Dry Creek. I had started too early for breakfast. I stopped at a sod cabin and spoke to an elderly man who was washing himself outside the door. I knew from his sod cabin he was a "sourdough" and had wintered here. I wanted to know from someone who had worked the beach what the prospects were for a tenderfoot.

"Come in and have some breakfast. I can't talk when I'm hungry, and I know you are hungry, too, by your looks."

The partner had the breakfast ready. They had hot and cold bread, bacon and eggs, tomatoes, butter, maple syrup and tea—surely, these men had made a stake, or they would not live like this. The miner was from Ohio—McKinley's town was his home. He was a near neighbor, and well acquainted with the president.

"The country is much greater and richer on the outside than it is here. The whole country is pocket. No big money will be made out of it except on the very rich claims on Anvil and Dexter. Good pay will be taken from Snowy Gulch and a few others. It takes hard, faithful work to make wages. The old miners are leaving Nome for other points. There is nothing here except for the fortunate few who have good claims. The crowds are here and they must eat and live, even if the government has to take them home. I feel sorry for the hard working, honest men who have made sacrifices to get here, expecting to make a fortune and will find it impossible to make an honest living.

"The few really good women who have come here allured by the big wages they supposed they would get in Nome will find there is not room enough in Alaska for them. There is really no likelihood of so many getting work as are coming to Nome with the rush. The miners as a rule are not marrying men. They believe all women marry for money. The Dawson men that brought women found they had picked up a burden they could not easily throw down. The example they have set will be remembered by the men here. There is no possible betterment in the situation. It's a good place to study humanity, but not a good place to make money in by the multitudes that have come here."

That man spoke the truth, as the sequel sadly proved.

It was a long walk and late in the day when I got back. I had thrown myself onto my blankets to rest. Blankets were spread on the wet sand. I was thinking of what McKinley's neighbor had told me, when a woman came in, and without any preface, only a few tears, commenced to tell me her awful condition. She was a poor, hard-working woman from San Francisco. She had taken all the meager savings of years to come to Nome. She believed she could easily make in a few months enough to buy her a little home. The wages were so low in 'Frisco she had despaired of ever getting enough ahead to buy a little place where she could rest once in a while, and not have to work all the time, but it's awful here!

She and her friend had sat in their camp chairs for two nights on the beach. Somebody had stolen her box of provisions, her tent and her blankets. Their trunks and camp chairs were all they had left. What to do she did not know. The first night they had stayed on the beach, a man came 'round and said to the watchman, pointing to them, "She-chokers [cheechakos]?"

"Yes, she-chokers."

"They both chuckled. I could stand it no longer. I said, 'hain't a she-choker as much a right to come to Nome as a he-choker, if she is trying to better her condition?' You ought to have heard the fools laugh. 'Oh, certainly, certainly, but—'"

"It can't be very pleasant for you to sit here in those chairs. Why don't you set up your tents?"

"Why don't I set up my tent? Because the thieves of Nome have stolen my tent, and everything else I've got."

"It's a hard case, sure, but there are hundreds here who do not have even a camp chair."

She told me that she had cooked the meals for some miners, and that they had given her board for her work. She now walked out as unceremoniously as she had come in. Next day she came in again.

"I have hunted for work all over this town, but I can't get a rap to do. These mining men are all right. I guess I would have starved to death if it had not been for the miners and now one has given me a tent and set it up for me. I am a near neighbor of yours."

She was quite hopeful. She had called on the preacher, and he had told her to come out to church; no doubt at all but he could put her in the way of a "position." In the meantime, she cooked for any of the miners who would give her a meal, a charity the church members of the denomination to which she belonged did not offer her. They probably thought as Mr. Conklin did. I had gone out to their tent one evening, and heard a man in one of the nearby tents groaning and coughing as though in great agony.

"What's the matter with your neighbor?" I asked.

Mr. Conklin replied, "I don't know, and what's more, I don't want to know. In Alaska everybody has enough to do to look out for himself."

The ladies were cooking dinner. His sister-in-law was slicing some bacon. I heard Mr. Conklin say, in a stage-whisper: "One piece apiece is enough." She kept right on with the slicing. This time a little more emphatic: "I tell you, one piece apiece is enough. Remember, you are in Alaska now."

"Remember you are in Alaska now," was a proverb with us, to use on all sorts of occasions. I left the Conklin's tent and, guided by the coughing, went on until I found the tent. It was a mosquito-proof tent. Somebody had gone out and left the string on the outside. Untying the string, I called, "May I come in?"

A hoarse voice said, "Come."

A great big giant of a man was stretched on a cot, an unkempt, forlorn looking specimen he was, too.

"What's the matter with you? You seem very sick." His voice choked, the tears ran down his cheeks. He soon choked them down.

"I have been very nigh death's door. The doctor says I have congestion of the lungs, and I am not out of danger yet." He looked at me, and a fresh gush of tears followed.

Looking at him seriously, I said, "If my looks are enough to make a big six-footer like you shed tears, I had better go. I can see you have congestion of some sort, for it's visible on your face, but soap and water will relieve that somewhat."

I washed his face and hands, brushed his hair, and all the time I was telling him about poor Mrs. Newman, his fellow townswoman, who had been robbed of all her supplies and had no work. He seemed to feel better as soon as his mind was taken from pitying his own condition. His name was Beatty. He had married a widow lady with considerable property, but he wanted to make some money of his own and so had come to Nome. I advised him, if he had a good home, to pocket his pride and go back to his family. He could still realize a good price for his horses and wagon, and by selling now, he could take one of the first boats home.

About a week afterward, I saw him down on the water front. He was all muffled up, and still coughing badly.

"I have taken your advice. I am going out on the first boat to 'Frisco."

Mrs. Newman went to church. The preacher could do nothing for her, and she was in despair. What will she finally do? What can a woman without money and without friends, as she was, do? There is always one way, and ninety-nine out of every hundred women situated as she was, find it. The Ohioan was right. Really good women who work for a living have no place in Alaska.

Clark decided that she would fall back on what she knew how to do—operate a roadhouse. She went twenty miles down the coast to a settlement called Port Safety and selected a site near where the schooners anchored and a ferry crossed the lagoon. Four days after she arrived, she was open for business.

As the title of her book suggests, Clark included stories about life on the trail that were related by the mushers who gathered around her fireplace on winter nights. She had kind words for the Alaskan Eskimos, calling them the original Americans. To her mind, the Natives were better off with their traditions, which would more likely result in happiness and well-being than the values being presented by newcomers calling themselves Christians.

An old Eskimo told Clark, "'Fore white man come, lots of fish, lots of seal, lots of fun. Now Eskimo die; all die! White man's boat scare fish, scare seal, scare whale. No fur, no eat, no fun, no nothing, but die."

Clark's response? "This about sums up the whole situation."[5]

After two years in Alaska, Clark went home to Washington and opened another roadhouse at Corkendale Creek. She resumed her female identity, became active in Seattle's circle of freethinkers, and was a proponent of natural law, believing that justice originates in nature rather than in society's laws. Writing as M. F. Clark, she published *The Span of Life* magazine in which the following poem appeared:

> This world is not so bad a world
> As some would like to make it,
> But whether good or whether ill,
> Depends on how we take it.[6]

Notes

Epigraph: M. Clark, *Roadhouse Tales; or, Nome in 1900* (Girard, KS: Appeal Publishing Company, 1902), 11.

1 Clark, *Roadhouse Tales*, 12.

2 M. Clark's biographical information was provided by her granddaughter, octogenarian Madrene "Tootsie" Clark, and her great grandson, Don Clark. The two continue what has become a family tradition of hostelry by operating the Skagit River Resort in Rockport, Washington. A flag that Matilda made from sewing scraps still hangs there. The Clarks have reprinted *Roadhouse Tales* and sell it at their lodge and on their website at www.northcascades.com.

3 Clark, *Roadhouse Tales*, 14.

4 L. H. French, *Nome Nuggets: Some of the Experiences of a Party of Gold Seekers in Northwestern Alaska in 1900* (New York: Montross, Clarke & Emmons, 1901), xxi.

5 Clark, *Roadhouse Tales*, 193.

6 Information about Clark's activities after her return to Seattle and the quote from *Span of Life* were provided by great-grandson Don Clark and his mother, Tootsie Clark, in an e-mail to the author dated July 24, 2010.

24

EDWARD J. DEVINE

The Great White Silence

In a mining camp, for obvious reasons, it is not considered good form to ask a man who he is or where he came from. So that it too often happens that when dead men are found on trails, or lying on the beach, no one knows who they are or anything about them.

When Canadian priest Edward Devine reached Nome in June of 1902, he was surprised to find shops, hotels, banks, and office buildings lining its plank street. Newsboys peddled papers and telephone and electric wires ran overhead. Someone suggested that the only things needed to complete the town were trolley cars and a university.

The Alaskan prospectors, as Devine observed, were cosmopolitan, with representatives from Holland, France, Japan, Sweden, England, Scotland, Ireland, Australia, South Africa, and other places. Although primarily of the Roman Catholic religion, few were interested in spiritual matters. Devine thus had plenty of spare time to devote himself to the study of Alaska's wildflowers. One might think that solitude would make miners receptive to religion, but Devine found that not to be the case. The prospectors he met in Alaska might call a priest to their bedside if they were near the point of death, but they "are altogether too delicate about troubling him when they are in health."[1]

Devine paid a visit to Council City, an outlying camp sixty or seventy miles away. The journey took a day and a half on something called a "horse boat," which involved an old nag pulling a long, flat boat through shallow rivers at the rate of two or three miles an hour. This gave the passengers plenty of time to jump out and explore the flowers and grasses along the shore. The rivers the boat had to travel were filled with fallen trees and limbs, but the horse plowed right through. If the "passengers escape with face and hands unscathed and clothes untorn, they put themselves down as lucky,"[2] Devine said.

Council City was a typical camp, with gambling and liquor establishments occupying "every point of vantage."[3] An Irish woman told Devine that gold hunting was "the honestest way of making a living"[4]—it involved taking, it was true, but only from God. Devine watched as miners trudged into the wilderness with their tents, bedding, and several months' food supply strapped to their backs in packs as big as "baby elephants."[5] He knew that some of them would be lost in the hills in summer, and others frozen to death in blizzards in winter.

Nome had no official police force but was nonetheless peaceful for the most part. However, it would have been a stretch to say, as one local newspaper did, that life in Nome was comparable "to a New England Sunday school."[6] There were drunken brawls, sporadic holdups, and the occasional "passing unpleasantness" in which the participants nearly lost their jugular veins.[7]

Like others, Devine noted the changes that were taking place in the lives of Alaska's indigenous peoples. The Eskimos had been simple and industrious but, since the incursion of the miners, were becoming dependent on the tea, milk, butter, and canned goods that they could get from the traders. One Native told Devine he would rather "open a can of Chicago corned beef than ... mend his nets and go a-fishing."[8] Besides this loss of ambition, the Eskimos were also losing their guilelessness. From the frequent tricks played upon them, they had learned to bite their money to test it before closing a deal.

As autumn came on, the question being asked of everyone was whether he or she planned to go "outside" for the winter. A "yes" meant that the respondent would be spending the winter in "some congenial spot" rather than remaining "hidden in snowdrifts"[9] at Nome. Once the Bering Sea iced up, it would be eight months before any steamer could get closer than seven hundred miles to Nome. One resultant hardship was the consequent disruption of mail delivery. In the summer, mail arrived at Nome by ship three months after it was sent. But once October came, there'd be no mail until January, when the Yukon River would have frozen over and mail could be brought by dogsled able to downriver from Dawson.

With the departure of the last boat in October, only the hardest heart could escape the feelings of loneliness and isolation that washed over Nome. Since winter travel was fraught with danger, those who stayed behind would spend most of the coming months hunkered down in town.

In this passage, Devine describes the long winter on the Seward Peninsula and an ingenuous new means of transportation, the "hot-air" stage.

EDWARD J. DEVINE

*The Great White Silence**

One must have had personal experience of eight months' isolation in an Arctic mining camp—with nearly three of the eight in comparative darkness, seeing nothing during all that time, on hill and tundra and sea, but snow and ice ten to fifteen feet thick, hearing nothing but the whistling of winds and the howling of Eskimo dogs—to know what winter life really means in that distant part of the world.

When navigation closed in the autumn, everyone began, in a practical way, to settle down for the winter. A stranger could see that the old-timers apprehended a season of intense cold, and a long siege of it, by the almost absurd precautions they were taking to bank their cabins with earth and to fill the chinks around their doors and windows.

Toward the end of October, the nights had become long and intensely dark, and we had to use artificial light earlier every afternoon. With the advancing season, the days grew short so rapidly that we began to ask when they were going to stop. In December, the darkness had eaten so deeply into the morning and evening, that we had barely three hours of sunlight. When the winter solstice arrived, December 21st, the sun just peeped over the horizon and then dropped into Bering Sea again. We were living in Arctic twilight. Darkness was complete at three o'clock in the afternoon; and nothing relieved the dreadful monotony, till ten o'clock the next day, but the large electric cross on our church-spire, whose graceful arms shed brilliancy over Nome twenty hours daily.

When I received orders to go to Alaska, one of my direct apprehensions was the rigor of the climate. How should I ever be able to stand the penetrating cold of an Alaskan winter? Having passed through two unscathed, I feel that I can write with some knowledge of the subject, at least as far as Seward Peninsula is concerned. The climate there is certainly severe, yet not at all to the degree that newcomers expect.

During my first winter, the thermometer registered 44° below zero only once, though we experienced a great variety of temperatures. No one seemed to mind the severe cold or the snow. The weather was rarely a topic of conversation—perhaps because we had so much of it.

*From *Across Widest America, Newfoundland to Alaska* (1905), 195–210.

There must be physical conditions besides latitude which affect the severity of climate. One feels the truth of this when one sees men living comfortably, through the long winter, in canvas tents and cabins heated only with small sheet-iron stoves. In Nome, children played in the streets even when the thermometer was 30° below zero. An afternoon walk out over the tundra on snowshoes or skis, when the temperature is between 30° and 40° below and the air is still and blue, is both pleasant and healthful. Now and then, one puts one's hands up to feel whether one's nose and ears are in their accustomed places; but this is mostly from the force of habit. As a result, there are few invalids in that country. It is the proud boast of Alaskans—and I am convinced there is some foundation for it—that their winter is the most invigorating in the world.

There is danger of freezing only when this intense cold is accompanied with wind and drifting snow. It is then that certain precautions must be taken; for blizzards are the great sources of danger in Northwestern Alaska. The miners who have been frozen to death in them were the imprudent or the inexperienced ones, who ventured out over the trails or across the hills when they should have followed the example of the natives and stayed under cover. One rarely hears of an Eskimo freezing to death.

The atmosphere is so dry that, after a storm, there is always a very large quantity of finely-powdered snow lying in drifts on the hills. When the wind blows, it drives this snow before it with terrific velocity, filling the air with clouds of it, blinding travellers and obliterating all trails in a twinkling. Objects fifty feet away become invisible; and under these circumstances darkness may set in.

When this happens, a miner loses his way, even though he may not be twenty feet from the trail. After circling around aimlessly for a few weary hours, undergoing meanwhile an excruciating mental agony—for he knows he is astray—his feet and legs grow numb, which is the beginning of the end. In a little while he sinks down, drowsy and exhausted, to rise no more.

I met several miners who had felt the symptoms of incipient freezing, and who would have succumbed had they not been rescued. They will carry all their lives vivid mental pictures of these moments. Invariably they saw lights flitting about, which deceived them as to distance; they heard sounds like bells, and sometimes delightful music, which drew their minds away from their danger. These pleasurable sensations are, strange to say, the result of hunger and exhaustion. Near the end, the pain of death by freezing resembles, they say, that of death by burning. But these sensations are of short duration;

the miner soon falls asleep and dies painlessly. Every year there are tragic instances of freezing to death. During my two winters, four or five were thus found on the trail cold and lifeless.

When men acquire some experience of conditions in that country, the element of danger disappears. An old-timer out on the trail will not face a blizzard. When there is no cabin or roadhouse close at hand, he digs a hole in the snowdrift and waits there till the storm has spent its rage. He has sometimes to stay two or three days hidden away in his furs or sleeping-bag, which gives him leisure to meditate on man's helplessness before nature's angry moods. It is well for him if he has food for this period of forced inactivity; sometimes he has not. A miner on Kotzebue Sound, who is also a physician, told me he was caught in a blizzard while on a sick-call during the previous winter. He had to burrow a hole in a snowdrift, where he stayed seventy-two hours. Hunger obliged him to consume portions of his furs and moccasins. He said he never tasted anything half so palatable.

Another miner met with a more tragic experience, a couple of years before. He had killed a bear and skinned him. A blizzard coming on, he rolled himself in the ample folds of the fur for protection, but this nearly proved his undoing. In a few hours, the bearskin, which was fresh from its owner's back, was frozen into a solid mass and almost smothered the hapless miner. His companions found him encased in a shell as hard as iron and had to use an axe to extricate his all but lifeless body.

Travelling in Alaska during winter is a problem that has not yet been fully solved, even by John Brower, the genius who invented what is known in that country as the "hot-air" stage. As a rule, prudent people stay at home in winter. The Eskimos rarely leave their igloos during the long white silence, and the typical miner has learned to follow their example. In autumn, when his work is finished on his "claim" and he decides to stay in Alaska, he sets to work to build himself a log-cabin. He fills the chinks with Arctic moss, cuts his season's firewood, buys his eight months' supply of Chicago canned goods, and then retires to his nest till the springtime. This is how thousands of men live through the long, dark winter. If a miner goes a-prospecting, he harnesses his team and travels over the snow-covered tundra, well supplied with food and furs. When night comes on, he digs a hole in the snow, or lies down on the lee side of his sled and dogs, then rolls himself in his furs, and goes to sleep. It is no extraordinary sight to see members of the gentler sex muffled in furs, trudging over the hills, from camp to camp, with their dog-teams and miners' outfits.

There is one woman miner in Nome who is quite famous in all Northwestern Alaska. She is familiarly known in the mining world as "Mother," a kindly name earned by her for the large, generous heart she carries under a weather-beaten, masculine exterior. This miner and her faithful dogs followed the two-thousand-mile stampede from Dawson during the first Nome excitement, and she secured large mining interests in the Solomon district. I met her on the Bering coast, one wintry afternoon, tripping along behind her sled and team as lightly as if twenty and not fifty years were weighing on her shoulders.

But women of this hardy stamp are not numerous in that country. Those who indulge in feats of endurance, in their "mushing" over the tundra, are the ones who have been in Alaska for three or four years, and who know just how venturesome they may be without risking their lives. But when recent arrivals—or "chechakos," as they are called—want to travel in winter, the dangers of the trail must be foreseen and guarded against. Newcomers, who do not take the conditions of the country into account, run the risk of being found frozen to death.

The introduction of the "hot-air" stage has made traveling relatively comfortable in Seward Peninsula, and a good deal of traffic goes on in winter between Nome and the different camps. Large, double sleighs, built like the time-honored emigrant prairie-schooners, have been introduced on the various trails. A double covering of thick canvas, enclosing a thin air space, covers the entire top and keeps in the warmth which is furnished by a small stove solidly bolted in one corner.

Of course, the old-timers, or "sour-doughs," ignore this way of travelling and still "mush" over the country with their dogs. The dog is the Alaskan miner's friend. Half a dozen harnessed to a sled will haul eight or ten hundred pounds of supplies twenty or thirty miles a day, without any difficulty. This is the reason why they are so useful in Alaska. There are few miners who do not own at least three, which they keep busy going from one mine to another during the winter months. In summer, the curs lie about the camps doing nothing. In Nome, you cannot walk ten steps without falling over one or more of them lying in your path, too lazy to move. They rest during the day, but during the night they keep you awake with their unearthly howling. During my first summer there, one of the large commercial companies blew a steam whistle, morning, noon and night. This was a boon, inasmuch as it enabled us to set our watches, and keep some sort of uniform time, but it was also a terrific nuisance, for it let loose the enervating yells of seven or eight hundred Eskimo dogs, which made the air vibrate, three times a day, with all the notes imaginable.

He is a beautiful animal and affectionate, but when his large, soft eyes are looking into yours so intelligently, when his great, bushy tail is wagging expression to the joy he feels at meeting you, keep an eye on your bundles. If your door is open, he steals your meat, preferring ptarmigan to reindeer. He lifts the lid of your fish-box, steals your fish, and then replaces the lid noiselessly. He reads the labels on tins of canned goods, so the miners say, for it is a well-known fact, that when two tins are put before him, he takes the meat invariably and leaves the fruit.

He is, for all that, the Alaskan miner's friend, and because he is such, many of his foibles are overlooked. He is faithful, even in death; many a time he has been found on the trail, plaintively sobbing and lying on the frozen body of his master, trying to give it warmth, long after the vital spark had fled.

Another miner's friend, an institution peculiar to Alaska, and a boon to lost or storm-bound travellers in winter, is the "road-house." On the trails to Council, Sullivan, Candle, and along the coast, about every ten miles, a log-cabin is built, or it may be only an abandoned native igloo, and fitted up with bunks and blankets. When the half-frozen miner, worn and fatigued, without food for himself or his dogs, sees a lantern at the end of a pole in some valley, or on a white hillside, he knows that he is safe from the storm. A roaring fire, a piping glass of toddy, or a red-hot cup of tea makes the blood flow freely in his veins and gives him back life and vigor. Road-houses on the Alaskan trail, during a blizzard, are more welcome to a miner than wells of sparkling water to an Arab on the Sahara. They are poorly kept—I speak from my experiences in five of them—but they are life-saving stations in an inhospitable climate; momentary homes in Alaskan fastnesses; oases amid the great white silence.

With dog-teams, hot-air stages and road-houses, life is not too miserable on the Alaskan trail. With the aid of the last two, I made several winter journeys to and from Council City. During one of these, I got my first taste of an Alaskan blizzard, the memory of which will remain as long as I live. A terrific storm overtook our party half-way between that camp and Nome. We had started from Topkuk, on the Bering coast, on the fourth day of our journey. We had not gone more than three miles when a brisk wind began to blow the dry snow across the trail and, in a few minutes, had completely blotted out every trace of it. The wind grew stronger and filled the air with tiny particles of snow, which beat pitilessly against the stage-driver's face with the pricking force of a thousand needles. His horses' eyes and nostrils were filled with this fine powder. They began to be smothered; they stampeded from side to side and refused to obey the reins. If they could be kept on the trail, the shelter of a hill or wooded spot would give them a respite from their tortures. But this seemed impossible. The air was thick and dark with snow which drifted rapidly up against the stage. Meanwhile the thermometer, which we carried with us, went down from 15° below to 40° [below] Fahrenheit. The wind grew fiercer and howled and whistled and threatened to tear away the canvas of the stage.

My travelling companion, an old German, and I were commiserating the poor driver outside, when the stage suddenly left the trail, gave a lurch to one side, and we felt ourselves going rapidly over. The force of the blizzard had done the work and, sooner than it takes to write it, we found ourselves on the broad of our backs on the floor of the stage. I myself was pinned down by a bale of compressed hay and a tool-chest, while the German began to call wildly for help, as the red-hot coal stove, bolted to the stage, was right over him, and he was in mortal dread lest a shower of lighted coals should come down on him. The driver rushed to the rear, opened the door, and extricated us none the worse.

The change from the warm air inside the stage to 40° below zero outside was anything but agreeable, but willy-nilly we had to face it. So we set to work to help the driver to unload his freight and lift the stage back on the trail. Among other articles, I picked up a box, iron-bound and covered with the word "Caution," which had fallen from the driver's seat into the snow. It turned out to be a box of dynamite and, fortunately, had struck a soft snow-drift. Had it reached the ice, a foot beneath, there is no telling how this Alaskan episode might have ended.

There was no tree within seventy-five miles of Nome, and in winter, the flat open land was covered with ten to twelve feet of snow, leading Devine to describe the countryside in winter as bleak. On top of that, a blizzard in the winter of 1902–3 was the worst ever recorded. The town's telephone wires were eighteen feet off the ground and suspended on poles, but that winter people were forced to duck beneath the wires as they walked from place to place. So much snow accumulated at neighboring Council City that the cabins were hidden from view, with only the stovepipes that stuck up through the snow giving a hint of the dwellings beneath.

The isolation and twenty-one hours a day of darkness at Nome made for long winters, but Devine found the summers delightful, with days of twenty-one hours of sunlight and wildflowers covering the landscape. Autumns, too, were gorgeous, with sunsets that could continue for three hours as their opalescent colors lit up the sky with azure, orange, crimson red, royal purple, and gold. Devine had an especially fond memory of the electrically lit steeple on Nome's Catholic Church, a fixture which served as a beacon for ships at sea as well as for travelers on land.

Devine concluded, after his two years at Nome, that ministering to prospectors would never be easy. While "the preacher is talking to them about the treasures which rust not, and which the moth cannot injure, they are thinking about … 'pay-dirt' and … the next 'clean-up.'"[10]

Notes

Epigraph: Devine, *Across Widest America*, 152.

1 Devine, *Across Widest America*, 276.

2 Ibid., 171.

3 Ibid., 173.

4 Ibid., 161.

5 Ibid., 151.

6 Ibid., 183.

7 Ibid., 184.

8 Ibid., 242.

9 Ibid., 182.

10 Ibid., 277.

25

ADDISON M. POWELL

The Alien God of Gold

> No more adapted to the vocation than a coyote would be to herd sheep.... men of talent and virility were on their way possibly to the sacrifice of everything, including their lives, among those mountains of solitude—and all for the alien god of gold.

Addison Powell was working in the US Surveyor General's office in San Francisco when the chief clerk recommended him for a job in Alaska. Captain I. N. West, a prospector, was looking for someone who, if necessary, could "rough it" alone in Alaska. West claimed to have found gold in the Copper River region and needed a surveyor to document his claim. He was willing to pay all expenses for the right person.

In preparing for his interview with West, Powell read Lieutenant Henry Allen's report of his exploration of the Copper River and talked to a professor from the local university who knew something about the subject. Based on what he'd learned, Powell doubted the veracity of West's story. As far as he'd been able to ascertain, the only white man who had successfully navigated the Copper River was Allen—and that had been thirteen years earlier. Armed with this information, Powell figured that, if West was a "sharper," he'd be able to trip him up.

It turned out that West, seventy-two years old and six feet tall, seemed to know what he was talking about—and, in fact, even corrected some of Allen's geography. Moreover, his story about a big find on Slate Creek sounded credible. He was leaving for Alaska right away, and Powell agreed to get his affairs in order and follow.

When Powell reached Valdez in May of 1898, it was only to find that West had left Alaska the day before. The captain had fallen ill in the back country, been hauled out on a sled, and shipped back south. Just before he sailed, West had said of Powell, "Oh, if I only could talk to him!"[1] The opportunity never came up, for West died on his way home.

Powell had arrived in Alaska with twenty-five cents in his pocket, but he had brought with him a year's worth of supplies and, with no other option, he decided to stay.

In the winter of 1897–98, thousands of would-be gold seekers arrived at Valdez. Anyone trying to get to the Alaskan goldfields by going through Canada was required by that country's government to bring along a year's worth of supplies—and Canadian officials collected a tariff on those goods at the border. Prospectors were anxious to avoid these issues and were thus looking for an "all-American route" to the goldfields of Alaska.

Rumors about an overland path from the coast of Alaska that led directly to the goldfields had been circulated. Many had gone to Valdez looking for that route but had landed only to learn there was no such trail. They would all discover, as did William Abercrombie and his men, that the only way to the goldfields was the deadly path across the glacier. Valdez was filled with cripples, the "Glacier Striders,"[2] who had attempted to cross the glacier and, on finding the task impossible, had turned back. Some of those who had made the attempt had been buried in avalanches, frozen in blizzards, or drowned in glacial streams. Others like Powell, who had spent everything they had getting to Valdez, were stranded with no way to get home.

"If the climate of Alaska is a tonic," Powell wrote, "many have lost their lives taking overdoses of it."[3]

In an effort to address the issue, the government had sent Abercrombie, whose account of his night on the Valdez glacier appears earlier in this collection. Since Powell's potential employment with West had evaporated, he went to work as a government surveyor, traveling some 600 miles in fifty-eight days with Abercrombie's right-hand man, Lieutenant P. G. Lowe, in the summer and fall of 1898.

In this excerpt, Powell describes some of the characters he met in the wilds of Alaska, including prospectors who had gotten wind of West's alleged discovery and who were looking for the same site that Powell was. Not having found the place, they became convinced West was a "humbug" who had never been anywhere near the site where he claimed to have found gold.

ADDISON M. POWELL

*The Alien God of Gold**

Napoleon's cavalry crossed the Alps and Abercrombie's crossed the Valdez glacier. This expedition, accompanied by several adventurous prospectors, left on the 5th of August. The amount of first-class profanity that gushed from ordinarily moral men, under the provoking circumstances, was astonishing. The same voluble profane prospector, who had been rescued from the snow-slide, was with us. He laboriously contended with the argumentative disposition of a donkey having a will of its own, and that fact added materially to the driver's already extensive vocabulary.

All day, we trudged on solid ice and jumped yawning crevasses. We camped on the ice during that short August night, as it was too dark to travel. The spring snow slides and glacial hydraulics had deposited huge boulders on this ice river, and they had melted large wells straight down. A few of those wells were closed or, like an inverted cone, had gradually narrowed to a point and now were filled with water. The rock that had formed this kind of a well had melted its way down, while the well had closed gradually behind it by freezing. Streams of water poured into the apparently bottomless ones, and into some of those we dropped large rocks, but never heard one strike bottom.

Those of us who had sleeping bags managed to secure a little sleep, but those without them were compelled to walk to and fro in the cold wind and rain to keep warm.

The next day, we crossed the divide at 5,000 feet altitude in a blinding snow storm. At this altitude and under these conditions, one's heart action is about as irregular as the stroke of a single-cylinder gas engine. In a similar blizzard, about a month later, a man by the name of Skelly, from San José, California, was frozen to death. I broke through a crust of snow that covered a crevasse, and with one leg swinging around in space beneath, declared I never again would attempt to cross that glacier. A strong wind pushed us along with almost irresistible force down the descent of the Coast Range, and at night we camped in timber near the foot of the glacier.

The profane prospector became very weary, and a man invited him to ride his saddle horse down the descent. The cinch became loosened, and when the saddle was on the horse's neck, the old man remarked that he believed he would alight. Just as he said this, he and saddle slipped over the horse's head.

*From *Trailing and Camping in Alaska* (1910), 37–46, 48, and 50–54.

After rolling and sliding some distance, the prospector managed to stand up and demonstrate that he was physically able to swear. He spread profanity all over that part of the glacier. It really dripped from his mouth when he stopped to get his breath.

This Coast Range stands on end. Geologists do not agree that it is the same mountain chain, because it has not the formation that the Coast Range possesses further down the coast. In respect to the meaning of the term Coast Range and their location of it, they are diverted in their opinions. A prospector who visits these mountains should bring a photograph of the sun with him, as well as a diving suit; but the most useful article would be a flying machine.

We traveled along the banks of a glacier stream where the water was colored milky, caused by the rock erosion, and was almost too dense and cold to swim in. Glacier water is just about as clear as mud. Alaskans claim that he who drinks of it takes upon himself ever after the reputation of being unable to tell the truth. At Valdez, a few of such initiated ones organized themselves into a mining company which they properly named "The Goldbrick Consolidated." When selecting a witness to verify my statements, I ascertain first if he has imbibed sufficiently of the glacier beverage.

We rested a day at a camp called Twelve Mile. A man was drowned there in two feet of water. The thick and swift glacier water rolled him over and over until he was drowned—and in sight of his companions. At this camp there were two headboards inscribed with the names of E. Vananthrope and J. Tournier, who died in the snow-slide of April 30, 1898.

We traveled along swamp hillsides, and then along a deep slough where we drowned a horse. We camped on August 12 in what was once a beaver pond, but, as the water had drained away, it was now a pasture of red-top grass as high as our horses' backs. A clear brook ran out of this, and there we caught many grayling trout. This was a romantic spot, such as would be conducive to poetical writing, if one were lyrically inclined.

We remained there and scouted for the best trail route. While I was crawling through brush and "devil club" that clung to me like debts, I heard the noise of a large animal breaking away. I soon arrived at an animal bed that was still warm. The long claw marks indicated that the recent occupant had been a grizzly. As my hands felt the warmth in the abandoned bed, I felt lonely and homesick, so I returned very deliberately to camp, occasionally looking back for the bear.

This camp was surrounded by a heavy forest of spruce that was on fire. At night, the flames would leap to the treetops with a roar, then calm down, and presently another tree's foliage would repeat the roaring, cracking and popping. This red glaring night scene was wild and enchantingly beautiful. We soon arrived at Klutena Lake and traveled along its shore for four days through timber and along gravelly beaches. This lake extends from spruce-covered hills on the east, to low spruce lands on the west, while back of the latter were high snow-capped mountains. Even the lake water was a milky color, but clear streams entered into it and up these ventured large red salmon. I stood on the bank while they ventured so near that I shot five from one position and soon had enough for supper for the whole crowd.

I visited a camp of some men who had been there since the winter rush. I asked one of them if ever he had known Captain West. I did this because West had told me in San Francisco that it was here he intended to leave the shore of the lake and cut across to the headwaters of the Chistochina River.

The man replied, "Know that old humbug! Well, I reckon I do! If it had not been for that old scoundrel we should not be camped here. We stopped here to dog his trail, as we had heard that he was after something he once had found. We kept a delegation in sight of his every move for a month. The old liar never saw this country, and we certainly should have shot him before he got out of it."

"Why, my dear fellow, he never asked you to follow him; besides, he might think the same of you for dogging his trail. You say he never was in the country, but I have heard that he piloted a crowd that got lost safely over the glacier when it—"

"Yes, but that was just an accident. If I had had my way, he never would have got out of this country alive."

That just shows how unreasonable some men can be, and indeed I found numbers of them who could not say enough against West. They pronounced him a humbug and a fraud who was working for the transportation companies.

The next day we traveled along the lakeshore, where gulls swooped and snipes flitted near the water, which was disturbed by the lashings of salmon. We arrived at a tent-town where there were a hundred and forty-six tents and eighty-four rowboats. The outlet was a deep, slow-running stream for about five miles, but from that point the rapids began. The occupants of that town were drying salmon, not prospecting. We found there Robert Hoffman, of Brooklyn, New York, with his jaw broken in five places by an enraged grizzly. Subsequently, he died from the injuries thus received.

About thirty miles below the rapids was another tent-town known as Copper Center. It was situated at the junction of Copper River and the Klutena and is to-day a trading post. Hundreds of outfits had been lost in attempting to boat through the rapids. A man who had been pulled from the water and laid on a drift pile to recuperate said afterwards, when relating his experience, that he had only recovered to realize that he was freezing.

"And, gentlemen, I also found that the Copper River fever had just left me."

We ascended about two hundred feet and traveled along the edge of a tableland. We were away from the humid coast climate, and our pack train kicked up a cloud of dust. The dense undergrowth of alder brush had disappeared, and we could ride out beneath the spruce trees. Wild rose bushes clustered here and there, and trellised over the little side gullies where they held out red-flowered greetings to us. As the weather was warm, we remained over a day at Copper Center, camped 'neath the shady trees and caught brook trout from a clear stream.

Among those who had arrived at Copper Center by pulling sleds and backpacking, many had neglected a previous examination for the necessary qualifications. When they now proved that prospecting was not their natural calling, and that Alaska's springtime did not bud gold leaves, their minds became semi-deranged. We had met a man near the lake who evidently was insane.

On being asked whence he came, he emphatically replied, "From California."

As I, being from California, was ridiculed about the answer, I explained that the transition from that state to Alaska was sufficient to affect the strongest minds. I felt, however, that my brains were not sufficiently scrambled to be addicted to mental storms.

At the rapids, we met another man who was mentally affected, and when asked from what state he hailed, he, too, replied, "From California."

The joke was becoming serious by this time, and a lunatic from some other state was in demand to divert insinuations and relieve suspicion.

At Copper Center, there appeared at our camp a man who talked in a very rambling manner. He was as crazy evidently as a rabbit in the third month of the year. The members of our expedition had gone to a near-by tent town, with the exception of a military officer and a New York sketch artist. They had remained, apparently, to see if this man would be asked the usual question which had recently resulted so embarrassingly to the interrogator. As they appeared so interested, I resolved to prove to them that there were deranged people who had come from other states beside California. With desperation, I asked the expected question.

He straightened himself to a dignified attitude, as he replied, "I am from Humboldt County, California."

In reply to his counter, I lied and said I was from Missouri and California was saved, as far as I was concerned.

At that time, Copper Center was one of those ephemeral towns where the occupants are here today and gone tomorrow. In the wild rush to this country, there were about two prospectors to every hundred invaders, and two others who were willing to learn, while the other ninety-six were waiting for a "strike," as they termed it. The latter busied themselves generally in holding miners' meetings over dog-fights and other such trivial matters. Most of them had never lived outside of the reign of written law and sheriffs and town marshals and mayors, so they held meetings and proceeded to elect those officials.

It was disgusting to a free-born American to see those who had been raised under a monarchical form of government approach Captain Abercrombie about their trivial disputes, as if he were a dictator or, possibly, Solomon. It was so annoyingly un-American that when they came to me inquiring for the Captain, I generally pointed out [Private] James Garrett as the man. He proceeded to fill them up with so much "bughouse" advice that I was obliged to caution him, fearing that he would advise the commission of some overt act done in the name of Captain Abercrombie and the United States of America.

A high clay bank opposite Copper Center had been prospected and found to be, from a monetary standpoint, defunct, bankrupt and busted. As guns and ammunition were plentiful and useless, those who were preparing to leave the country spent whole days in doing nothing but shooting the inoffensive bank, and some day a lead mine may be found there.

The wastefulness of shooting the ammunition away was a characteristic trait of those who had always lived in civilization. A frontiersman never would have done such a thing, but would have given it to those who intended to remain with the country or have cached it in some dry place where at some time it might be of some use to others. This is only one instance. Another was the burning of a large outfit of provisions by some individuals who had become disgusted and were leaving. They had worked hard to pull it there and, rather than leave it to be of some use to wandering wayfarers, they preferred to burn it. Alaska was better off when that sort of people departed.

A short distance from the din and rattle of the "shooters" and the chopping and falling of trees, could be heard the voice of an auctioneer saying, "Now, gentlemen, what am I offered for this article?" Those who had come into the country with two and three years' outfits were selling them for a pittance, and that, too, before they had been there six months.

"I am a married man, and this is no place for me!" said one of their number. "My wife thinks I'm a peach, a blossom, and a hero!"

Then he straightened up, tightened his belt a hole, stroked his unkempt bear, strutted up and down the trail with his hands on his hips and flirted his ragged coat-tails until he had lowered my estimation of his wife's opinion about ninety per cent.

"She thinks I am a loo-loo bird," he continued, "and I feel through my whole system that I ought to be at home *doing* something! You can't imagine how my wife loves me, my person and my ways! Don't talk to me of imaginary millions! I don't want riches, but am going home! Behold, today you see me and tomorrow I'll be gone, flown, vamoosed! Ta, ta, adios!" and that ragged, bedraggled specimen of humanity disappeared down the trail, in a "dog trot." Surely his wife must have been a lovebird of the rarest sort if, behind those whiskers, tangled like last year's nests, she could have recognized any sort of bird, "loo-loo" or otherwise.

Powell again worked with Abercrombie the following year, surveying the trail that was being blazed that summer from Valdez through Keystone Canyon, and then stayed in Alaska for nine more years, alternately surveying and looking for gold.

During his time in the bush, Powell once "winged" a grizzly just as he realized he had used the last round in his .44. The angry bear charged, and Powell took off running. He dove over an embankment as the bear stopped, sniffed the air, and—luckily for Powell—kept going. On another occasion, Powell was caught between a mother bear and her cubs. When the mother charged, it took Powell three minutes to run down the mountain it had just taken him three hours to climb.

In 1899, while searching for the site of West's supposed claim, Powell's shoes gave out, and he wrapped his feet in sacks and kept searching. In the depths of the winter, he finally found Slate Creek—a different Slate Creek from the one of that name near Coldfoot—but the snow was deep, and he had no means of melting water to wash gravel. Realizing that he was risking his life, Powell turned back toward Valdez and, when he came to a trading post, was so starved that he and his companion ate fourteen pounds of moose meat at a single sitting.

The following summer, Powell went back to Slate Creek only to find the site had been overrun with prospectors. While the miners were at a meeting, Powell walked along the deserted creek, where he saw thousands of dollars in dust and nuggets lying around in gold pans and tin cups. Powell would later meet dozens of men on the trail who had only recently heard of Slate Creek and were headed for it. These people had no way of knowing that—long before the news had reached them—all the claims had been staked, and that "they were just going in there to look at other men's gold."[4]

Notes

Epigraph: Powell, *Trailing and Camping in Alaska* (New York: Wessels & Bissell, 1910), 22.

1 Powell, *Trailing and Camping in Alaska*, 21.

2 Ibid., 25.

3 Ibid., 21.

4 Ibid., 225.

26

ARTHUR ARNOLD DIETZ

On the Other Side of Disenchantment Bay

Hardships came to be a matter of course and nothing that happened surprised us in the least. Nothing interested us but gold, and although we had not seen a sign of the precious metal, yet our supply of optimism seemed to be inexhaustible.

After reading the newspaper accounts of "untold treasures" in Alaska, New Yorker Arthur Dietz contracted what he called the "craze." He placed an advertisement for a partner or two to join him on a trip north and, by the following morning's mail, received more than forty responses from clerks, policemen, firemen, even women—with more letters arriving in the afternoon.

From the replies, Dietz selected seventeen men who met and agreed to form the New York and Bridgeport Mining Company. Members included Dietz's physician brother-in-law, a mineralogist, three tool makers, five office clerks, a factory superintendant, a tinsmith, a mail clerk, two civil engineers, and two policemen. The group met on Sundays to make plans and to discuss the works of explorers Perry and Scott, and trained their St. Bernard and Newfoundland dogs to pull sleds loaded with lumber around the city. When the group left the city in February of 1897, they were dressed in matching outfits—heavy sweaters, sombreros, corduroy trousers, and leather boots. Given their costumes and the dogs, the group drew quite a bit of attention as they traveled across the country.

When they reached Seattle, they found it "a maelstrom of raving humanity driven half insane by the desire for gold."[1] Pickpockets and gunmen hung around "like flies about a cider jug,"[2] and houses of ill repute were on every block. "Fakers" hawked worthless contraptions and imitation goods, such as the hundred pounds of dehydrated eggs Dietz and his company bought that turned out to be yellow cornmeal.

Any ship headed for Alaska had been booked long in advance. The New Yorkers had made no prior arrangements and feared that they would be stranded at Puget Sound, but they located a condemned brigantine, the *Blakely*, and joined with others in having it repaired. Once the refurbished ship was loaded with its hundred passengers, each of them traveling with 1,000 pounds of baggage, water almost reached the *Blakely's* decks; but everyone was so anxious to get underway that no one questioned the ship's seaworthiness.

Out at sea, the *Blakely* "rolled and dipped and rode the waves in a bewildering manner."[3] The sailing was so torturous that one man died of seasickness while others lay debilitated in their bunks, unable to escape their own filth. The captain got drunk and closeted himself in his cabin until his liquor ran out, and the ship took on so much water that the passengers and crew were forced to operate mechanical and hand pumps around the clock to keep it afloat. Hurricane-force winds blew twenty-foot waves across the deck, drenching everything above and below and, as was later discovered, ruining much of the cargo. Crates stamped "*Blakely*" were washed overboard and found by passing sailors who, assuming the worst, reported the ship lost at sea.

Despite this troubled passage, Dietz and his companions reached Yakutat in high spirits. Their destination lay toward the McKenzie River, a thousand miles inland in Canada. The local Indians, the Yakutats, advised the men to travel to Disenchantment Bay and then to cross the Malaspina Glacier. After buying additional dogs and sleds from the Indians, the party set out with two guides, Koomanah and Koodleuk.

To get to the glacier, each man had to transport his personal load of a thousand pounds as well as some portion of the communal supplies and equipment. One item the party had with them was an eight-hundred-pound motor with which they planned to generate electricity. As they struggled on foot through forests and ravines, they relayed their outfit on their backs, heads, and shoulders. A decade later, Dietz said that his back still bore the indentations of his pack straps from this part of the journey.

Once on the glacier, four men wearing snowshoes broke trail while the rest of the party followed, each man on a sled pulled by four dogs. By day's end, they were exhausted after covering only ten or fifteen miles. They hunkered down during a blizzard and woke to find they were buried in snow.

With all that reading and advance planning, the members of the New York and Bridgeport Mining Company believed that they had prepared for all contingencies. As Dietz explains here, the glacier would teach them otherwise.

ARTHUR ARNOLD DIETZ

*On the Other Side of Disenchantment Bay**

Imagine, if you can, a rolling sea of ice which stretches away to meet the horizon on all sides. There is nothing above but the light blue sky, nothing below but the snow-covered ice, modeled into hills and hollows, much the same as a treeless stretch of rolling landscape. The surface of the glacier is always windswept, so that here and there, where the ice is bare, the dazzling whiteness of the snow is augmented by the blinding brilliancy of the reflected light from these ice mirrors.

At first, this brilliant scene seemed to fascinate us but, as we toiled heroically on, the glinting flashes of reflected light gradually revealed to us the desolation that surrounded us and threatened to devour us.

Although we all wore blue or smoked glasses made like automobile goggles, some of the men began to feel the effects of snow-blindness within a short time after we reached the glacier. At first, we began to lose control of our feet. Unable to see ahead on account of the piercing glare of reflected light, we tried to walk on blindly and found it impossible. Whenever we managed to open our eyes, the surface of the ice seemed only to be a few inches away and we were completely bewildered.

We tried to reinforce the glasses by covering our faces with red handkerchiefs in which two small holes were cut for eyes. This plan gave little relief and we were unable to refrain from rubbing our eyelids, which caused them to become very much inflamed and sore. At times, the pain became almost unbearable. My eyes felt just as if someone was rubbing sand into them, and my head became giddy. I have been told that men often go insane with the pain, and had our party not come prepared with a large assortment of glasses of different colors, I am sure some of us would have met this fate. Even the natives who live in the arctic regions are not immune from the attacks of snow blindness and, not being able to secure smoked glasses, often suffer more than white men.

The only life that is seen anywhere on the glacier is the ptarmigan, or fool-hen as they are known, a sort of morbid species of chicken. Its eyes are protected by being surrounded by a black disk fringed with red. In attempting to prevent snow blindness, the natives use nature's plan and paint a portion

*From *Mad Rush for Gold in Frozen North* (1914), 105–15 and 118–26.

of their faces around their eyes with black soot and stain the edge with the juice of berries. Some of the men of our party tried this plan, but did not find it was [as] good as the smoked glasses. When the natives painted their faces in this way, they presented an extremely horrid appearance and looked like demons as they trudged along.

In the middle of the day, when the sun was highest, the air became comparatively warm, but the temperature near the ground was very cold. At times, we tugged at the sleds with the dogs and perspired freely with no clothing except a thin shirt about the upper portion of our bodies, but our legs would always have to be covered with heavy "mucklocks" [mukluks] or moccasins.

During the first two or three days we were on the glacier, we could hear water gurgling under the surface, but not a drop could be seen anywhere. In places, these subterranean streams would cut deep crevasses in the ice under the surface and we had to be very careful to test the ice with sticks before venturing ahead in order to prevent breaking through. From the very first, we had many narrow escapes because we did not take the necessary precautions.

After we had traveled over the very rough and hummocky ice for at least fifteen miles, we left these gurgling streams behind, but the crevasses in the ice were ever present. Some of them were no more than a few inches or a foot wide, and we could step across them with ease.

In other places, the crevasses and cracks were much wider and were packed full of snow, forming a bridge, and we were able to cross them in safety. The snow never completely filled the crevasses but was plugged tight in the mouth for several feet. Sometimes we could push a stick down through the snow, but it was packed together tightly enough that we could walk over it safely with snow-shoes.

Of course this was a very dangerous piece of business, but we were both ignorant and fearless and, up until that time, did not take risks into consideration. Whenever we saw a streak of snow across the ice, we knew it filled the mouth of a crevasse.

At times, when our entire party would cross a snow-plugged crevasse at the same point, the snow in the center would sag down several feet and, although we realized it would only be a question of time before someone would go through, we plodded on doggedly without giving such a possibility so much as a passing thought.

The attitude of our Indian guides, whose names were Koomanah and Koodleuk, toward us in our ignorance and foolhardy risks, gave us a good insight into their character. They could not understand why we did not know as much as they did regarding the ice and snow and were loath in giving us information.

Although they were very cautious themselves, they paid no attention to us whatever and, if we attempted something in our ignorance of conditions that was extremely hazardous, they never warned us or paid any attention to us whatever. Then, when we would ask them a question and they could not answer it, they would not say they did not know but would stand mute. Until we learned to understand their peculiarities, we were often very much provoked at their strange actions. After a time, we learned to watch how they did things and then attempt to imitate them.

Another condition that made the first stages of our journey very laborious was the fact that we were continually traveling up grade. Where the grade was real heavy, the dogs were unable to draw all our goods at one time and we were compelled to leave a portion of them cached behind and then go back after them. This doubled the amount of work to be done and greatly hindered our progress. At times, the surface was very rough and we were compelled to choose our path carefully in order to avoid the continual overturning of the sleds.

It is almost impossible to set down in cold type the hardships we endured at this time. We were all so intent upon getting gold that nothing else seemed to enter into the scheme of our lives. Each man lived for himself alone.

During the first week or more on the glacier, we toiled on and it was seldom that one man spoke to another. We would travel along for six or eight hours without a word being spoken except to the dogs, which would usually be "All right dogs," or "Go ahead, dogs." Then, when we stopped for rest, everyone seemed too weary to talk or enjoy any social intercourse with the others of the party. At that time, we very much resembled a party of deaf mutes.

After we had been on the glacier a week or more, our habits began to assume a definite plan and a sort of daily program was carried out. Once a day, we stopped and put up a tarpaulin to act as a shield against the cold winds that were constantly blowing over the surface of the ice. Fire was started in our cooking lamps and the day's cooking done, which consisted in heating some beans and making flapjacks. After the meal, we usually were ready to retire, and when we did not take time to pitch our tents, we would crawl into our sleeping bags and sleep on the loaded sleds out in the open.

Every few days, and sometimes every other day, we would pitch our tents and cook some evaporated potatoes and beans and make coffee. I have no doubt now that our rations were very poor, but after a hard day's work, everything that was fit to eat always tasted good and we thoroughly enjoyed our meals.

From the first, I avoided eating bacon or pork to any extent, having heard of sailors being terribly afflicted by scurvy in this way. Our cooking on the glacier was done with oil lamps, which we secured from the natives and which seemed to produce more smoke than heat. After a pot had been hanging over a blaze long enough to cook some food, there would be an accumulation of half an inch of soot on the bottom. Every time we moved our tent, this soot was scraped off and left on the top of the snow. The relief that this one black spot in the landscape gave to our eyes can hardly be imagined. I got more satisfaction out of seeing those dirty black spots of soot than anything else on the glacier.

Already we began to find our supply of oil for cooking purposes getting low, and we had not yet reached the summit or backbone of the glacier which was somewhere near the center. Because of this fact, and our desire to make as few stops as possible, many of our men started to eat our evaporated articles uncooked. This caused them to get very thirsty and, as they walked along, they got in the habit of eating snow. Almost every member of the party developed bad attacks of sore throat, which at that time could be partly relieved by my brother-in-law, the physician of the party, who had brought a large quantity of medicines along.

Snow blindness also caused us much trouble at this time, which, unlike the sore throat, could not be relieved. Some of the men howled with pain, and I feared they would go insane. When the sunlight began to fade, we would be relieved somewhat, but the semi-darkness was very short. During this time, the Aurora Borealis was so brilliant that it was almost as bright as day and it was difficult to sleep at any time.

On April 25th, an accident happened that awakened us from the indifferent stupor into which the gold craze had plunged us and, for the first time since we started, we found time for reflection. The snow had covered the ice completely, making it very hard for us to pick our way. We had been plodding on doggedly with no thought of danger with the heaviest loads ahead of us so that, in case of a breakdown, the lighter loaded sleds could come up and help out. My brother-in-law, the physician, who had a light load consisting of the medicines and the more valuable parts of our equipment, was two sleds ahead of me, and six sleds were ahead of him.

The sleds were about a hundred feet apart and no one paid any attention to those ahead or behind and no noise broke the silence except the creaking of the loaded sleds and the occasional shout of a man to his dogs which, on account of the stillness, could be heard for a great distance.

About noon, as we were going up a steep incline, suddenly, in front of me, I heard the howl of dogs and then a man shout. I looked up just in time to see my brother-in-law's sled disappear. It just seemed to drop out of the landscape in a flash. I realized what had happened—my sister's husband lost! His four dogs and sled containing all our valuables gone!

The awfulness of the tragedy seemed to settle upon us in an instant; then when I recovered and tried to make haste to the spot, it seemed to retard me. Cheered on by one last forlorn hope that we might be able to rescue him, I rushed forward and within a moment came to the hole in the snow that covered the mouth of that treacherous crevasse. The opening was about ten or twelve feet in diameter and, as we looked down into that terrible abyss, all our hopes sank within us. My first glimpse made me feel sick at heart. I was convinced that nothing could be done, yet I could not help looking down into that cavern with a glimmer of hope that was worse than torture.

I will not attempt to say how deep that crevasse was. We could see down probably two hundred and fifty feet. Below this, there was nothing but a hopeless blackness which, as our vision arose, faded into dark green which grew lighter as you looked up, and near the top was a beautiful shade of emerald.

But the beauty of the thing was a hollow mockery! As we looked, we thought we could hear faint distant sounds, which, as we listened, raised and lowered the last glimmer of our hopeless hope. There before us was that cold lifeless thing, immovable and commonplace, as if nothing had happened.

We decided to let down a rope and, after much trouble and delay, due to our unnerved condition mostly, we got the work started. Before we had let down a hundred feet of the rope into the hole, it began to get very heavy and required several men to hold it. We let all of our five hundred feet of rope down, and that yawning gulf still said "more, more." Who could have said how much more? It was no use.

We had to give up. Our oil was getting short and we had to be moving or we would all be lost on the glacier, which was beginning to crack badly with the snow melting. We had trouble tearing ourselves away from the scene of the tragedy and leaving my brother-in-law behind to his fate. What a fate!

While the men were still on the glacier, a second man, Weiden, went insane from the pain of snow blindness and the lack of proper food, and then fell into a crevasse. Each man became driven by the idea of self-preservation and thought only of himself and no longer of the group. When a third member of the party was lost in another crevasse, the men realized it was useless to attempt a rescue and quickly resumed their onward trek. After fifty days of crossing the glacier, the men reached the far edge of it and resumed their constant talk of gold.

Back on dry land, they lashed the giant motor to poles and carried it like a "Soudan" chair. They grew tired and built a wagon to transport it, but the wagon's wheels bogged down in the mucky ground and, in the end, they abandoned the engine somewhere in the wilderness. They then made better time relaying their goods, in stretches of five and ten miles, up the trail.

The company was by then no longer headed for the McKenzie River but had turned northwest toward Alaska's Tanana River. Some of the party, convinced that gold covered every surface in Alaska, dug into the sides of mountains along the trail. However, anything the men presented to the group's mineralogist turned out to be merely "fool's gold." They blazed their trail through alders and brambles, and shot game and caught fish to supplement their supplies. Another man died of what the men feared was typhoid fever contracted from the ubiquitous mosquitoes that fell into their food.

As winter approached, the party stopped and built a cabin on what they hoped was the Tanana River. They spent the following seven months holed up, telling stories and confessing secrets they'd never revealed to anyone. As winter wore on, the darkness was so extended that Dietz thought that the sun had burned out. The men became depressed, staying cocooned in their sleeping bags, too enervated to change out of their dirty clothes, emerging only for meals. Some of the group turned to prayers and Bible reading, straining eyes already afflicted with snow blindness. Three of the group asked for their share of the supplies and headed downriver toward Dawson, never to be heard from again. Dietz's only comfort was in the companionship of his St. Bernard, Kodiak, who served alternately as a pillow and foot warmer on cold nights.

With the coming of spring, the company's eagerness for gold hunting was renewed, and the men began to prospect in earnest. They burned wood to thaw the dirt, dug shafts in the ground below, hauled mud out with a windlass, and operated a crib and rocker to wash for gold. Then the mineralogist died of an inexplicable illness, and three other men, who disappeared while out prospecting, were never found.

By the time their second winter in Alaska set in, the company's food supplies were depleted and their clothes and boots were worn out. Only eight members of the original group of eighteen survived, and they became obsessed with one thought—reaching home alive. They waited for the river to freeze, dressed in clothing belonging to their deceased companions, and wrapped their feet in rags. In November or December—Dietz had lost all sense of time—they set out.

By happenstance, they met a Swede who was living with a party of Indians, and the Swede advised them to follow the Copper River down to the coast. Dietz's map was the best available but was so inaccurate that he never found the river. Instead, he and his companions came to another glacier and knew they would only reach the coast if they crossed it. When Dietz remembered that he had stashed seven hundred dollars behind a log in the cabin, he shrugged off the loss. By then, money and gold had lost their value. "I am firmly convinced that if we had accidentally struck the richest gold mine in the world, we would have left it untouched. What was gold to us now? Gold was simply a yellow metal."[4]

In the six weeks the group spent crossing this second glacier, another man died of frostbite. Their flour ran out, and they killed and ate some of their dogs. At the Pacific Ocean, they ate rotten fish they found on the beach, then slaughtered and ate Dietz's St. Bernard, Kodiak.

When a US revenue cutter spotted their driftwood fire and picked them up, only four of the party were alive, three others having died in their ragged sleeping bags. In Seattle, Dietz read in the newspaper that he had returned with a half million dollars in gold. At his home in New York, he learned that his family had received word that the *Blakely* was lost at sea and had long believed him dead.

Dietz concluded that the stories of Alaska's limitless gold had been circulated by "some inhuman brute [who] organized that mad gold-rush for selfish gain."[5] He moved his family to Los Angeles, where he became a YMCA physical education director. Although he suffered from snow blindness the rest of his life, he considered himself lucky. Two of the other survivors were totally blind.

Notes

Epigraph: Arthur Arnold Dietz, *Mad Rush for Gold in Frozen North* (Los Angeles: Times-Mirror Printing and Binding House, 1914), 160.

1 Dietz, *Mad Rush for Gold*, 21.

2 Ibid.

3 Ibid., 29.

4 Ibid., 225.

5 Ibid., 13.

27

JOHN F. STACEY

Twenty-One Days from Rampart City

When a friend of mine came to me and said, "Why don't you go to Alaska?" I said I thought I was too old to take such a trip. I was fifty-three at that time.... When I talked it over with my wife, she said ... "If you really want to go, I will try and get along some way, for I don't want to put anything in your way."

With the newspapers filled with stories of riches in Alaska, John Stacey was inspired to answer an advertisement for the Moulton Klondike Mining Company of Manchester, New Hampshire. He and eleven other men were accepted and each put up a thousand dollars to finance the trip.

The "Moultons," as Stacey called his group, were scheduled to sail from Seattle on the twentieth of May but received word that the steamship company wanted them in Seattle on the tenth of April. They hustled across the continent only to find that, at Puget Sound, no boat awaited them. To pass the time, they explored the city, parts of which were so dangerous that a person took his life into his hands if he ventured there. Crooks abounded, one of whom approached the Moulton men and offered to get them to "Juno" faster than they would get there on the boat they were scheduled to sail on.

When their ship, the *Laurador,* did arrive, three hundred and thirty-six ticketed passengers were waiting to board. Transportation of liquor to Alaska was illegal, and, when officials found crates of spirits onboard, they ordered them off the boat. Just before the boat sailed, the same boxes of spirits were reloaded, the same officials came onboard, and, after inspecting the cargo, declared all in order and allowed the boat to sail. "In some way," Stacey wrote, "their eyes seemed to have been blinded since the last inspection."[1]

The ship reached Dutch Harbor, where the verdant growth and rolling landscape reminded Stacey of Minnesota. A local storekeeper told him that it never froze there and that the temperature never varied more than ten degrees, summer and winter. Stacey thought the place would be good for farming, but the storekeeper told him the daily rains kept the ground so wet that nothing could grow. Well, Stacey suggested, surely cattle could be grazed in that place. That, too, was impossible, the storekeeper said. He could turn his two cows out for only an hour each day before he had to bring them in so that they wouldn't die of hoof rot.

At St. Michael, the *Laurador's* passengers had to offload their own provisions. Thus, the Moulton group helped unload eight hundred tons of jumbled cargo in order to get at their own twenty tons—with the last item off the boat a sack of their beans. Meanwhile, a customs officer came onboard and seized the liquor, but it was brought onboard again, supposedly under the governor's orders. Governor's orders or not, Stacey wrote, it was still illegally transported liquor.

The Moultons loaded their supplies onto a riverboat and started up the Yukon. Five minutes into the trip, the boat struck a rock that knocked a hole through its bottom, just beneath the space where the Moultons' outfit was stored. They hauled their twenty tons ashore while repairs were made, then loaded them back onboard again.

"Floating" sandbars in the Yukon River changed position overnight, so even the best pilots couldn't know where they'd be located. Vessels on the Yukon often ran aground and had to be towed off. The Moultons had been planning to go all the way to Dawson, but, as their riverboat was being towed off yet another sandbar, they realized that, at the speed they were going, they would never get there before freeze-up. Thus, they decided to get off at nearby Rampart City.

Once ashore, they found an empty knoll that they christened Knob Hill. They carried their twenty tons of goods to the top and set up their tents. The prospectors who had already settled at Rampart City had cut down all of the trees in the vicinity, and the nearest still standing were five miles away—four miles up the Yukon, and another mile up the Big Minook—so that's where the Moultons went. They cut down a hundred and sixty-five spruces, floated them back to Rampart City, and, at the base of Knob Hill, looked up the quarter-mile slope that led to the top.

"Boys," said Al Moulton, the group's president, "we are not used to this kind of work, but just the same, we will look at these hundred and sixty-five logs and then look up the hill and keep up our courage and we shall get it done."[2]

They tied ropes around their bodies and built slings from which they suspended the logs so that they could claw their way uphill with their hands. Some logs were so heavy it took four men to carry one, but in three days, they had completed the task.

To figure out how to build a cabin, the men looked around at those constructed by their neighbors. They chinked the sidewalls with mud and moss and built the roof of poles with a layer of birch bark covered with moss and mud. The warmer bunks were on top, but Stacey drew one on the bottom in the corner, where he felt the cold "very acutely on many a night."[3] The party set up their two Yukon stoves, sawed boards for a floor, a table, and doors, and stored their two-year supply of beans, bacon, flour, canned milk, and dried fruit in a second cabin, nicknamed "the shack."

Stacey surprised his fellows with his baking—pies of apricots, peaches, and raisins; yeast breads; and doughnuts fried in bacon grease. Away from the warmth of the cabin, meals were more basic. In the winter, Stacey and his friend Freeman were working out of a smaller cabin the men had built farther from town, closer to the diggings. Out on the trail, they were blowing on frozen biscuits so that they could gnaw off a bite. "If my wife could see me now and she didn't cry," said Freeman, "I would never speak to her again."[4]

Winter prospecting—with all that wood cutting, fire building, thawing, and digging—was hard work, and, by the time spring arrived, the Moulton Klondike Mining Company had found no gold. Al Moulton and some of the men wanted to stay, but others, like Stacey, were homesick and ready to leave. Stacey decided he'd travel out with a man whose last name, like the group's leader, was Moulton, but Stacey's companion was "Old Man" Moulton.

In the following passage, Stacey describes part of his journey down the Yukon as he left the goldfields and headed for home.

JOHN F. STACEY

*Twenty-One Days from Rampart City**

Freeman did his best to persuade me to stay over till another fall and then we would begin early in the season and work that hole and see what there was there. But I simply could not stay another year. I had left a wife and small

*From *To Alaska for Gold* (n.d.), 59–67.

daughter at home and I must get back to them. We all went in to Rampart City to the big cabin on the Yukon, just managing to get all our stuff in on sleds before the snow went, otherwise we should have had to carry it all in on our backs.

The twenty-second of May, the Yukon broke up and it was a grand sight. The ice was anywhere from five to six or seven feet thick and, when the water coming down from above and from the mountains around got under the ice, there was a sound as of the booming of many cannons. The ice formed a dam below us so that the water rose fifty-five feet that night right in front of our cabin, but it did not reach to where we were. One large cake thirty-five feet wide and probably seventy-five feet high was left standing on end in front of a man's store. It had to be blown up by dynamite for fear when it melted it might fall over on someone.

Now we could begin to think of starting home. Al Moulton and five others were going to stay, but, as for the rest of us, the quicker we could get started the better we were suited. There was a man who had a small schooner who would carry men down to St. Michael for twenty-five dollars if they boarded themselves. I had partly made a trade with him when I had another proposition offered. Mr. Mills, the man who had the drop in the shaft and broke his ankle and was still on crutches, had a small flat-bottomed boat, eighteen feet long and three feet beam, and he wanted to know if I would not go down with him.

So old man Moulton and I agreed to go with him as soon as the ice was cleared out enough to be safe. We talked with the old settlers and they thought the fifth of June it would be safe, and of course the whole town knew we were going to start with this small boat on the thousand-mile trip down the Yukon with all our luggage. When mine was weighed later it proved to amount to two hundred and twenty pounds and, with that of the other men and our own weight, the boat settled down into the water until there was only about four and one-half inches from the water line to the edge of the boat.

Everybody was there to see us start. The Yukon is anywhere from four to twenty-five miles wide in different places. In some places it is calm and in some others it is just like the ocean with monstrous waves. We had thought we could drift with the current but it was not safe to get into the current.

It was the fifth of June when we finally felt sure the ice would be out of the river and made our start. It was a beautiful morning when we got under way about ten o'clock, but in half an hour it was raining hard and the wind began to blow. We had to keep close to the shore and had to row all the time.

Where we were at this time, the sun was visible about eighteen hours out of every twenty-four and it was daylight all the time. The first night, the other men lay down for about six hours while I rowed alone. I had to keep close to the shore and be on my guard all the time to keep us right side up, as we were so heavily loaded. It was a lonesome night as I thought of those at home and wondered if I should ever reach there.

The next day, we came to a place where the river took a turn to the left. We were following along the right shore and, as it was about five or six miles across the river at this point, we thought we could save considerable by cutting across the corner, instead of keeping with the shore. It was calm and we tried it, but just as we got about halfway across, the wind came up, and how it did blow! It kept us busy heading waves so as not to be swamped and we did not land just where we expected to. But we managed to get back to the right hand shore and around the curve after a struggle.

When we left Rampart City, they told us to keep to the right side of the river. The Yukon is full of small branches which they call slues [sloughs] and, in following the shore, one is apt to get into one of these instead of keeping on the main river and perhaps get off the course before he discovers it. All the slues leading off from the right side, they assured us, would lead us back to the Yukon sooner or later, if we should get into any of them. But if we should get into any on the left they would take us off into Bering Sea. So for this reason we tried to keep to the right all the way.

As I had not had any rest for some time and everything seemed quiet, I thought, after we got around the curve, I would lie down for a little sleep and let the other two look after the boat. I don't know how long I slept, but they woke me up in a hurry for my help. There had been a shower (we often had several in a day, but not severe ones) and then the wind had risen and now we were nearing one of the slues we had heard about. At this point, the main river followed the left shore while the right shore, where we were, led off into the branch river. The point of land in between curved around in such a manner as to cause a regular whirlpool where the water came down from above and struck against it. We didn't like to get into this whirlpool and remembering what the man had told us we decided to take the slue, for we should probably come back into the Yukon a little further down.

We did but it took twenty-six hours hard rowing and then we had made five miles. We estimated we had traveled nearly one hundred miles in and out among the mountains. It was worse than the detours one finds in the main roads of today. We were working hard and going one hundred miles to make five. It made us rather discouraged but the water was fine and the river also and we got in one whole day's travel without special event.

Then we struck a shower. At first it rained on shore, but in a little while we went into it, and it rained on the water but not on the shore, and we got wet. Then we came to another slue. And this time the whirlpool was worse than before and spray flew in all directions. We didn't know what to do, but Mills said, "Don't go there; go to the right." So to the right we went. The mouth of this slue was a half mile wide and it was a pretty good-sized river.

We saw a man on the shore at this lonely place and asked him where he was going.

"Going to H——," was his reply, and it didn't encourage us greatly. We asked him if he had any folks at home and he said he had a wife, but the last letter she wrote him, she told him not to come home until he struck it. We also asked him if he had heard or seen anything of the small schooner I had intended to come down on. He told us she had gone all to pieces in the middle of the river, near where we were. Said he saw her just break up all of a sudden without any apparent cause and the men swim around in the water a while and then go down. We could see some of the wreckage at a little distance. So we went on, thinking we might be worse off after all.

As we went into this slue, we found ourselves facing a big snowcapped mountain and the river was so crooked and winding that we found ourselves facing this same mountain three times in the next three days. For it took us three days this time to get back into the Yukon. And we had made about twenty-five miles on our journey.

During all that time, we rowed by shores that were perpendicular, sometimes of rock and sometimes dirt, but always perpendicular. No place could we land. We came to one quiet bay we had to cross. We thought it looked about four miles across, but it took us over four hours to reach the other side, and the natives there told us it was between nineteen and twenty miles. They also said it was at times a very wild and treacherous piece of water, but when we crossed it was still as a mirror.

In this native camp so far from all civilization, we were surprised to see a white woman. She was tall and good-looking and we thought we would speak to her and see if there was anything we could do for her. But she would make no answer to our questions and showed no interest. We could even take her hand and she would not resist but seemed to be perfectly passive. We could not solve the mystery of her presence there, where there was no other white person, and with her mind apparently a blank. We thought she must have been abandoned there by some white man and that her situation had driven her insane.

We were glad of the chance here to get some meat, as we had not been good enough shots to get any ducks or geese as we had planned. So we bought a red salmon from a native. It measured a little over three feet in length, and we paid him two quarts of flour for it. He took his bandana handkerchief from his neck and spread it out for us to put the flour in and, picking it up by the corners, went off well pleased with his bargain.

After making a good supper from half this fish, I remarked to the others that I was going to row all night. I was really the only able-bodied man there. Mills was still disabled from his broken foot and could only handle the rudder, and old man Moulton was not very strong for rowing. The night that followed was one of the hardest of my experience. We were following absolutely perpendicular shores and all along the shore was driftwood. The wind, which usually had blown up stream, now changed to an oblique direction, and it took all the strength I possessed to keep the boat off the driftwood. I had to pull for the center all the time and Mills helped all he could with the rudder. We expected any minute to be smashed to pieces and, if we had been, we could not have gotten ashore. After two hours and fifteen minutes of this harrowing experience, we found a small cove and we went in and tied up our boat. It was the first chance we had had for a good sleep, and Mills and I lay right down in the boat and slept, while Moulton went on shore and made a fire and slept by that.

Sometime in the night, I heard away off to the right a whistle that sounded like a river boat whistle. In the morning, I took a walk through the woods and after about four miles of tramping came to another river which I was told was the Andreafski and a tributary of the Yukon.

We stayed another day and night in our cove before we dared to go out on the river again. By this time, the wind was again blowing up stream. We went about two miles, when we came to the mouth of the Andreafski, and I told the others I had rowed against the wind as long as I wanted to. Now, I had found a river that went with the wind and I was going to take it wherever it went. So we went up the Andreafski River. And up there about four miles, we found the very river boat whose whistle I had heard a few nights before.

I went on shore and inquired for the captain. He was pointed out to me and I asked him what he would take three men, their baggage and boat down to St. Michael for.

"Five dollars apiece and board yourselves," was his answer. I jumped at the chance. "Come around about five o'clock and the boys will help you on board," he said.

I went back and told the boys we must eat a good meal, as we should have no chance to get anything more for thirty-six hours. We had one hundred and thirty-five miles more to go. So we cooked the rest of the salmon and ate as much as we could. About five o'clock, they helped us aboard. Mills and I found a small boat covered with canvas up on the upper deck and in this we spread our blankets and had a good sleep.

The first thing we heard the next morning was when someone called out, "Come on, you boys, wake up, if you want any breakfast."

Another voice said, "Oh, they are going to board themselves."

About half past ten, we got up and washed. At dinner time they all formed in line and we stood with the rest and marched in to dinner. They had a grand good dinner. I had the first piece of fresh meat I had tasted for over a year. We amused ourselves till supper time and then went to supper. We expected to pay extra for the meals, but nothing was ever said about it.

As soon as we got in to St. Michael, they helped us off with our boat and we rowed ashore, just twenty-one days after we left Rampart City.

Before he had gone to Alaska, Stacey had been in poor health, but, while in the north, he slept outside in temperatures below zero and never had so much as a cold. When he returned home, he was stronger and in better health than when he'd left. Nevertheless, he said, good health was the only thing he "brought with [him] from that cold region."[5]

Notes

Epigraph: John F. Stacey and Mrs. John W. Davis, *To Alaska for Gold* (n.p., n.d.), 11.

1 Stacey and Davis, *To Alaska for Gold*, 18.

2 Ibid., 34.

3 Ibid., 35.

4 Ibid., 45.

5 Ibid., 42.

Captain W. B. Brightman's House at Killisnoo, n.d.
Alaska State Library, P1-103.
Vincent Soboleff Photograph Collection.

Man with Native women and children standing outdoors in front of log cabin, ca. 1886–1887. Alaska State Library, P88-044. William H. Partridge Collection.

EPILOGUE

A Cabin on the Edge of the Forest

"Alaska," says Hennessey, friend and chorus to Mr. Dooley, "is nawthin' but an iceberg with a few seals roostin' on it" and, in making this pithy statement, he quite correctly reflects the view of the great majority of the citizens of the United States concerning this great, though still so-little known province.

Anna Shane Devin,
"Homes and Home-Makers of Alaska," 1906

In June of 1909, a glitzy affair known as the Alaska Yukon Pacific Exposition (AYPE) opened in Seattle. By the time its gates closed in mid-October, 3.7 million people—three times the population of the state of Washington—had attended.[1] In spite of a grand diversity of attractions, the fair's underlying purpose was "to extol the riches, wonder, and beauty of Alaska."[2] The show was so spectacular that anyone who—at that late date—still believed that Alaska was nothing more than "an iceberg with a few seals roostin' on it" would have surely been convinced otherwise.

The 250 acres of fairgrounds were covered with imposing structures—some in the classical style and one built entirely of massive logs—specially constructed to highlight countries and states on the Pacific Rim and beyond. Buildings were devoted to subjects such as music, education, good roads, and agriculture. In the course of a single day, an attendee could take in a cattle show, ride in a hot-air balloon, and observe a reenactment of the Battle of Gettysburg. Exotic dance shows were so racy that a morality police patrol periodically shut them down.[3]

Alaska was well represented at the exposition, with an Alaska Monument, an Arctic Brotherhood Building, and an Alaska Building. On a visit to the fair,

Myra Tweedale, Dolly Bourn, and others in front of Mrs. Steven's (?) log house, Skagway, ca. 1899. Alaska State Library, P99-188. F. B. Bourn Photograph Collection.

President William Howard Taft toured the Alaska Building and panned for gold. There were displays of Alaska's minerals and ores, fish canneries, Indian and Eskimo artifacts, and Native crafts. The unofficial fair mascot, someone named Caribou Bill, had mushed overland from Valdez to Seattle and was on hand with his team of Huskies. At the Eskimo Village, fairgoers watched Native dancers, visited igloos, and took dogsled rides. A heavily guarded cage holding a million dollars' worth of Alaska's gold dust and nuggets was lowered each night into an underground vault,[4] and the Pay Streak amusement area featured the "Fairy Gorge Tickler," where patrons paid a dime to race through a plaster mountain then career downhill in carts that rotated and zigzagged down a rickety hillside.

But the rosy picture presented in Seattle was only part of the story. No matter how elaborate the fair's exhibits and displays were, they could convey a mere fraction of Alaska's majesty. Besides, the exposition made no mention of Alaska's implacable realities—a largely inhospitable environment; extreme variations in temperature and weather; rugged, even treacherous terrain; a paucity of arable land; and an intensely short growing season. Was it any wonder that Alaska was having a hard time attracting, much less retaining, settlers?

Few of the writers in this collection, except for Caroline Willard and Hudson Stuck, could be considered Alaskans. Addison Powell was in Alaska for ten years before he returned to what he called "the dyspepsia of civilization."[5] Robert Dunn and John Muir each made multiple trips north, and William Abercrombie and Josiah Spurr returned in the scope of their duties. They were visitors, nonetheless. Like Joseph Grinnell, they wrote about Alaska "for the folks at home."

In 1904, D. A. McKenzie, a prospector from Coldfoot, told a delegation of touring US congressmen that the miners of Alaska weren't like those down south. In California, a man could take his family with him, plant a garden, settle down. The Alaskan prospector owned what he could load on his sled and often travelled alone. He had to deal with the high cost of living, the fact that his supplies all had to be shipped in, and the dearth of available women. The congressmen asked McKenzie how many of the miners he knew would remain in Alaska. "We all intend to get out as soon as we can get a stake,"[6] he said. And, if anyone needed confirmation of what McKenzie said, he or she only had to look around at the abandoned cabins and deserted mining camps that littered the countryside.

Despite this dire prediction, some people were choosing to stay in Alaska.

Single-story log house of J. Morrow, ca. 1905–1909.
Alaska State Library, P137-143.
Alfred G. Simmer Photograph Collection.

In the years between 1869 and 1910, the number of Native peoples in Alaska had remained at roughly 25,000. In the same period, the population of non-Natives had grown from 2,000 to 30,450—and some of those new residents were undoubtedly miners or former miners, since they comprised the majority of those who had gone to Alaska during those years.

In her 1906 article for *Pacific Monthly* magazine, Anna Shane Devin wrote about some of the "larger and more commodious" homes being built in Alaska. She assured her readers that people actually were settling in the far north, for "there are many who already love Alaska and would not leave it."[7] One cottage in Sitka, described by Devin as "the apotheosis of a log-cabin," was set in a clearing on the edge of the forest. It had a thriving garden with "brave blooming" flowers, a sitting room with a bay window, oak wainscoting, and windows hung with dimity curtains. An open fireplace "gave promise of leaping flames … and one could readily imagine how the dark-red carpet would catch and reflect the glow of the fire."[8]

Such cozy domestication was taking place on another level elsewhere in Alaska. Hudson Stuck described 1904 Fairbanks as a place "of feverish trade and feverish vice," where stores were "open all day and half the night, and dance-halls and gambling dens open all night and half the day."[9] The town had been so wild and wooly that local prostitutes had presented a diamond star to the chief of police and the weekly cleanup of gold had to be guarded by armed horsemen as it was carried in from the creeks.

A mere six years later, Fairbanks had changed. The miners had cleared out, and the gambling dens and dance halls had disappeared. Shops were shut down early, and a railroad and a telegraph connected the creeks to town. Fairbanks had become a "substantial place" with a library, two hospitals, "good business houses," and electrically lit, steam-heated homes. The populace was so cultivated that "the local choral society [was] lamenting the customary dearth of tenors for its production of 'The Messiah.'"[10]

By 1910, there were other changes in Alaska. The dispute over the boundary between British Columbia and Alaska had been resolved. Although the map would continue to be drawn well into the twentieth century,[11] Alaska's contours—its mountain ranges and rivers—were more defined. Trails and roads were being built, and the focus was shifting from gold to copper, oil, and coal. A telegraph line united Alaska with the rest of the nation and brought contemporaneous news.

Some of these new Alaskans may have been busily grafting the civilization they had known and loved in whatever places they had left behind onto their new lives in Alaska. But there were others who had little use for news or roads or maps and whose fondest dream was to get as far away as possible from those dimity curtains and the *Messiah*. These were the descendents of Huckleberry Finn, who, in lighting out for the territory, had no intention of ever looking back. If their kind wanted only independence, solitude, and peace, they needn't have worried. For them, Alaska offered something special.

In 1903, Jack London wrote in the *Atlantic Monthly* of the endurance and single-mindedness of the sort of "grizzled"[12] pioneers who went to Alaska and got hooked. They couldn't leave, for "the spell of it gripped hold of them and would not let them go."[13] Flinty loners plodding out into the wilds, they were incapable of being cured. If they tried to quit Alaska, they invariably went back. London was writing at the dawn of the twentieth century, but in certain measure his words hold true today:

> A man may wander from the trail for a hundred days, and just as he is congratulating himself that at last he is treading virgin soil, he will come upon some ancient and dilapidated cabin and forget his disappointment in wonder at the man who reared the logs. Still, if one wanders from the trail far enough and deviously enough, he may chance upon a few thousand square miles which he may have all to himself.[14]

That is Alaska.

Notes

Epigraph: Anna Shane Devin, "Homes and Home-Makers of Alaska," *Pacific Monthly* (June 1906), 680.

1 *Alaska Yukon Pacific Exposition: Seattle's Forgotten World's Fair,* written by Christina Ruddy, produced and directed by John Forsen (Fidget, 2009), DVD.

2 Shauna O'Reilly and Brennan O'Reilly, *Alaska Yukon Pacific Exposition* (Charleston, WV: Arcadia Publishing, 2009), 11.

3 *Alaska Yukon Pacific Exposition,* DVD.

4 O'Reilly and O'Reilly, *Alaska Yukon Pacific Exposition*, 62–64, and 76.

5 Addison M. Powell, *Trailing and Camping in Alaska* (New York: Wessels & Bissell, 1910), 379.

6 US Congress, Senate, Committee on Territories, *Conditions in Alaska* (Washington, DC: Government Printing Office, 1904), 3–4.

7 Devin, "Homes and Home-Makers of Alaska," 680.

8 Ibid.

9 Hudson Stuck, *Ten Thousand Miles with a Dog Sled: A Narrative of Winter Travel in Interior Alaska* (New York: Charles Scribner's Sons, 1914), 251.

10 Ibid., 252.

11 Morgan B. Sherwood, *Exploration of Alaska, 1865–1900* (New Haven: Yale University Press, 1965), 181.

12 Jack London, "The Gold-Hunters of the North," *Atlantic Monthly* (July 1903): 44.

13 Ibid.

14 Ibid., 43.

Chronology of Alaska History through 1910

14,000 Before Present Era+
Paleolithic people hunt wooly mammoths in Beringia, a 1,000-mile-wide land bridge that spans the fifty or so miles between Alaska and Siberia

ca. 12,000–9,000 BPE
Ice Age ends; Beringia refloods; further migration stops

1728 Vitus Bering sights islands east of far northeast Siberia

1741 Bering and Aleksei Chirikov independently sight North America; returning to Kamchatka, Bering is shipwrecked

1743 Russian fur trappers, the *promýshlenniki*, begin to hunt in Aleutian Islands using Natives as forced laborers

1778 English captain James Cook sails into Cook Inlet, then through Bering Strait into Arctic Ocean

1784 First Russian settlement at Three Saints Bay, Kodiak Island

1792–94 English captain George Vancouver surveys and maps Alaska's coast from Strait of Juan de Fuca to Cook Inlet; English exploration of Northwest America is curtailed by English involvement in the French Revolution and the Napoleonic Wars

1799 Tsar Paul I charters the Russian American Company with a monopoly on exploitation and trade in North America

1802 Russian fort at old Sitka is destroyed by Tlingit Indians

1804 Alexander Baranov destroys Tlingits' village, banishes them from Sitka Island, and establishes post at New Archangel, site of present-day Sitka

1815 Otto Kotzebue charts northwestern Alaska's coast and provides first descriptions of Northern Eskimo Inupiats

1817 Baranov is removed as manager of Russian American Company due to decreased profits, lax management, and mistreatment of Russian and Native laborers

1821 Second Russian American Company charter; Russia bars foreign ships from Russian areas of Northwest America

1824 Russo-American Treaty opens Russian areas of Northwest America to foreign vessels; Russian explorers discover Kuskokwim, Yukon, and Koyukuk Rivers

1825 Anglo-Russian Treaty vaguely defines boundaries of Alaska, leading to later dispute between the United States and Britain

1835–40 Tlingit population of 16,000 in southeastern Alaska is reduced by perhaps half due to smallpox epidemic resulting from white incursion

1840s Fur market collapses; Russian American Company enters agreement with Hudson's Bay Company to eliminate liquor trade along Alaska's coast; New England whalers enter Arctic Ocean

1853 Oil seeps are found in Cook Inlet

1850s A San Francisco company exports lake ice from Alaska and, by mid-1860s, is capable of shipping 20,000 tons annually to California, Mexico, and Central and South America; demand fizzles with better transportation methods from Sierras and invention of artificial ice

1858 Gold discoveries in lower British Columbia's Fraser River

1861 Prospectors find gold on Stikine River in Canada; minor rush ensues

1864 Surveyors map route for Western Union telegraph line through Alaska to Siberia and Europe; project is abandoned two years later

1867 Profits from fur trade continue to fall and, recognizing impossibility of supplying and defending Alaska, Russia offers to sell it to the United States; some scoff at William Seward for proposing the idea, but US Senate votes thirty-seven to two in favor of Charles Sumner's motion to ratify treaty; Alaska's 586,000 square miles purchased from Russia for $7.2 million (around two cents per acre)

October 18, 1867
Formal transfer to United States; US commander at Sitka reports Tlingits unhappy over transfer of their territory by one country that didn't own it to another; flurry of American settlers temporarily swells non-Native population to around 900

1868 Nine months after taking possession, US House approves payment of Alaska's purchase price to Russia

1869 Seventy-year-old Seward visits Alaska and pronounces it good; with only 2,000 non-Natives living among 25,000 Natives, Seward recommends Alaska be designated a military district and placed under control of US Army; Chilkats ask Seward to kill nine members of another tribe in retaliation for deaths of three of their number, and Seward persuades them to accept thirty-six blankets instead; Army Corps of Engineers informs British trader at Fort Yukon that he has been squatting on what was Russian and is now American soil; trader departs, leaving no Caucasian on the Yukon River

1870 Alaska Commercial Company granted twenty-year lease of seal harvest on Pribilof Islands; company soon expands commercial operations to Kodiak, Aleutian Islands, and Yukon River valley

1872 Gold discovered near Sitka and in British Columbia

1874 George Holt is first Caucasian to cross Chilkoot Pass to look for gold; thirty-two white men living on three major rivers in Alaska: Yukon, Kuskokwim, and Tanana

1877 President Hayes withdraws US troops and sends them to fight Nez Percé Indians in Idaho; one government official, a customs officer, remains in Alaska; Tlingits argue their country was stolen, invade Sitka, tear down parts of stockade, and occupy abandoned buildings

1878 First Presbyterian boarding school established at Sitka; first canneries opened at Klawock and Sitka

1879 Tension between Caucasians and Natives at Sitka leads to violence and deaths; US fails to respond; after desperate Sitkans implore British to come to their aid, HMS *Osprey*

sails north from Victoria; embarrassed US Navy begins patrols of Alaska's waters with revenue cutters; John Muir travels to Alaska and finds perfection in the wilderness

1880 Joe Juneau and Richard Harris discover gold near what would become Juneau; US census counts 435 non-Natives in territory; Alaska Commercial Company pays 100 percent dividend to shareholders, much of it from fur seal profits

1881 Henry Villard charters steamer *Idaho* and pioneers the classic tourist route through the Alexander Archipelago and on to Glacier Bay

1883 Lt. Frederick Schwatka crosses Chilkoot Pass and travels the length of the Yukon River, providing publicity for Alaska and a map to future goldfields

1884 Congress enacts legislation that allows staking of mining claims on federal lands, appropriates $15,000 to educate Native children, and appoints Rev. Sheldon Jackson as general agent of education; Alaska named a "district" but not a territory

1885 Exploration of Copper, Tanana, and Koyukuk Rivers by Lt. Henry T. Allen; "Jack" McQuesten brings fifty tons of mining supplies from San Francisco and transforms Yukon trading stations from fur trading and Indian clientele to supplying goods to miners

1886 Gold found on Fortymile River on American soil; settlement of Forty Mile arises on Canadian soil

1887 Lay missionary William Duncan and his thousand Tsimshian followers migrate from Canada to New Metlakatla

1890 Native population decimated by diseases brought in by outsiders; US census counts Alaska's population: 4,298 whites, 23,531 Natives, 1,823 mixed, and a few others; most non-Natives live at Juneau and Douglas and are employed in the Treadwell mines

1891 Congress authorizes survey and sale of town lots to private citizens

1893 Gold discovered on Birch Creek by two Creoles, Pitka Pavalof and Sergei Cherosky; settlement of first mining camp in interior Alaska at Circle City

1896 George Washington Carmack, Skookum Jim, and Tagish Charlie find gold on Rabbit (Bonanza) Creek in Canada; prospectors rush to the Klondike from Alaska

Summer 1897

Excelsior arrives in San Francisco and *Portland* in Seattle with nuggets, dust, prospectors, and news of Klondike; 1890s economic depression and sensational journalism incite mass hysteria; many Americans, some believing the Klondike is in Alaska, make plans to go

By summer of 1898

Estimated 100,000 to 200,000 travel north to seek gold; 40,000 of them cross White and Chilkoot Passes or travel up the Yukon River; some, disappointed in Dawson, continue on to Alaska

1898 Forty-three killed in snow slide near Chilkoot Pass; gold found at Nome; construction of White Pass and Yukon Railway begins; Homestead Act provides for eighty-acre home sites

1899 Congress authorizes civil and criminal codes for Alaska, creates judicial districts, and increases number of federal judges from one to three; 2,000 men and women, their claims the length of their shovel handles and possessed only so long as they stand in place, take two million dollars in gold from the beaches of Nome

1900 Nome's population swells to 20,000; US Census counts a little more than 30,000 non-Natives and a little less than 30,000 Natives; Congress authorizes civil government; fifty canneries are in operation; influenza and measles epidemic in western and northern Alaska kills a quarter to a third of Natives

1902 E. T. Barnette sails the *Lavelle Young* up the Tanana River, runs aground, and founds trading post at the place that becomes Fairbanks; Italian Felice Pedroni (Felix Pedro) discovers gold in creeks flowing into Chena River near its confluence with Tanana River

1903 More gold found in the Tanana River valley and rush ensues; Fairbanks supersedes Circle City as "largest log-cabin town in the world"

1904 Congressional delegation visits Alaska and travels 6,600 miles, 111 of that on land; completion of Alaska telegraph line connects non-Native communities to Seattle; national wire service transmissions provide newspapers with direct link to outside world

1905 Trail between Valdez and Fairbanks develops into wagon road; provides first transportation of freight and passengers from coast to interior

1906 The Guggenheims, J. P. Morgan, and others form syndicate to mine Alaska's copper; resolution of ongoing dispute over boundary between Alaska and Canada; year of highest gold recovery in Alaska, with Fairbanks district producing 3.8 million ounces and Seward Peninsula, 2.7 million ounces; capital moved from Sitka to Juneau; President Theodore Roosevelt withdraws all coal deposits on public lands until orderly federal development plan can be confected

1907 Construction begins of Copper River and Northwestern Railway between copper mine at Kennecott and port of Cordova on southern coast; survey of international boundary starts in south and works north; upon completion (years down the road), American and Canadian surveyors take a dip in the Arctic Ocean; President Roosevelt designates much of southeast Alaska as the Tongass National Forest

1908 Former federal judge James Wickersham elected Alaska delegate to US Congress and begins to press for territorial legislature; President Roosevelt designates twenty-three million acres along Prince William Sound as Chugach National Forest

1909 Alaska Yukon Pacific Expedition in Seattle

1910 US Census counts 30,450 non-Natives and 25,331 Natives

Bibliography

Works of the Anthology

Abercrombie, Captain William R., and Captain Edwin F. Glenn. "Report of Captain W. R. Abercrombie." Adjutant-General's Office. *Reports of Explorations in the Territory of Alaska (Cooks Inlet, Sushitna, Copper, and Tanana Rivers), 1898.* Washington, DC: Government Printing Office, 1899.

Aldrich, Herbert L. *Arctic Alaska and Siberia; or, Eight Months with the Arctic Whalemen.* Chicago: Rand, McNally and Company, 1889.

Allen, Lieutenant Henry T. *Report of an Expedition to the Copper, Tananá, and Kóyukuk Rivers in the Territory of Alaska in the Year 1885.* Washington, DC: Government Printing Office, 1887.

Clark, M. *Roadhouse Tales; or Nome in 1900.* Girard, KS: Appeal Publishing Company, 1902.

Collis, Septima M. *A Woman's Trip to Alaska; Being an Account of a Voyage Through the Inland Seas of the Sitkan Archipelago in 1890.* New York: Cassell Publishing, 1890.

Devine, Edward J. *Across Widest America: Newfoundland to Alaska, with the Impressions of a Two Years' Sojourn on the Bering Coast.* Montreal: The Canadian Messenger, 1905.

De Windt, Harry. *Through the Gold-Fields of Alaska to Bering Straits.* New York: Harper Brothers, 1898.

Dietz, Arthur Arnold. *Mad Rush for Gold in Frozen North.* Los Angeles: Times-Mirror Printing and Binding House, 1914.

Dunn, Robert. *The Shameless Diary of an Explorer.* New York: The Outing Publishing Company, 1907.

Grinnell, Joseph. *Gold Hunting in Alaska.* Elgin, IL: David C. Cook Publishing Company, 1901.

Hallock, Charles. *Our New Alaska; or, the Seward Purchase Vindicated.* New York: Forest and Stream Publishing Company, 1886.

Herbert, Agnes, and a Shikári. *Two Dianas in Alaska.* London: J. Lane, 1909.

Hine, C. C. *A Trip to Alaska: Being a Report of a Lecture Given with Stereopticon Illustrations.* Milwaukee: King, Fowle and Company, 1889.

Hitchcock, Mary E. *Two Women in the Klondike: The Story of a Journey to the Gold-Fields of Alaska.* New York: G. P. Putnam's Sons, 1899.

Ingersoll, Ernest. *In Richest Alaska and the Gold Fields of the Klondike.* Chicago: The Dominion Company, 1897.

Kirk, Robert C. *Twelve Months in Klondike.* London: William Heinemann, 1899.

Muir, John. "Notes of a Naturalist." *San Francisco Daily Evening Bulletin,* September 6, 1879.

Powell, Addison M. *Trailing and Camping in Alaska.* New York: Wessels & Bissell, 1910.

Seton Karr, H. W. *Shores and Alps of Alaska.* London: Sampson Low, Marston, Searle & Rivington, 1887.

Spurr, Josiah Edward. *Through the Yukon Gold Diggings: A Narrative of Personal Travel.* Boston: Eastern Publishing Company, 1900.

Stacey, John F., and Mrs. John W. Davis. *To Alaska for Gold.* N.p., n.d.

Stuck, Hudson. *Ten Thousand Miles with a Dog Sled: A Narrative of Winter Travel in Interior Alaska.* New York: Charles Scribner's Sons, 1914.

Sullivan, May Kellogg. *A Woman Who Went to Alaska.* Boston: James H. Earle and Company, 1902.

Taylor, Charles M., Jr. *Touring Alaska and the Yellowstone.* Philadelphia: George W. Jacobs & Co., 1901.

Willard, Mrs. Eugene S. *Life in Alaska: Letters of Mrs. Eugene S. Willard.* Eva McClintock, ed. Philadelphia: Presbyterian Board of Publication, 1884.

Winchester, J. D. *Captain J. D. Winchester's Experience on a Voyage from Lynn, Massachusetts, to San Francisco, Cal., and to the Alaskan Gold Fields.* Salem, MA: Newcomb and Gauss, 1900.

Primary Sources

Abercrombie, Captain W. R. "Report of Captain W. R. Abercrombie." *Copper River Exploring Expedition, 1899.* Washington, DC: Government Printing Office, 1900.

———. "Supplementary Expedition into the Copper River Valley, Alaska." US Congress, Senate. Committee on Military Affairs. *Compilation of Narratives of Explorations in Alaska.* Washington, DC: Government Printing Office, 1900.

Aldrich, Herbert. "Eskimo Whaling." *Outing Magazine* 18, no. 1 (1891): 13–18.

American Geographical Society Bulletin. "Exploration of Central Alaska." *The Alaska and Northwest Quarterly* 1, no. 4 (January 1899): 66–69.

Amery, C. F. "An American Penal Colony (Would Make Alaska the Botany Bay of the US)." *North American Review* (August 1887): 212–14.

Babcock, Walter. "Report of First Lieutenant Walter C. Babcock." In *Copper River Exploring Expedition, 1899.* Washington, DC: Government Printing Office, 1900.

Badlam, Alexander. *The Wonders of Alaska.* San Francisco: Bancroft Company, 1890.

Ballou, Maturin Murray. *The New Eldorado: A Summer Journey to Alaska.* Boston: Houghton, Mifflin and Company, 1891.

Bancroft, Hubert H. *History of Alaska, 1730–1885.* San Francisco: A. L. Bancroft and Company, 1886.

Broke, Horatio George. *With Sack and Stock in Alaska.* London: Longmans, Green and Company, 1891.

Brooks, Alfred Hulse. "History of Explorations and Surveys." In *Alaska and Its History*, ed. Morgan Sherwood, 21–44. Seattle: University of Washington, 1967.

Bruce, Miner. *Alaska, Its History and Resources, Gold Fields, Routes and Scenery.* New York: The Knickerbocker Press, 1899.

Chicago Record. *Klondike: The Chicago Record's Book for Gold Seekers.* Chicago: Monarch Book Co., 1897.

Clark, W. E. "Ten Years of Progress in Alaska." *World's Work* (August 1909): 11941–44.

Collis, Septima M. *A Woman's War Record.* New York: G. P. Putnam's Sons, 1889.

Craig, Lulu Alice. *Glimpses of Sunshine and Shade in the Far North; or, My Travels in the Land of the Midnight Sun.* Cincinnati: The Editor Publishing Co., 1900.

Devin, Anna Shane. "Homes and Home-Makers of Alaska." *Pacific Monthly* 15 (June 1906): 680–82.

De Windt, Harry. *From Paris to New York by Land.* London: Thomas Nelson & Sons, n.d.

Dunham, Sam C. *The Alaska Gold Fields and the Opportunities They Offer Capital and Labor.* Bulletin No. 16. Washington, DC: Department of Labor, May 1898.

Dunn, Robert. "Across the Forbidden Tundra." *Outing Magazine* 43, no. 4 (January 1904): 459–71.

———. "The Fallacies of Roughing It." *Outing Magazine* 46, no. 6 (September 1905): 643–52.

———. *World Alive.* London: Robert Hale Limited, 1958.

Elliott, Henry Wood. "Ten Years' Acquaintance with Alaska: 1867–1877." *Harper's New Monthly Magazine* 55, no. 330 (November 1877): 801–16.

Fell, Sarah. *Threads of Alaskan Gold.* N.p., 1904.

Field, Kate. "Rum in Alaska." *Kate Field's Washington,* February 26, 1890.

Fitzgerald, William G. "The New El-Dorado on the Klondike." *The Strand Magazine* 14, no. 82 (October 1897): 419–31.

French, L. H. *Nome Nuggets: Some of the Experiences of a Party of Gold Seekers in Northwestern Alaska in 1900.* New York: Montross, Clarke & Emmons, 1901.

Gannett, Henry. "The General Geography of Alaska." *National Geographic* 12, no. 5 (May 1901): 180–96.

Georgeson, C. C. "The Possibilities of Alaska." *National Geographic* 13, no. 3 (March 1902): 81–85.

Gray, William Cunningham. *Musings by Camp-Fire and Wayside.* Chicago: F. H Revell Co., 1902.

Hall, James A. *Starving on a Bed of Gold; or, The World's Longest Fast.* Santa Cruz, CA: Press of the Sentinel, 1909.

Haskell, William B. *Two Years in the Klondike and Alaskan Gold Fields, 1896–1898.* 1898. Reprint, Fairbanks: University of Alaska Press, 1997.

Heilprin, Angelo. *Alaska and the Klondike: A Journey to the New El Dorado with Hints to the Traveler.* New York: D. Appleton and Co., 1899.

Herron, Joseph S. *Explorations in Alaska, 1899, for An All-American Overland Route from Cook Inlet, Pacific Ocean, to the Yukon.* Washington, DC: Government Printing Office, 1909.

Hine, C. C. *Mrs. Leary's Cow: A Legend of Chicago.* New York: The Insurance Monitor, 1872.

Jackson, Sheldon. *Alaska and Missions on the North Pacific Coast.* New York: Dodd, Mead and Company, 1880.

Keeler, N. E. *A Trip to Alaska and the Klondike in the Summer of 1905.* Cincinnati: The Ebbert & Richardson Co., 1906.

London, Jack. "The Gold-Hunters of the North." *Atlantic Monthly* (July 1903): 42–49.

Lukens, Matilda Barns. *The Inland Passage: A Journal of a Trip to Alaska.* N.p., 1899.

McKee, Lanier. *The Land of Nome.* New York: The Grafton Press, 1902.

McLain, John Scudder. *Alaska and the Klondike.* New York: McClure, Phillips & Co., 1905.

Muir, John. *Stickeen.* Boston: Houghton Mifflin Company, 1913.

———. *Travels in Alaska.* Boston: Houghton Mifflin, 1915.

Pierce, W. H. *Thirteen Years of Travel and Exploration in Alaska.* Lawrence, KS: Journal Publishing Co., 1890.

Radclyffe, C. R. E. [Charles Robert Eustace]. *Big Game Shooting in Alaska.* London: R. Ward, 1904.

Rickard, T. A. *Through the Yukon and Alaska.* San Francisco: Scientific and Mining Press, 1909.

Schwatka, Frederick. *Along Alaska's Great River.* New York: Cassel and Company, 1885.

———. "King of the Continent." *New York Times,* October 19, 1886.

Scidmore, Eliza Ruhamah. *Alaska: Its Southern Coast and the Sitkan Archipelago.* Boston: D. Lothrop and Company, 1885.

———. *Appletons' Guide-Book to Alaska and the Northwest Coast.* New York: D. Appleton and Company, 1893.

Shepard, Isabel S. *Cruise of the U.S.S. Steamer "Rush" in Behring Sea, Summer of 1889.* San Francisco: The Bancroft Company, 1889.

Stanley, William M. *A Mile of Gold: Strange Adventures on the Yukon.* Chicago: Laird and Lee, 1898.

Sullivan, May Kellogg. *The Trail of a Sourdough.* Boston: Gorham Press, 1910.

Sumner, Charles. *"Speech of the Hon. Charles Sumner on the Cession of Russian America to the United States, 1867."* Washington, DC: Government Printing Office, 1867.

Swineford, A. P. *Alaska: Its History, Climate, and Natural Resources.* Chicago: Rand, McNally and Company, 1898.

Tuttle, C. R. *The Golden North.* Chicago: Rand, McNally and Company, 1897.

US Congress, House. *Annual Report of the Governor of Alaska, 1888.* H. Ex. Doc. 1, 50th Congress, 2nd Sess., 1888, pt. 5 in vol. 12.

US Congress, Senate. Committee on Military Affairs. *Compilation of Narratives of Explorations in Alaska.* Washington, DC: Government Printing Office, 1900.

US Congress, Senate. Committee on Territories. *Conditions in Alaska.* Washington, DC: Government Printing Office, 1904.

US Public Land Commission. *The Public Domain, Its History with Statistics.* H. Misc. Doc. 45, 47th Congress, 2nd sess., 1880, pt. 4 in vol. 19.

Wardman, George. *A Trip to Alaska.* San Francisco: Samuel Carson & Co., 1884.

Whymper, Frederick. *Travel and Adventure in the Territory of Alaska.* London: John Murray, 1868.

Wickersham, James. *Old Yukon: Tales—Trails—and Trials.* Washington, DC: Washington Law Book Co., 1938.

Woodman, Abby Johnson. *Picturesque Alaska: A Journal of a Tour among the Mountains, Seas, and Islands of the Northwest, from San Francisco to Sitka.* Boston: Houghton, Mifflin and Company, 1893.

Young, G. O. *Alaskan-Yukon Trophies Won and Lost.* Huntington, WV: Standard Publications, 1947.

Secondary Sources

Alaska Historical Society. *The Alaska 67: A Guide to Alaska's Best History Books.* Walnut Creek,

CA: Hardscratch Press, 2006.

Alaska Yukon Pacific Exposition. Written by Christina Ruddy. Produced and directed by John Forsen. Fidget, 2009. DVD.

Berton, Pierre. *The Klondike Fever: The Life and Death of the Last Great Gold Rush*. New York: Alfred A. Knopf, 1972.

Campbell, Robert. *In Darkest Alaska: Travel and Empire Along the Inside Passage*. Philadelphia: University of Pennsylvania Press, 2007.

Carlson, L. H. "The Discovery of Gold at Nome, Alaska." In *Alaska and Its History*, ed. Morgan Sherwood: 352–80. Seattle: University of Washington, 1967.

Cole, Terrence. Introduction to *Along Alaska's Great River*, by Frederick Schwatka. 1885. Reprint, Anchorage: Alaska Northwest Publishing Company, 1983.

———. *Crooked Past: The History of a Frontier Mining Camp, Fairbanks, Alaska*. Fairbanks: University of Alaska Press, 1991.

———. *Nome, "City of the Golden Beaches."* Anchorage: Alaska Geographic Society, 1984.

———. Introduction to *Two Women in the Klondike*, by Mary E. Hitchcock. 1899. Reprint, Fairbanks: University of Alaska Press, 2005.

Conroy, Sarah Booth. "She Painted the Town Pink." *Washington Post*, February 1, 1999, A1.

Engberg, Robert, and Bruce Merrell, eds. *Letters from Alaska by John Muir*. Madison: University of Wisconsin Press, 1993.

Farb, Peter. *Man's Rise to Civilization (as Shown by the Indians of North America from Primeval Times to the Coming of the Industrial State)*. New York: E. P. Dutton, 1968.

Golder, Frank A. "Mining in Alaska Before 1867." In *Alaska and Its History*, ed. Morgan Sherwood: 149–56. Seattle: University of Washington, 1967.

Grauman, Melody Webb. "Kennecott: Alaskan Origins of a Copper Empire, 1900–1938." *Western Historical Quarterly* 9, no. 2 (April 1978): 197–211.

Gruening, Ernest. *The State of Alaska*. New York: Random House, 1954.

Haycox, Stephen. *Alaska, An American Colony*. Seattle: University of Washington Press, 2002.

———. *Frigid Embrace: Politics, Economics, and Environment in Alaska*. Corvalis: Oregon State University Press, 2002.

———. "Sheldon Jackson in Historical Perspective: Alaska Native Schools and Mission Contracts, 1885–1894." *The Pacific Historian* 28, no. 1: 18–28.

Haycox, Stephen W., and Mary Childers Mangusso, eds. *An Alaska Anthology: Interpreting the Past*. Seattle: University of Washington Press, 1996.

Hayes, Derek. *Historical Atlas of the Pacific Northwest: Maps of Exploration and Discovery*. Seattle: Sasquatch Books, 1999.

Heintz, Clara Burke. *Doctor Hap*. New York: Coward-McCann, 1961.

Hinckley, Ted C. *The Americanization of Alaska, 1867–1897*. Palo Alto, CA: Pacific Books, 1972.

———."The Inside Passage: A Popular Gilded Age Tour." *Pacific Northwest Quarterly* 56, no. 2 (April 1965): 67–74.

———. "Sheldon Jackson and Benjamin Harrison." In *Alaska and Its History*, ed. Morgan Sherwood: 293–312. Seattle: University of Washington, 1967.

Hinckley, Theodore C., and Caryl Hinckley, eds. "Ivan Petroff's Journal of a Trip to Alaska in 1878." *Journal of the West* (January 1966): 25–70.

Hoagland, Edward. Introduction to *The Shameless Diary of an Explorer,* by Robert Dunn. 1907. Reprint, New York: The Modern Library, 2001.

Holeski, Carolyn Jean, and Marlene Conger Holeski, eds. *In Search of Gold: The Alaskan Journals of Horace S. Conger, 1898–1899.* Anchorage: The Alaska Geographic Society, 1983.

Hulley, Clarence Charles. *Alaska, 1741–1953.* Portland, OR: Binfords and Mort, 1953.

Hunt, William R. *Arctic Passage: The Turbulent History of the Land and People of the Bering Sea, 1697–1975.* New York: Charles Scribner's Sons, 1975.

———. *North of 53 Degrees: The Wild Days of the Alaska-Yukon Mining Frontier, 1870–1914.* New York: Macmillan, 1974.

Keithahn, E. L. "Alaska Ice, Inc." *Pacific Northwest Quarterly* 36 (April 1945): 1–16.

Lopez, Barry. *Arctic Dreams: Imagination and Desire in a Northern Landscape.* New York: Charles Scribner's Sons, 1986.

McLean, Isabel C. "Eliza Ruhamah Scidmore." *The Alaska Journal* (Autumn 1977): 238–43.

McPhee, John. *Coming into the Country.* New York: Farrar, Straus and Giroux, 1977.

Mergler, Wayne. *The Last New Land: Stories of Alaska, Past and Present.* Seattle: Alaska Northwest Books, 1996.

Moessner, Victoria Joan, and Joanne E. Gates, eds. *The Alaska-Klondike Diary of Elizabeth Robins, 1900.* Fairbanks: University of Alaska Press, 1999.

Moore, Terris. *Mt. McKinley: The Pioneer Climbs.* 2nd ed. Seattle: The Mountaineers, 1981.

Murie, Margaret E. *Two in the Far North.* 2nd ed. Anchorage: Alaska Northwest Publishing Company, 1978.

Murphy, Claire Rudolf, and Jane G. Haigh. *Gold Rush Women.* Anchorage: Alaska Northwest Books, 1997.

Nash, Roderick. "Tourism, Parks, and the Wilderness Idea in the History of Alaska." In *Alaska in Perspective,* ed. Sue E. Liljeblad. Anchorage: Alaska Historical Commission / Alaska Historical Society 4, no. 1 (1981): 1–27.

———. *Wilderness and the American Mind.* 3rd ed. New Haven: Yale University Press, 1967.

Naske, Claus M., and Herman E. Slotnick. *Alaska: A History of the 49th State.* 2nd ed. Norman: University of Oklahoma Press, 1987.

Nelson, Richard. Introduction to *Travels in Alaska,* by John Muir. 1915. Reprint, New York: Penguin Putnam, 1997.

Neufeld, David, and Frank Norris. *Chilkoot Trail: Heritage Route to the Klondike.* Whitehorse, Yukon: Lost Moose Publishing, 1996.

O'Reilly, Shauna, and Brennan O'Reilly. *Alaska Yukon Pacific Exposition.* Charleston, WV: Arcadia Publishing, 2009.

Sherwood, Morgan B., ed. *Alaska and Its History.* Seattle: University of Washington Press, 1967.

———. "Ardent Spirits: Hooch and the *Osprey* Affair at Sitka." *Journal of the West* (July 1965): 301–44.

———. *Exploration of Alaska, 1865–1900.* New Haven: Yale University Press, 1965.

Starr, Frederick S. "Why Did Russia Let Seward's Folly Go on the Cheap?" *Smithsonian* (December 1979): 129–44.

Sullivan, Micahel Sean. Introduction to *An Expedition to the Copper, Tanana, and Koyukuk Rivers in the Territory of Alaska, in the Year 1885,* by Lieutenant Henry T. Allen. 1887. Reprint, Anchorage: Alaska Northwest Publishing Company, 1985.

The Gold Rush. Produced, written, and directed by Charlie Chaplin. United Artists, 1925.

Tryck, Keith. "Rafting Down the Yukon." *National Geographic* 148, no. 6 (December 1975): 830–61.

US Department of the Interior. National Survey of Historic Buildings. *Theme Twenty-One: Political and Military Affairs, 1865–1910.* Special study, *Alaska History, 1741–1910,* by Benjamin F. Gilbert. Typewritten manuscript, 1961.

Webb, Melody. *The Last Frontier.* Albuquerque: University of New Mexico Press, 1985.

Weeden, Robert B. *Alaska: Promises to Keep.* Boston: Houghton Mifflin Company, 1978.

Wharton, David. *The Alaska Gold Rush.* Bloomington: Indiana University Press, 1972.

Wickersham, James. *A Bibliography of Alaskan Literature, 1724–1924.* Fairbanks: Alaska Agricultural College and School of Mines, 1927.

CPSIA information can be obtained
at www.ICGtesting.com
Printed in the USA
BVHW040214161122
652073BV00004B/113